In memory of my father, Roy May

SOCIAL RESEARCH

Issues, methods and process

SECOND EDITION

Open University Press
Celtic Court
22 Ballmoor
Buckingham
MK18 1XW

and
1900 Frost Road, Suite 101
Bristol, PA 19007, USA

First published 1993
Reprinted 1993, 1994, 1995, 1996

First published in this second edition 1997

A catalogue record of this book is available from the British Library

ISBN 0 335 20005 2 (pb) 0 335 20006 0 (hb)

Library of Congress Cataloging-in-Publication Data
May, Tim. 1957–
    Social research : issues, methods and process / Tim May. — 2nd
ed.
        p.   cm.
    Includes bibliographical references and index.
    ISBN 0-335-20006-0 (hc.). — ISBN 0-335-20005-2 (pbk.)
    1. Social sciences—Research.   2. Social sciences—Research–
–Methodology.   3. Sociology—Research.   4. Sociology—Methodology.
I. Title.
H62.M325   1997
300'72—dc21   97-20094
                                                                  CIP

Typeset by Type Study, Scarborough
Printed in Great Britain by Redwood Books, Trowbridge

Contents

Acknowledgements		ix
Preface to the second edition		xi
Introduction		1
Part I	**Issues in social research**	5
1	**Perspectives on social science research**	7
	Schools of thought in social research	7
	Objectivity	9
	Positivism	9
	Empiricism	10
	Realism	11
	Subjectivity	12
	Idealism	13
	Building bridges	14
	Postmodernism	15
	Feminist criticisms of research	17
	Challenging the scientific cloak	17
	Reason and emotion	20
	The critique of 'disengagement'	20
	Biography	20
	Feminist epistemologies	21
	Women, race and research	24
	Summary	25
	Questions for your reflection	26
	Suggested further reading	26
2	**Social theory and social research**	27
	Exploring the relationship between social theory and social	

research | 28
Linking theory and research | 30
Situating social theory and research | 34
Summary | 40
Questions for your reflection | 41
Suggested further reading | 41

3 Values and ethics in the research process | 42
Values and social research | 42
What are value judgements? | 43
Values in the research process | 45
The connection between values and research | 49
Ethics and their relation to social research | 53
What are ethics? | 54
Relations between ethics and social research | 56
Summary | 60
Questions for your reflection | 61
Suggested further reading | 62

Part II Methods of social research | 63

4 Official statistics: topic and resource | 65
Sources of official statistics | 65
The social construction of crime statistics | 67
Official statistics: the debates | 74
Summary | 78
Questions for your reflection | 80
Suggested further reading | 80

5 Social surveys: design to analysis | 81
The logic of survey method | 83
Sampling | 85
Probability samples | 85
Non-probability samples | 87
Stages in constructing a survey | 88
Preliminary work | 88
Types of questionnaires | 89
Designing and testing questions | 92
Types of questions | 94
Coding | 95
Attitude scales | 96
Question wording | 98
The analysis of questionnaires | 101
Levels of measurement | 101
Relationships between variables | 102

Surveys in critical perspective   103
Summary   107
Questions for your reflection   108
Suggested further reading   108

6   Interviewing: methods and process   109
Interviews in social research   109
   Structured interview   110
   Semi-structured interview   111
   Unstructured or focused interview   112
   Group interview   113
Conducting interviews in social research   114
   Common prescriptions for interviewing practice   114
   The practice of focused interviews   118
   Feminist approaches to the process of interviewing   121
   The analysis of interviews   124
Issues in interviewing   128
Summary   130
Questions for your reflection   131
Suggested further reading   131

7   Participant observation: perspectives and practice   132
Participant observation and social research   133
   The Chicago School and participant observation   133
   Muddying the waters   136
The practice of participant observation   138
   The researcher's role   138
   Access   141
   Utilizing flexibility   142
   Field notes   144
   Subjective adequacy   145
The analysis of observations   147
   Writing ethnography   152
Issues in participant observation   153
Summary   155
Questions for your reflection   155
Suggested further reading   156

8   Documentary research: excavations and evidence   157
The place of documents in social research   157
   Sources of documentary research   159
The process of documentary research   162
   Conceptualizing documents   162
   Using documents   166

Approaching a document   169
The analysis of documents   171
    Quantitative and qualitative approaches   171
    A note on presentation of findings   175
Issues in documentary research   176
Summary   177
Questions for your reflection   177
Suggested further reading   178

9 **Comparative research: potential and problems**   **179**
Globalization and comparative social research   180
    The place of comparison in social research   182
The process of cross-national research   184
    The potential of comparative research   185
    Problems in comparative research   189
    Potential and problems: an overview   192
Summary   193
Questions for your reflection   194
Suggested further reading   194

Bibliography   195
Author index   219
Subject index   222

Acknowledgements

As I look back over the seven years since I began my full-time academic career, I have met a number of people who have been supportive and helpful, as well as good company. Lyn Bryant, in particular, has been a supportive friend in the competitive environment of modern academia. In this respect, I would also like to thank Ken Parsons, Carole Sutton, Tracey Bunyard, Malcolm Williams, Louise Ackers and David Denney.

My love and gratitude to Dee. In the recent past we have lived through all but one of the events which are regarded as the highest predictors of stress. Had our relationship not been so close, those alone would have led to us completing the lot, so we would certainly agree with the validity of that analysis! Also, my love to both Calum and Cian whose spirits demonstrate that we have as much to learn from children, as they do from us.

My thanks also to Sarah Goff, Margaret Bell, Steph Lawler, Tim Strangleman, Nick Ellison and David Chaney at Durham. Finally to Justin Vaughan at Open University Press for his continuing encouragement and support, as well as to Sue Hadden, Christine Firth, Jacinta Evans, Janet Howatson, Jeremy Lloyd, Maureen Cox and Gaynor Clements for all the work they performed during the production of this book.

Preface to the second edition

I was very pleased to learn that this book has been so successful as to warrant a second edition. Many people have been very supportive in their comments and letters regarding its aims, structure, style and content. Students, lecturers and researchers alike found the book to be accessible and comprehensive. It was, therefore, with some trepidation that I approached the writing of a second edition.

This book, as with all books, has its limitations, as well as strengths. However, when it came to taking critical comments onboard in an attempt to rectify any shortcomings, published reviews, while complimentary, were mixed in relation to its intended audience. All agreed that it was aimed at undergraduates, but noted that it was suitable for postgraduates. I also found that while lecturers were defining it as a 'textbook', they were often consulting it in order to update themselves on current thinking, as well as quoting from it to justify or expand upon their own investigations.

With these messages in mind, where was I to start? In the end I decided that the structure of the book should remain intact and it can be read at different levels. What I thought was required were additions to the content of each chapter in order to render further justice to ideas on the research process in general, as well as aspects of its practice in particular. Given this decision all chapters have been revised and expanded and I have added suggested further readings to the end of each chapter.

When it came to the chapter on questionnaires, it is now five years since I have undertaken, first-hand, survey research through the stages of design, administration and analysis. This does not reflect so much a methodological preference, but the ebbs and flows to which one is subjected in the first years of an academic career, as well as the costs associated with large-scale survey research. Quite simply, you are not in a position to refuse opportunities that come your way and these have involved more qualitative aspects of research practice. Thus, although I have acted in an advisory capacity on survey research projects, Malcolm Williams, an experienced quantitative researcher and friend with whom I have worked on several occasions, kindly agreed to assist me in expanding and updating that chapter.

Overall, the end result is a new edition which takes into consideration recent developments in the field of social research. In so doing it is hoped that readers find it as accessible and comprehensive as the first edition and it renders further justice to a rich and varied field of perspectives and practices. Its basic philosophy, however, remains the same: that is, reflexive researchers will produce the most insightful research into the social worlds which we inhabit, while the social sciences are central for understanding social relations and explaining the workings of societies in general.

Introduction

Research methods are a central part of the social sciences. They constitute an important part of their curricula and provide a means through
which their intellectual development is enhanced. Indeed, their status as
'sciences' are often justified by alluding to the technical aspects of
research methods, while the very term 'science' carries with it ideas of
areas of study which are accessible only to those who have undergone a
lengthy training process in order to understand their inner workings. At
the same time there are also those within these disciplines who might
characterize themselves as 'theorists' rather than 'researchers'. The latter
concentrate on the process and products of research, while the former
might argue that they gain an advantage in being 'distanced' from the
empirical world which they seek to understand and explain.

There is some merit in both of the above views, but they are not the
dichotomies that some of their respective protagonists often claim to be
the case. After all, both innovative thinking and a meticulous attention to
the detail of data gathering and analysis characterize the practice of social
research. Theory, methodology and methods are all part of the issues and
processes that surround and inform the discipline. These differences,
however, frequently lead to disputes, as well as confusions, over the
nature of research and the methods which it should employ in pursuance
of its aims. For this reason, in the first three chapters of this book, there
is an examination of the ways in which we gain our knowledge of the
social world, the relationships that are held to exist between theory and
research, and the place of values and ethics in research practice. While
these issues are complicated, they are also fundamental to an understanding of research methods. Without this, issues and methods can
become separated and practitioners left with the impression that they
simply have to learn various techniques in order to undertake research.

A technicist attitude to research practice perpetuates the idea that
theory, ethics, values and methods of social research are distinct topics
and that researchers, despite living and participating in the societies that

they study, are somehow distinct from the social world which is the object of their investigations. This distance between them and the subjects of their study permits a limited idea of value-freedom to be maintained. As will become evident in Part I, this position is open to considerable debate, for our very membership of a society, it may be argued, is a necessary condition for understanding the social world of which we are a part, as well as being a fact of life from which we cannot escape. Indeed, such participation may itself be a prerequisite of objectivity. In having an understanding of these debates and the applicability of different methods of research, improved research and more inquiring and confident researchers will be the end result. To this extent, it is important to be aware of not only the strengths of particular methods of social research, but also their limitations.

The aim of the book

This discussion forms the starting-point for the philosophy which underlies this book: that is, that issues and methods cannot be simply separated and that we, as researchers, will produce more systematic understandings of the social world by being aware of these debates, their implications for research and our place within them. That said, this book is also intended for those who do not have a detailed knowledge of the issues within social research and its practices. Therefore, these debates are presented in a way that does not assume a great deal of prior knowledge on the part of the reader, while additional readings are provided for those who have the time and inclination to pursue areas of interest in greater depth.

The book itself is divided into two parts. Part I examines the issues and Part II discusses the methods used in research. Because the aim is to produce an accessible text, there is a limit to which the connections between Parts I and II can be developed. For this reason both sides of a debate are presented and parallels are drawn between Part II and the earlier discussions in Part I. All too often, however, reading can be a passive exercise in which we, as the readers, act as the recipients of the text, but do not engage with it by criticizing, analysing and cross-referencing the materials covered (May 1995). To help in this process, I have written questions at the end of each chapter which are intended to assist you in reflecting upon its content.

An overview of Part I

Part I introduces the debates involved in and around the research process. This part of the book is based on the belief that values, prejudices and prior beliefs affect the way we all think about an event, person or subject. An awareness and consideration of how these relate to the research process is therefore assumed to be able to sharpen and focus our decisions and choices in research work.

Towards this end, Chapter 1 covers the different perspectives which exist on social research by examining their arguments and intellectual foundations. To use a building analogy, if we do not understand the foundations of our work, then we are likely to end up with a shaky structure! Terms such as 'realist', 'empiricist', 'idealist', 'positivist', 'subjective', 'objective', 'postmodern' and 'poststructuralist' require clarification in order to consider their implications for research practice. Towards this end, Chapter 1 also introduces the reader to the wide-ranging criticisms that have been made of methodology from feminist perspectives.

Chapter 2 develops the points raised above by examining the relationship between social theory and social research and Chapter 3 discusses the place of values and ethics in social research. These topics are often thought to present such intractable problems for the researcher that they take a backstage position in the research process. The development of theory, however, is a necessary part of the intellectual development of social research, while ethics are a fundamental component of the idea of a 'discipline' and the confidence which people have in the actions of its members. The place of values in social research is also central and an understanding of the nature and effect of values a necessary part of its practice. As I hope will become evident, to ignore these issues does not mean that they are no longer an influence, for they routinely inform and affect research practice.

An overview of Part II

Chapter 4 begins the second part of the book by considering the main sources of official statistics that researchers use, followed by an account of their strengths and weaknesses. By tracing the issues which surround the production of crime statistics, the questions regarding their place in contemporary social research and, more generally, the use of other official statistics, can be considered.

Chapters 5–8 examine the process and methods of analyses involved in the major techniques used in social research. These cover questionnaire design, interviewing, participant observation and documentary research. In order to provide for ease of comparison between these different methods, each of the chapters follows a similar structure. First, the chapter begins with a discussion of the place of the method in social research which makes links with the discussions in Part I. Second, there is an examination of the actual process of undertaking research using the method, and third, the techniques of data analysis for each method are discussed. My intention at this point is to enable you to consider the different ways of approaching your data and to direct you to specific sources for further investigation of the topic. Therefore, should you decide to utilize the method for your own research, you will be aware not only of the ways in which the data are collected, but also of the methods employed for their analysis. Finally, each of these chapters ends with a critique of the method. By comparing this last section in each of the four chapters, together with the other sections and the issues covered in Part I, the advantages and disadvantages of each method can be assessed.

Chapter 9 is an introduction to comparative research. While the idea of comparison has long been used in social sciences, a growth in information technology and institutions such as the European Union has led to an increase in funding for comparative research. As such, there are important developments taking place in this field. Awareness of both the potential and problems involved in these developments and the methods of comparative research is therefore an important part of social research.

Within the text, references are used to other works on social research. The bibliography is a resource intended for you to use in exploring themes and topics in greater depth. Research is an exciting and fundamental part of the practice and future of the social sciences and an important component in understanding and explaining human relations. It only remains for me to say that I hope this book achieves a greater understanding of the methods and issues involved in social research.

PART 1 Issues in social research

CHAPTER **1** **Perspectives on social science research**

Schools of thought in social research
    Objectivity
    Positivism
    Empiricism
    Realism
    Subjectivity
    Idealism
    Building bridges
    Postmodernism
Feminist criticisms of research
    Challenging the scientific cloak
    Reason and emotion
    The critique of 'disengagement'
    Biography
    Feminist epistemologies
    Women, race and research
Summary
Questions for your reflection
Suggested further reading

The aim of this chapter is to introduce perspectives which assist in understanding the aims and practice of social research. Importantly, these perspectives do not determine the nature of research practice itself, for there is a constant interaction between ideas about the social world and the data collected on it. Nevertheless, a discussion of the main debates between these schools of thought, together with the key terms used, will enable a consideration of their arguments and the assumptions which each make about how we can come to know the social world and what properties it contains. These may then be linked with discussions in Part II on the actual practice of research methods.

Schools of thought in social research

A science is often thought of as being a coherent body of thought about a topic over which there is a broad consensus among its practitioners. As Alan Chalmers notes of the popular view of science:

> Scientific knowledge is proven knowledge. Scientific theories are derived in some rigorous way from the facts of experience acquired by observation and experiment. Science is based on what we can see and hear and touch, etc. Personal opinion or preferences and speculative imaginings have no place in science. Science is objective. Scientific knowledge is reliable knowledge because it is objectively proven knowledge.
>
> (Chalmers 1982: 1)

However, the actual practice of science shows that there are not only different perspectives on a given phenomenon, but also alternative methods of gathering information and of analysing the resultant data. While these differences do affect the natural sciences, we are concerned here with the history and practice of the social sciences.

Differences of perspective appear to many to be problematic. After all, if there is no consensus within a discipline then surely that is because its methods and theories simply do not work? However, perhaps we should challenge the idea that science is an all-embracing explanation of the social or natural world beyond our criticism. Instead, why do we not see the methods and theories of science as the outcome of disciplines which are contested because there are political and value considerations which affect our lives and are therefore a central part of their practice? These are not within the power of science to alter, nor in any democracy should they be. Their role in society is to understand and explain social phenomena, to focus attention on particular issues and to challenge conventionally held beliefs about the social and natural worlds:

> Scientific work depends upon a mixture of boldly innovative thought and the careful marshalling of evidence to support or disconfirm hypotheses and theories. Information and insights accumulated through scientific study and debate are always to some degree *tentative* – open to being revised, or even completely discarded, in the light of new evidence or arguments.
>
> (Giddens 1993: 20, original emphasis)

In the social sciences, theories which challenge our understanding of the social world and the systematic gathering of data are a central part of its practice. However, while this characterization might appear attractive, the disputes within social science are more complicated (and more exciting) than any single definition could encompass: for example, what constitutes a 'science', the nature of its methods and the types of data which it should collect are open to dispute. In order to see how this situation arises, an excursion into the main ideas and debates within social science is required, before moving on (in Chapter 2) to examine the relationship between social theory and research.

Objectivity

The Introduction noted that objectivity, along with generalization and explanation, were considered as fundamental characteristics of a science. To many researchers, debates around these questions are considered peripheral to their activities. However, if we are to hold to the view that social science research offers us knowledge about the social world which is not necessarily available by other means, then we are making some privileged claims about our work. Research then becomes more than the simple replication of our opinions and prejudices: it substantiates, refutes, organizes or generates our theories and produces evidence which may challenge not only our own beliefs, but also those of society in general.

It is at this point that the debate over objectivity in the social sciences enters. It is often assumed that if our values do not enter into our research, it is objective and above criticism. Objectivity is therefore defined as

> the basic conviction that there is or must be some permanent, ahistorical matrix or framework to which we can ultimately appeal in determining the nature of rationality, knowledge, truth, reality, goodness, or rightness.
>
> (Bernstein 1983: 8)

After all, many people accept what scientists say is the 'truth'. On the other hand, the subject matter of the social sciences is social life itself. People are obviously fundamental to social life and the question is now raised that as social researchers and as members of a society, is it possible or desirable for us to suspend our sense of belonging? Different perspectives have provided answers to this question.

Positivism

We may argue that people react to their environment much as molecules which become 'excited' when heat is applied to a liquid. Clearly, science does not have then to ask the molecules what they think. So is it necessary that we, as social scientists, ask people? We may, of course, be interested in people's opinions in terms of their reactions to events that affect their lives, but only in so far as they are reacting and we wish to explain and predict their behaviour accordingly. However, don't we all believe that we possess something called free-will? That is we can, to some extent, control our own destinies rather than have it controlled, like the molecules, by a change in our environment. In other words that we can 'act on', as well as behave in 'reaction to', our social environments. Some social science experiments do take the form of altering the environment and seeing how people react to it. Is social life really like that? Surely experiments in a laboratory are artificial and do not reflect the complications, decisions and contradictions involved in social life?

If we believe ourselves to be the product of our environment – created by it – then to some extent we are the mirror image of it. It defines our nature, or our being. We do not have to refer directly to the people themselves because we can predict how they will behave. Simply expressed, this is the position of two schools of thought in social research: behaviourism and positivism. For a positivist, the social scientist must study social phenomena 'in the same state of mind as the physicist, chemist or physiologist when he probes into a still unexplored region of the scientific domain' (Durkheim 1964: xiv).

Objectivity is defined by positivism as being the same as that of natural science and social life may be explained in the same way as natural phenomena. We can characterize this tradition in the same terms as the aims of natural science: the prediction and explanation of the behaviour of phenomena and the pursuit of objectivity, which is defined as the researcher's 'detachment' from the topic under investigation. The results of research using this method of investigation are then said to produce a set of 'true', precise and wide-ranging 'laws' (known as covering laws) of human behaviour. In fulfilling these aims, we would then be able to generalize from our observations on social phenomena to make statements about the behaviour of the population as a whole. In this process, positivism explains human behaviour in terms of cause and effect (in our example above, heat is the cause and the effect is the molecules becoming excited as the liquid increases in temperature). 'Data' must then be collected on the social environment and people's reactions to it. Given this attention to the detail of data collection by researchers, positivism shares similar ideas to another perspective on the research process: empiricism.

Empiricism

If the aim of positivism is to collect and assemble data on the social world from which we can generalize and explain human behaviour through the use of our theories, then it shares with empiricism the belief that there are 'facts' which we can gather on the social world, *independently* of how people interpret them. As researchers, we simply need to refine our instruments of data collection in order that they are neutral recording instruments as the ruler might measure distance, or the clock measure time.

The fundamental difference between empiricism and positivism is in the realm of theory. As will be developed in Chapter 2, data within positivism is theory-driven and designed to test the accuracy of the theory. Empiricism, on the other hand, is a method of research which lacks, or more usually has not referred explicitly, to the theory guiding its data collection procedures:

'empiricism' refers to a conception of social research involving the production of accurate data – meticulous, precise, generalisable – in which the data themselves constitute an end for the research. It is summed up by the catchphrase 'the facts speak for themselves'.

(Bulmer 1982b: 31)

At this stage, it is important not to confuse the words empirical and empiricism. The word empirical refers to the collection of data on the social world to test or generate the propositions of social science, while, as Bulmer's quote indicates, the empiricist school of thought believes that the facts speak for themselves and require no explanation via theoretical propositions.

While there are differences between positivism and empiricism, the former does rely on the methods of the latter. They also both assert that there are facts about the social world which we can gather. Objectivity is then defined in terms of researchers' detachment from the social world, as well as the accuracy of their data collection instruments. Therefore, there is a world out there that we can record and we can analyse independently of people's interpretations of it. This follows the 'correspondence theory of reality' which holds that a belief, statement or sentence is true as long as there is an external fact that corresponds to it. This, as we shall see below, is a highly disputed contention that is problematic to maintain.

Realism

This tradition shares with positivism the aim of explanation; beyond that, the similarity ends. Realism has enjoyed a particular boost in the social sciences with the works of Roy Bhaskar (1975; 1989a; 1989b; 1993) who states:

Normally to be a realist in philosophy is to be committed to the existence of some disputed kind of being (e.g. material objects, universals, causal laws; propositions, numbers, probabilities; efficacious reasons, social structures, moral facts).

(Bhaskar 1993: 308)

Realism has a long history and may be associated with the works of Karl Marx and Sigmund Freud (see M. Williams and May 1996: 81–8). Marx, for example, constructed his typology (a method of classification) of capitalism on the basis that there are certain essential features which distinguish it from other economic and political systems. Within this economic system there exist 'central structural mechanisms' and the task of researchers is 'to organize one's concepts so as to grasp *its* essential features successfully' (Keat and Urry 1975: 112, original emphasis).

In referring to underlying structural mechanisms, an important argument within this perspective is being employed. If researchers simply content themselves with studying everyday social life, such as conversations and interactions between people, this will distract them from an investigation of the underlying mechanisms which make those possible in the first instance. The task of researchers within this tradition is to uncover the structures of social relations in order to understand why we then have the policies and practices that we do. Similarly, Sigmund Freud argued that our consciousness was determined by our subconsciousness. Thus people's neuroses are the visible manifestations of their sexual and aggressive desires that are repressed in their subconscious. Psychoanalytic theory then attempts to trace a line 'from certain adult or adolescent activities to certain infantile experiences' (Wollheim 1977: 156). While people may not be directly aware of these experiences, they still affect the way that they act.

Realism argues that the knowledge people have of their social world affects their behaviour and, unlike the propositions of positivism and empiricism, the social world does not simply 'exist' independently of this knowledge. As such, causes are not simply determining of actions. However, people's knowledge may be partial or incomplete. The task of social research is not simply to collect observations on the social world, but to explain these within theoretical frameworks which examine the underlying mechanisms which structure people's actions and prevent their choices from reaching fruition: for example, how schools function to reproduce a workforce for capitalism (P. Willis 1977).

The aim of examining and explaining underlying mechanisms cannot use the methods of empiricism as these simply reflect the everyday world, not the conditions which make it possible. Therefore, along with others in this tradition (Sayer 1992), Keat and Urry (1975) argue that realism must utilize a different definition of science to positivism. In particular, a realist conception of social science would not necessarily assume that we can 'know' the world out there independently of the ways in which we describe it. For these reasons, there are those within this tradition who have built bridges between the idea that there is a world out there independent of our interpretation of it (empiricism and positivism) and the need for researchers to understand the process by which people interpret the world. Before discussing those who have attempted this, I shall first examine the perspectives which argue, contrary to positivism and empiricism, that there is no social world 'beyond' people's perceptions and interpretations.

Subjectivity

Up to now, we have spoken of the ways in which our environment or its underlying structures – of which we are not necessarily aware – structure us, or create us as objects (positivism) or subjects and objects (realism). Perhaps you are not happy with the idea that you are created or formed in this way. We like to believe that we exercise free-will and make judgements which alter the courses of our lives. Positivism does not pay much attention to the detail of people's inner mental states. Realism, on the other hand, may refer to people's consciousness in so far as it reflects the conditions under which they live, how structures are reproduced and their desires are frustrated.

When we refer to people's consciousness we are concerned with what takes place – in terms of thinking and acting – within each of us. These subjective states refer to our 'inner' world of experiences, rather than the world 'out there'. To concentrate on subjectivity we focus on the *meanings* that people give to their environment, not the environment itself. Contrary to the contentions of positivists we, as researchers, cannot know this independently of people's interpretations of it. The only thing that we can know with certainty is how people interpret the world around them. Our central interest, as researchers, is now focused upon people's understandings and interpretations of their social environments.

Idealism

Some schools of thought emphasize our creation of the social world through the realm of ideas, rather than our being simply conditioned or created by it. They would argue that our actions are not governed by cause and effect, as in the case of molecules in a test tube, but by the rules which we use to interpret the world. As natural science deals with matter which is not 'conscious', researchers of this persuasion argue that its methods cannot deal with social life and should therefore be discarded from its study. To speak of cause (heating of molecules, for example) and effect (excitement of molecules) is not applicable to researching social life for people, unlike molecules, contemplate, interpret and act within their environments. For these reasons, the methods of the social sciences are fundamentally different from, but *not* inferior to, the natural sciences. It is the world of ideas in which we are interested as social researchers:

> human beings uniquely use complex systems of linguistic signs and cultural symbols to indicate to themselves and to others what they intend and mean to do. Such a viewpoint suggests that human activity is not behaviour (an adaption to material conditions), but an expression of meaning that humans give (via language) to their conduct.
>
> (Johnson *et al.* 1990: 14)

Rules exist in social action through which we understand each other. Rules, of course, are often broken and also subject to different interpretations. For that reason, we cannot predict human behaviour. People are constantly engaged in the process of interpretation and it is this which we should seek to understand. In other words, researchers should concentrate upon *how* people produce social life. Social life cannot simply be observed (empiricism), it can be understood only as the result of examining people's selection and interpretation of events and actions. Understanding these processes and the rules which make them possible is the aim of research for schools of thought within this tradition. It is not explaining why people behave in certain ways by reference to their sub-conscious states or environmental conditions, but how people interpret the world and interact with each other. This process is known as *inter-subjectivity*. The idea of an external social 'reality' has now been aban-doned because the meanings which we attach to the world are not static, nor universal, but always multiple and variable and constantly subject to modification and change. Our accounts of the social world must therefore be 'internalist': that is, arising from within the cultures we are studying. As one advocate of this view puts it in relation to meaning and language use: 'To give an account of the meaning of a word is to describe how it is used; and to describe how it is used is to describe the social intercourse into which it enters' (Winch 1990: 123).

In order to produce systematic studies of society, there are those within this tradition who argue that researchers need to employ 'hermeneutic principles'; hermeneutics referring to the theory and practice of interpre-tation. We are no longer proclaiming our 'disengagement' from our sub-ject matter as a condition of science (positivism), but our 'commitment' and 'engagement' as a condition of understanding social life. As William Outhwaite puts it in a discussion of the German hermeneutic theorist Hans-George Gadamer: 'understanding is not a matter of trained, methodical, unprejudiced technique, but an encounter . . . a confron-tation with something radically different from ourselves' (Outhwaite 1991: 24).

Our sense of belonging to a society and the techniques which we use for understanding are not impediments to our studies. The procedures through which we understand and interpret our social world are now necessary conditions for us to undertake research. In the process we both utilize and challenge our understandings in doing social science research. Contrary to positivism and empiricism, the social researcher now stands at the centre of the research process as a requirement of understanding social life. The idea of science is now very different from positivism and empiricism. After all, hermeneutics was 'determined to show that the gen-eralising of the natural science model of knowledge to all spheres of knowledge was unacceptable' (R. Anderson *et al.* 1986: 65).

For these reasons, as will be noted in Part II, there is a tendency in this tradition of social thought to prefer methods of research such as partici-pant observation and focused interviewing.

Building bridges

There are those who have attempted to synthesize some aspects of these major perspectives. One social theorist, in particular, has argued that our everyday actions are meaningful to us, but they also reproduce structures which both enable and constrain our actions (Giddens 1976; 1984; 1996). The insights of psychoanalysis and linguistics have also been employed to argue that while human actions are meaningful and variable, this does not mean that we cannot then agree on what is valid or 'true' about the social world. This bridge-building attempt fuses the twin aims of 'how' (understanding) and 'why' (explanation) in social research (Habermas 1984; 1987; 1989; 1990).

In addition to the above there is the school of 'poststructuralism', which includes the French philosopher Jacques Derrida, as well as Michel Foucault until his death in 1984. Foucault's thought, in particular, evolved in reaction to both the subjectivism of some social science perspectives and the naive empiricism imported from the natural sciences (Foucault 1977; 1980). His work is then characterized as moving beyond structuralism and hermeneutics, towards an 'interpretive analytics' (Dreyfus and Rabinow 1982). In the process, Foucault considers knowledge and power to be constructed within a set of social practices. The result is to question the concept of truth as separable from the exercise of power:

> contrary to a myth whose history and functions would repay further study, truth isn't the reward of free spirits, the child of protracted solitude, nor the privilege of those who have succeeded in liberating themselves. Truth is a thing of this world: it is produced only by virtue of multiple forms of constraint. And it induces regular effects of power. Each society has its régime of truth, its 'general politics' of truth.
>
> (Foucault 1980: 131)

While an exposition of these ideas and their implications for research are well beyond the stated aims of this book, I have deliberately included them so you can refer directly to their works, or studies about their works (see M. Dean 1994; May 1996; Morrow with Brown 1994). They demonstrate the ingenuity with which some theorists have attempted to tackle issues which are so central to social research.

Postmodernism

Before moving on to the section on feminist research, we need to consider a perspective about which there is much discussion, but often little clarification. It shares, with feminist relativism (see pp. 22–3), the belief that knowledge is both local and contingent and there are no standards beyond particular contexts via which we may judge their truth and falsity.

Although there are those who are labelled as postmodernists who exhibit clear differences in their perspectives, postmodernism refers to a cultural perspective or movement and/or epistemology, while postmodernization relates to a process that is said to lead to the historical epoch known as postmodernity (see Lyon 1994; May 1996). Therefore, it is important to note that one does not necessarily have to become a postmodernist in order to accept some of its insights regarding the changing times through which we are living (Bauman 1988).

Postmodernists are anti-foundationalist. Whether talking about implosions of meaning with the consequence that the world becomes devoid of any meaning (Baudrillard 1983a), or of the computer age and the severing of the link between knowledge and legitimacy (Lyotard 1984), or of the potential for dialogue within a liberal consensus in which scientific claims to truth about the social and natural worlds have little place (Rorty 1989), postmodernists exhibit the same underlying tendency: that is, that there are no universal standards against which science may lay claim in order to validate its standards. Quite simply, objectivity gives way to relativism with the result that not only science, but also truth, goodness, justice, rationality, etc., are concepts relative to time and place:

> For the relativist, there is no substantive overarching framework or single metalanguage by which we can rationally adjudicate or univocally evaluate competing claims of alternative paradigms . . . the relativists claim that we can never escape from the predicament of speaking of 'our' and 'their' standards of rationality.
>
> (Bernstein 1983: 8)

This challenge aims at the heart of systematic social and natural scientific research practice. What have been termed the 'repressed rivals' of science – religion, folk knowledge, narrative and myth – are now said to be returning to 'take their revenge' (Seidman 1994). Not without significance, it is within the humanities and the area of cultural studies that these views have found their greatest legitimacy. Yet how this translates into a practical research programme, without contradiction, is a matter of some difficulty, let alone considerable dispute. Take, for example, the idea of truth which underlies research. Must not all communities, including those conducting research, assume a truth which lies beyond that which they propagate and adhere to in order to legitimize their beliefs and practices in the first instance? If so, relativism must presuppose the existence of a truth that is beyond itself. Throughout the book, I shall return to issues such as these in order to render what are important, but difficult debates, more intelligible.

In considering all of the above perspectives, the waters are far more muddy than suggested. For instance, Durkheim is often termed a positivist but would not simply deny the place of subjectivity in social life, nor would an idealist necessarily deny objectivity defined as 'detachment' from the social world and Foucault possessed clear elements of positivism in his work (see M. Dean 1994). However, there is a fundamental difference between idealists and positivists in terms of the methodology of social research: that is, social science is not the same as natural science and human actions, unlike the observed effects of molecules when heated, are meaningful and involve a process of interpretation of events by conscious actors. For this reason, they must utilize different methods of investigation. That said, they are not inferior as a result, simply different.

Feminist criticisms of research

All of the thinkers whom I have mentioned so far have been men. Does this matter? If these men have produced valid theories and research results which enable us to understand social relations, then it would remain a matter of concern if more women wished to become theorists and researchers, but were prevented from doing so because men, either intentionally or otherwise, stood in their way and occupied key positions in social research centres. On the other hand, if these theories and research results did not advance our understanding, but reflected a deep-rooted male bias which defined society and science in terms of male values, then not only would the aims of research be incomplete, but also its results would be a distorted representation of the social world. What we take to be science would reflect this state of affairs by collecting so-called facts on the social world (empiricism) and is so doing would perpetuate the subordination of women by providing a scientific cloak behind which unequal status's and positions between men and women are justified.

These contentions form the starting-point of feminist criticisms of science. Perhaps the first point which should be made is that, like the social sciences in general, feminist perspectives are not a unified body of thought and it is more accurate to talk of 'feminisms' (Humm 1992). However, in the following discussions it should be borne in mind that they do share several beliefs. First, women and their fundamental contributions to social and cultural life have been marginalized and this is reflected in research practice. Second, the norms of science perpetuate and disguise the myth of the superiority of men over women and reflect a desire to control the social and natural worlds. Third, gender, as a significant social category, has been absent from our understandings and explanations of social phenomena in favour of categories such as social class. Clearly, these characterizations do not convey the depth and sophistication of arguments employed by different schools of feminism (see Tong 1989; Harding 1991; Evans 1995). At the same time, these extensive and cogent criticisms cannot be ignored. Therefore, in order to add to our understanding of social life in general and research methods in particular, it must occupy a centre-stage position in any discussion of research perspectives.

Challenging the scientific cloak

As noted in the first section of this chapter, the claims of objectivity, explanation and understanding are a central part of the social sciences.

However, what if these claims are based on limited ideas? In order to illustrate how this occurs, a brief excursion into dominant aspects of social and political thought is required.

Our notions of the roles, relations and forces within society are, according to feminist critiques, built upon unexamined assumptions about women which are then reproduced in our theories about society. When the roles of women are considered in social life, they are characterized as passive and emotional. Although this assumption has long been challenged by groups of women, their voices were lost by a selective reading of historical events (Spender 1982). In particular, there is the reference to something called 'human nature': that is, a belief in the fundamental characteristics of people regardless of their history or social context. Social thinkers have provided many a justification for the belief that social roles are natural, rather than the product of social and political manipulation by men over women. An influential philosopher, John Locke (1632–1704), for example, believed people to be innately 'reasonable' (a view of human nature). At the same time he saw a need for a 'social contract' so that order could be brought to what would otherwise be a chaotic social and political world.

From these positions of reasonableness and the need for a social contract he then took a 'leap' to argue that because of their reproductive capacity, women were 'emotional' and were also unable to provide for themselves so were 'naturally' dependent on men. As in contemporary society, property rights were crucial in Locke's ideas and due to women's natural dependence, he argued that they do not then possess such rights. Marriage was a contract they entered in order to produce sons who can then inherit property. The contract of marriage thus ensures that property rights are stable within society and men have sons in order to perpetuate their lineage.

As feminist scholars have noted (Sydie 1987) Locke equated 'rights' with the capacity to be reasonable which he then argued that women did not possess. This splitting of so-called natural differences, feminists argue, occurs throughout western thought and provides the foundation upon which we base our thinking and scientific practice. Buried within these assumptions are not scientific statements, but deep-rooted biases against women by male thinkers. The German philosopher Hegel (1770–1831), for instance, believed that women's position in the family, as subordinate to men, was the natural realm for their 'ethical disposition'. Similarly, Darwin (1809–82) believed he had found a scientific basis for traditional assumptions about the division of labour between the sexes. Again, we are led to believe that these are natural differences. If we believe them to be natural, then tampering with them would upset the 'natural order of social life'. However, this is precisely the point of contention. Feminists argue that women's position within society is not a natural phenomenon, but a social, political and economic product which is reflected and perpetuated by the bias of 'science' (Okin 1980; Lieven 1981; Harding 1986).

According to feminist critiques, sociology, social policy and other social sciences have, like the natural sciences, perpetuated this myth (J. Dale and Foster 1986; Pascall 1986; Sydie 1987; Stanley and Wise 1993). For instance, in the earlier studies on the family and work, before feminist research had some impact on dominant practices, women were 'wives', 'mothers' or 'housewives', but not people in their own right. The American sociologist Talcott Parsons (1902–79) believed that the major 'status' of an urban, adult woman was that of a housewife. Her status in this domestic sphere was, in turn, determined by the status of the husband or, as is also commonly referred, head of household. The positivist Emile Durkheim, who so adhered to the idea of a natural science of society, did not in fact produce a scientific account of society, but a moralizing one hidden behind the guise of science. His views on the family were, according to what is probably the most authoritative study of his life and work, an 'alliance of sociological acumen with strict Victorian morality' (Lukes 1981: 533). The use of the term 'family' in social policy research is also criticized for being a 'unit of analysis in which women's particular interests are often submerged' (Pascall 1986: 4).

If our claims to theorize about social life simply function to disguise such moralizing, they will be distortions of the social world. In the separation of the 'public' from 'private' social worlds, men have become the people of action in the public realm, while women are subordinated to the private realm of the family and their status determined accordingly. For feminists, perspectives on social life have either reflected this political phenomenon or attempted to justify it as a natural state of affairs.

Our understanding of social life is thereby limited by this silencing of women's voices and the perpetuation of particular and narrow ideas of science. Social research often focuses selectively in the public realm: it is men who paint pictures; men who think about the world; men who make money and men who shape our destiny. If the contribution of women is acknowledged, it is in terms of being the 'power behind the throne', 'the boss in the house' or what has been described as 'drawing-room manipulation'. In research on the world of work, for example, we operate according to definitions which remain unchallenged:

> Workplaces are generally thought of as strictly demarcated from the home and family life. Similarly, we think of workers as people who leave home in the morning to travel to work and who work a certain number of hours. . . . These conceptions of work and workers would seem to be an accurate characterization of some kinds of paid work. However, they are not very satisfactory as a characterization of women's paid work.
>
> (Beechey 1986: 77–8)

Researchers have not only provided evidence for some changes to this dominant model of work (Hörning et al. 1995), but its gendered nature is of central importance (Adkins 1995). Theories of the social world and practices of research are thus argued to be *androcentric*. What we call science is not based upon universal criteria which are value-free, but upon male norms and, in particular, the mythical separation of reason (men) and emotion (women):

> From an androcentric perspective women are seen as passive objects rather than subjects in history, as acted upon rather than actors; androcentricity prevents us from understanding that both males and females are always acted upon as well as acting, although often in very different ways. Two extreme forms of androcentricity are gynopia (female invisibility) and misogyny (hatred of women).
>
> (Eichler 1988: 5)

Reason and emotion

Men are assumed to be reasonable and women emotional. Yet definitions of words are interpreted by individuals or groups in certain ways and their political translation takes subtle forms. The nature of this is rendered highly problematic by the fact that women are excluded from scientific practices by virtue of men saying they are incapable of 'reason'. As Lloyd (1984) puts it: 'our ideas of Reason have historically incorporated an exclusion of the feminine, and . . . femininity itself has been partly constituted through such processes of exclusion' (quoted in Whitford 1988: 110). From this idea we then base science upon reason and reason is based upon truth. Feminists, on the other hand, argue that you cannot separate reason and emotion in simple ways. Therefore, certain ideas of disengagement, or aloof detachment by the researcher from the researched, are criticized by feminist thought.

The critique of 'disengagement'

The idea that 'rigorous research' involves the separation of researchers from the subject of their research simply reflects the idea that reason and emotion must be separated. Instead of seeing people in the research process as simply sources of data, feminists argue that research is a two-way process. Frequently, however, textbooks speak of not becoming 'over involved' with participants. Over-identifying with the 'subject' of the research is said to prevent 'good' research. The researcher should be detached and hence objective. According to feminists, this is not only a mythical aim, but also an undesirable one which disguises the myriad of ways in which the researcher is affected by the context of the research or the people who are a part of it.

Biography

In much the same way as the ideas of disengagement and objectivity are challenged, so too is the idea that a researcher's biography is not important or relevant to the research process. Both the researcher and those people in the research carry with them a history, a sense of themselves and the importance of their experiences. However, personal experience is frequently devalued as being too subjective, while science is objective. There is much to be gained from exploring the lives and experiences of women in understanding society and correcting the silence which surrounds women's voices. As will be apparent in Part II, this is a fundamental aspect of research methods in, for example, interviewing and oral histories. Researchers should be aware of the ways in which their own biography is a fundamental part of the research process. It is both the experiences of the researched *and* researchers which are important. Despite this, it is a subject in social research frequently reserved for separate publications (see C. Bell and Newby 1977; C. Bell and Roberts 1984; Roberts 1990; D. Bell *et al.* 1993; Hobbs and May 1993).

Feminist epistemologies

We now have the critique of disengagement, the critique of the absence of gender as a significant social category in social research and the critique of the nature and methods through which science is constructed based upon a male perspective and limited ideas of what constitutes reason. These add up to a considerable indictment of the practice of science. A question now remains: what alternatives have feminists proposed which are of importance to us as researchers? This brings us round to questions of *epistemology* and *ontology*.

These are complex subjects, but for the purposes of our discussion, they refer to the ways in which we perceive and know our social world and the theories concerning what 'exists'. Therefore, without explicitly saying as much, we have examined the epistemologies and ontologies of positivism, empiricism, realism and idealism. Feminists, on the other hand, start with the above critiques of science and their responses may be considered under three headings: empiricist, standpoint and relativist epistemologies.

Standpoint feminism has developed in contrast to many of the dominant ways of viewing knowledge (Hartsock 1987; D. Smith 1988). Its basis lies in taking the disadvantage of women's exclusion from the public realm by men and turning that into a research advantage. Because women are 'strangers' to the public realm and excluded from it, this provides them with a unique opportunity for undertaking research:

> The stranger brings to her research just the combination of nearness and remoteness, concern and indifference, that are central to maximizing objectivity. Moreover, the 'natives' tend to tell a stranger some kinds of things they would never tell each other; further, the stranger can see patterns of belief or behaviour that are hard for those immersed in the culture to detect.
>
> (Harding 1991: 124)

A female researcher is thus able to operate from both an oppressed position as a woman and a privileged position as a scholar (Cook and Fonow 1990). A woman's biography and experiences become central to the production of unbiased accounts of the social world. However, it is not experience itself which provides the basis of claims to objectivity by standpoint feminists. While experience is a fundamental starting-point, experiences themselves are reflections of dominant social relationships. Experience is a beginning point to research, but for standpoint feminists this must then be situated within the wider context of women's lives in general. However, male-science overrides experience. Thus, in order that the theorist does not then become the expert on people's lives, as is the usual hierarchical way in which science proceeds, any thinking about women's lives by the researcher must take place in a democratic and participatory way through involving other women.

Two emphases within standpoint epistemology are apparent from this discussion. First, women's experiences are an excellent starting-point upon which to base research as they occupy a marginalized position within society and can therefore 'look in' as the stranger might to a new social scene. As Sandra Harding puts it, the aim

> is not so much one of the right to claim a label as it is of the pre-requisites for producing less partial and distorted descriptions, explanations, and understandings.
>
> (Harding 1987b: 12)

Second, an emphasis on the scientific study of society whose aim is to place women's experiences within a wider theory of their location in society. For this reason, there are parallels between feminist standpoint epistemologies and realism (see Cain 1990). Although the idea of science is maintained, its norms have changed. It becomes a feminist stance and one which does not marginalize, but promotes the cause of women in general.

These two contentions form the starting-point for the differences between feminist standpoint and feminist relativist epistemologies. First, feminist relativists, and these would include those influenced by postmodernism, would reject the idea of any type of science for this would be just another way in which women's experiences are sequestrated by those who claim to be experts:

> the inconvenient fact that much human behaviour cannot be described, let alone understood, in unexplicated categorical terms is largely ignored, or rather 'resolved' by treating people's experiences as faulty versions of the theoretician's categories.
>
> (Stanley and Wise 1990: 24)

To treat people's experiences as 'faulty' is argued to be a dominant approach to theory. Second, they would also reject the view that knowledge or 'truth' about women's position in society is possible.

Instead there are many versions of social reality, all of which are equally valid. Women's experiences become a starting *and* finishing point for research which aims to assist the process of 'breaking out' of a positivist paradigm:

> Women's lives, women's bodies, women's experiences, demonstrate that the social (and physical) world is complicated. 'Reality' is shown to be multidimensional and multi-faceted. But 'reality' is constructed as one reality, simple and unseamed. And thus the necessity to suppress, distort, use, oppress, women's differences. Women's lives demonstrate that 'the circle' is a collection of gaps and broken links, not iron-clad and inviolate at all.
>
> (Stanley and Wise 1993: 183)

To impose some theoretical idea on the social world conspires with this suppression of difference. Women's experiences and feelings are not limited in this perspective, but are valid in themselves. The means by which research is undertaken should then be made available for all to see as part of this process of validating experiences. However, are all experiences equally valid and not limited and/or biased? Is the opinion of the middle-class woman who says women are not oppressed, the same as the working-class woman who says they are?

For some feminists the answer to assessing this question has been to accept the basis of science, but to move away from its male-centred perspective and place women at its centre. With the tension between difference and essentialism and relativism and objectivism in mind, particularly when it comes to the actual practice of feminist research (Acker *et al.* 1991), there are those who now argue for a 'fractured foundationalism' (Stanley and Wise 1993) or a 'strategic essentialism' (Grosz 1994).

Those feminists who fall under the category of feminist empiricism would 'see themselves as primarily following more rigorously the existing rules and principles of the sciences' (Harding 1991: 111). Margrit Eichler's (1988) work, for example, provides a series of technical steps that the researcher should avoid in order to produce research which does not fall into the four 'traps' of malestream research. These are androcentric practices, the over-generalization of research findings which are solely based on men's experiences, an absence of explanations for the social and economic influences of gender relations, and finally, the use of 'double standards', for example, in terms of language the use of 'man' and 'wife', when we should refer to 'woman' and 'man'. The aim is to produce less partial and more accurate accounts of social life. In other words, its criticism is focused not so much on the *foundations* of science, but upon its *practice*. For this reason, it has been criticized for replicating male norms of scientific inquiry which, according to other feminist epistemologies, should be both challenged and changed.

There are, as with research perspectives in general, a number of viewpoints from which feminists approach issues in social research.

Nevertheless, we can take the following lessons for research practice. As researchers, we should seek to avoid the age-old fallacy of a woman's reproductive capacity as being a hindrance to her participation in society. The important questions are first, how the fact of women's reproduction is manipulated in the organization of social life. Second, how women are marginalized in the public sphere. Third, a greater understanding of the fundamental contribution which women make to cultural, political and economic life. Fourth, the implications of feminist analysis for research in particular and social life in general. Fifth, a general challenging not only of androcentric thought, but also of heterosexist assumptions within our society. For these reasons

> feminism does not start from a detached and objective standpoint on knowledge of the relations between women and men. Even the most moderate advocates of women's rights must take the view that men have rights which are unjustly denied to women. This commitment does not mean that feminist knowledge is not valid knowledge, but it does entail asking what we mean by knowledge, and why some forms of knowledge are seen as more valid than others. Feminism implies a radical critique of reason, science and social theory which raises questions about how we know what we think we know.
>
> (Ramazanoglu 1990: 9)

Women, race and research

Feminisms, while correcting the class-based accounts of research, have faced similar criticisms as research in general, for its neglect of the issue of race. The ways in which sexual and racial stereotypes cut across each other has been documented by researchers (Ackers 1993). An exclusive concentration on gender and class within research, however, is to the detriment of differences which exist between women on ethnic and racial lines:

> The oppression of women knows no ethnic nor racial boundaries, true, but that does not mean it is identical within those differences. Nor do the reservoirs of our ancient power know those boundaries. To deal with one without ever alluding to the other is to distort our commonality as well as our difference.
>
> (Lorde 1992: 139)

Angela Davies (1981) documents the racism of the early women's movement with its assumptions concerning the intellectual inferiority of black men and women. Class-based accounts of society, on the other hand, have been criticized for being economically determinist and ignorant of the political dimensions of gender and race. In our research and within the limits of our power, we should be aware of these issues and how they relate to the research process (Phoenix 1993). For instance, in her criticisms of the discipline of criminology, Marcia Rice notes that it has been both racist and sexist in a 'machocentric' frame of reference which she defines as

> a discourse which is male-centred. It represents 'masculinity' as the primary defining characteristic and as qualitatively different from 'femininity', but it is more extreme than the normal usage of masculinity as aggression is central to it.
>
> (Rice 1990: 68, n.1)

Not only does she consider that criminology is male-centred, but also she criticizes feminism for its ethnocentricity. As a result, she suggests the following ways of overcoming the limitations of this approach. First, researchers should avoid racist stereotypes and ethnocentric approaches to research for this is not only an inaccurate representation of the social world, but also ignores important differences between people's experiences. This would avoid what Fiona Williams (1989) calls the 'danger of homogenization' whereby the use of terms such as 'blacks' and 'women' which do not specify their composition, assumes such categories are universal and therefore do not allow for the diversity of people's histories, cultures and experiences. Second, there should be an increase in research which examines the ways in which 'gender roles and differential opportunity structures are affected by racism as well as sexism' (Rice 1990: 68). Third, an increase in comparative studies of the dimensions of race, class and gender would assist in our understanding of the operation of power and discrimination within society. Fourth, empirical studies, in order to enhance understanding, should be situated within a wider sphere of social, political and economic contexts. Finally, as with feminism in general, the experiences of those researched should not be separated from the researchers. An exchange based on consultation and participation should take place in which each learns from the other.

Summary

This chapter has provided an introductory tour of major perspectives in social research. We have moved from the idea that social science should reflect the aims and methods of natural science, through a critique of these methods as inapplicable to social research, to feminist criticisms of the foundations and aims of science as being male-centred and hierarchical, finishing on a critique of research practice as ethnocentric and racist.

The debates themselves are complicated, but no less important for that. Yet we should note that these perspectives do not simply dictate the nature of research itself, nor how it is conducted; although the issues will inform how the aims, methods and process of social research are considered. As Jennifer Platt has written in a history of research methods in North America:

research methods may on the level of theory, when theory is consciously involved at all, reflect intellectual *bricolage* or *post hoc* justifications rather than the consistent working through of carefully chosen fundamental assumptions. Frequently methodological choices are steered by quite other considerations, some of a highly practical nature, and there are independent methodological traditions with their own channels of transmission.

(Platt 1996: 275, original italics)

That said, research which is not only aware of the issues raised in this chapter, but also then acts reflexively, is more likely to produce an enhanced and systematic study of social life.

Questions for your reflection

1 What are the differences between the terms subjectivity and objectivity?

2 How do empiricism, positivism and realism differ in their ideas on the basis and practice of social research?

3 How have feminist researchers sought to overcome the problems that their critiques make of social research and science in general?

4 What five main issues raised in this chapter would inform your practice as a researcher and why?

Suggested further reading

Blaikie, N. (1993) *Approaches to Social Enquiry*. Cambridge: Polity.

Dickens, D. R. and Fontana, A. (eds) (1994) *Postmodernism and Social Inquiry*. London: UCL Press.

Fonow, M. M. and Cook, J. A. (eds) (1991) *Beyond Methodology: Feminist Scholarship as Lived Research*. Bloomington and Indianapolis: Indiana University Press.

Williams, M. and May, T. (1996) *Introduction to the Philosophy of Social Research*. London: UCL Press.

CHAPTER 2 Social theory and social research

Exploring the relationship between social theory and social research
    Linking theory and research
Situating social theory and research
Summary
Questions for your reflection
Suggested further reading

What exactly is the role of theory in social research? Is it a neutral medium through which we interpret our findings? Should it be a critical endeavour which challenges our dominant ways of thinking about social phenomena? Should the data we produce about the social world and its relations refute our theories or generate them? In the process of discussing these issues, questions will be raised concerning the place of values in social research. Chapter 3 thus moves on to explore this topic in more depth.

Before moving on, it may be of help to ask what we can and cannot expect of social theory. Social theory, along with social research, is of central importance in the social sciences. Social theory is of use for the interpretation of empirical data. However, it also enables a more general orientation in relation to political, historical, economic and social issues, as well as providing a basis for critical reflection on the process of research itself and social life and social systems in general. This necessitates a two-way relationship in which there is a challenge to both ideas and practices.

Given this critical and productive relationship, social theory should fall under our gaze in order that its own presuppositions are open to scrutiny. From this point of view, to gain the most from its explanations requires an open and inquiring attitude. The study of social theory and social research is a reflexive endeavour in which to assume that one theoretical paradigm, as an enclosed system of thought, is capable of fully explaining the social world is rendered suspect. Monolithic social theories and one-dimensional approaches to research cannot fully explain the workings of societies or understand social relations. Instead, we have a constant relationship between social theory and social research in which both endeavours are modified through a combination of reflection, experience and practice.

The practising social scientist requires insights into both theory and research. Nevertheless, as noted in the Introduction, there is often a problematic dichotomy between these disciplines. Practically speaking, it is difficult enough just to keep up with trends in research methods, let alone those in methodology, the philosophies of social and natural sciences and social theory. This chapter recognizes this difficulty and seeks to provide an account of the main issues which should be considered in examining the relations between social theory and social research.

Exploring the relationship between social theory and social research

The idea of theory, or the ability to explain and understand the findings of research within a conceptual framework which makes 'sense' of the data, is the mark of a mature discipline whose aim is the systematic study of particular phenomena. In our case, as social researchers, these phenomena are the dynamics, content and context of social relations. We aim, with our own research training and experiences in mind, together with the perspectives which guide our thinking, to explain and understand the social world. This requires the development and application of social theory.

Social theory informs our thinking which, in turn, assists us in making research decisions and sense of the world around us. Our experiences of doing research and its findings, in its turn, influences our theorizing; there is a constant relationship that exists between social research and social theory. The issue for us as researchers is not simply *what* we produce, but *how* we produce it. An understanding of the relationship between theory and research is part of this reflexive project which focuses upon our abilities not only to apply techniques of data collection, but also to consider the nature and presuppositions of the research process in order that we can sharpen our insights into the practice and place of social research in contemporary society.

While social theory is taken to be a grand enterprise, the problems which preoccupy theorists are not so different from those that often occupy 'non-theorists'. That said, they can appear to be abstract as they attempt to situate concerns and issues within a more general framework of understanding. Jürgen Habermas has this in mind when he wrote:

All social theories are highly abstract today. At best, they can make us more sensitive to the ambivalences of development: they can contribute to our ability to understand the coming uncertainties as so many calls for increasing responsibility within a shrinking field of action. They can open our eyes to dilemmas that we can't avoid and for which we have to prepare ourselves.

(Habermas 1994: 116–17)

What is different, and for our purposes as researchers, important, is the approach of theorists to those questions that concern us. Some appear to float over the social landscape as if unfettered by the problems and realities of everyday life. This ability to transcend or abstract theories from everyday life allows us to have a perspective on our social universe which breaks free from our everyday actions and attitudes with which we are, understandably, preoccupied. Such theories allow us to make links from our own specific fields of interest to those of other researchers, as well as locate our research findings within a general theory of the workings of society. As such, there is more to assessing social theory than in terms of its empirical utility. It might also be assessed in terms of its logical coherency, the kinds of problems that it generates and the insights that it offers; insights and issues that empirical researchers may have overlooked (Giddens, in Mullan 1987: 102).

On the other hand, while these theories may enable us to break free from everyday thinking, we should also recognize that their level of generality may be of little use in researching particular areas of social life, as well as reflecting limited perspectives. There have been those who are disparaging of the inability of 'grand theorists' to grasp the social problems which are important to specific 'historical and structural contexts' (Mills 1959: 42). So abstracted are these theories seen from the dynamics of social relations, they are sometimes regarded as little more than the 'philosophization of social theory' (Rex, in Mullan 1987: 19).

An alternative to such abstraction or generality is, in the words of one book on this subject, to 'ground' social theories in our observations of everyday life (Glaser and Strauss 1967). As researchers, we should seek to render the attachment between theory and data as close as possible (unlike grand theory which is stated at such a general level we could not possibly match data to theory). Instead of descending upon the social world armed with a body of theoretical propositions about how and why social relations exist and work as they do, we should first observe those relations, collect data on them, and then proceed to generate our theoretical propositions.

Another option is to ignore the idea of theory altogether and presuppose, along with the empiricists, that facts speak for themselves. Our aim would then be to act as technicians who concentrate on detailed techniques of research and data collection. This is exactly what often occurs in research practice. However, to choose this course of action does not mean our research is then more 'relevant', if by relevance we mean that it suits the ends of particular interests. It simply means that our presuppositions about social life remain more hidden, but still influence decisions and interpretations. Furthermore, an involvement in present problems divorced from theory is argued to be a sign of 'immaturity' as it severs the link which exists between the present and the development of humanity across time (Elias 1987).

We are now back to the same issue – except at a different end of the spectrum from which we left grand theory. If we assume that we can neutrally observe the social world we shall simply reproduce the assumptions and stereotypes of everyday actions and conventions. We need to understand and acknowledge these influences in our own thinking and that of society in general. Facts, in other words, do not speak for themselves and theory 'is everywhere . . . intimately connected to issues of problem, method and substance' (Plummer 1990: 122). Thus, for social research both to intellectually develop and to be of use in understanding or explaining the social world, we need theory and theory needs research. There is a 'mutual interdependence' between the two (Bulmer 1986a: 208). It is argued that for a discipline to be conferred the status of a 'science' the assumption that there is an object world beyond the descriptions that it employs to understand and explain it, must hold. In realist terms this can be expressed in the following manner:

> Things exist and act independently of our descriptions, but we can only know them under particular descriptions. Descriptions belong to the world of society and of men; objects belong to the world of nature. . . . Science, then, is the systematic attempt to express in thought the structures and ways of acting of things that exist and act independently of thought.
>
> (Bhaskar 1975: 250)

Linking theory and research

In the process of research, we embark on empirical work and collect data which either initiates, refutes or organizes our theories and then enables us to understand or explain our observations. Bearing in mind the above references to 'grounded' and 'grand' theories, we may proceed to achieve this by using one of two routes. First, we might consider a general picture of social life and then research a particular aspect of it to test the strength of our theories. This is known as *deduction* where theorizing comes before research. Research then functions to produce empirical evidence to test or refute theories. On the other hand, we might examine a particular aspect of social life and derive our theories from the resultant data. This is known as *induction*. Research comes before theory and we seek to generate theoretical propositions on social life from our data. I shall now examine both induction and deduction and their relationship to theory.

Induction has a long history in the philosophy of science. It is based on the belief, as with empiricism, that we can proceed from a collection of facts concerning social life and then make links between these to arrive at our theories. The first point of consideration in this process refers to the relationship between theory and data in order to demonstrate that the 'facts' can speak for themselves and are distinct from the interpretation of researchers. An example will help to explain how this relates to social theory.

Consider the proposition, once maintained by the results of psephological research (D. Butler and Stokes 1969), that 'more manual workers vote labour than they do conservative'. This is an empirical generalization about the voting behaviour of a particular group within society. However, it is not a theory or explanation of the pattern of behaviour observed, but a statement of observation on voting behaviour collected by asking people, via surveys, about their voting intentions. However, for it to be explained (in other words, *why* manual workers vote Labour) we need a theory. This might take the form of explaining voting behaviour in terms of the different primary and secondary socialization processes that manual workers undergo in comparison to non-manual workers. Alternatively, we might say that manual workers tend to vote Labour because they believe that party best represents their interests in maintaining material securities such as housing, employment prospects, etc. Now, while the connection between class position and voting behaviour has diminished since Butler and Stokes's research (Dunleavy and Husbands 1985), this illustrates that we require a theory to interpret the findings of social research. As social researchers, our findings on the social world are devoid of meaning until situated within a theoretical framework.

A question still remains: why do researchers decide to collect such data in the first place? They might be representing particular interests who are funding the research, or are personally interested in this area and have access to resources to test ideas which they have on the relationship between class membership and voting behaviour. Whether the research is 'pure' or 'applied' in this sense, interests have guided our decisions *before* the research itself is conducted. It cannot be maintained that research is a neutral recording instrument, whatever form it might take. As a result, researchers should make their theories, hypotheses or guiding influences explicit and not hide behind the notion that facts can speak for themselves. The very construction of a field of interest is itself a matter of academic convention that should be open to scrutiny (Bourdieu and Wacquant 1992). This is not a situation from which researchers can escape for their interpretations are an inevitable part of the research process. An alternative to induction is thus to make the theories or hypotheses which guide our research explicit.

Deduction rejects the idea that we can produce research on the basis of initially rejecting theory or, to put it another way, that there is a simple distinction to be made between the language of theory and the language of observation. It seeks to fuse the empiricist idea that there are a set of rules of method by which we proceed as researchers, with the ideas of deductive reasoning which hold that if our hypothesis or ideas about social life are 'true', then they will be substantiated by the data produced. In order for this to take place, data collection is driven by theoretical interests, not the other way round. Thus according to one famous exponent of this tradition: 'scientists try to express their theories in such a form that they can be tested, i.e., refuted (or else corroborated) by such experience' (Popper 1970: 654–5). A theory concerning social life must not only be based upon empirical evidence, but also be capable of being *falsified* by such evidence: '*it must be possible for an empirical scientific system to be refuted by experience*' (Popper 1959: 41, original emphasis).

The attraction with this system is that it acknowledges, unlike inductivism, that data are theory-driven. It also sustains social theory only in so far as it is corroborated by empirical evidence. Therefore, it proceeds on the same basis as the methods of natural scientific inquiry to enable the production of a 'science of society'. Attractive as this sounds, we are still left with some issues. First, if our empirical evidence falsifies a theory, is this a sufficient reason for rejecting it? We might simply assert that we have found a deviant or exceptional piece of evidence which does not falsify our theory as such. Second, there is a pragmatic point for us to consider as researchers. Until a new theory comes along to explain our research findings, we are unlikely to abandon existing theories which still assist us in understanding or explaining social life. Scientists, in general, are likely to hold on to core elements in their theoretical armoury that are not open to the process of falsification (Lakatos and Musgrave 1970). Finally, deductivism is still, like inductivism, assuming that we can derive theories of the social world independent of our preconceptions or values due to its adherence to a natural scientific method of research.

The idea that we might derive our theories on the social world, independent of our preconceptions, is thus highly problematic. Theorists, for instance, take for granted certain aspects of the social world which are not subjected to empirical falsification (the assumptions concerning the 'natural' roles of women in society for instance). As noted in Chapter 1, we research a social world which people are already interpreting and acting within. To assume that we can separate these activities from scientific fact may be not only an impossibility, but also undesirable for the production and practice of science itself.

In accepting this, our focus of attention is now transferred away from the procedures of generating or testing theories, to the influences which inform theorizing and research. This provides us with a starting-point for examining a seminal contribution on the way in which science has developed – as opposed to how it should develop according to the rules of deduction and induction.

Thomas Kuhn's work was a historical study of scientific progression (Kuhn 1970). He argued that science does not progress according to the criteria of falsifying theories, as Popper would maintain. On the contrary, evidence which does not support theories is regarded as only a temporary problem to which future research is directed. In this way theories are not falsified, but become the subject of continuous research. It is this that Kuhn calls 'normal science':

'normal science' means research firmly based upon one or more past scientific achievements, achievements that some particular scientific community acknowledges for a time as supplying the foundation for its further practice.

(Kuhn, quoted in B. Barnes 1991: 87)

Given that any deviant data serve as the basis for future research, the theory is never falsified because there will always be evidence which both supports and refutes it. Kuhn therefore refers to scientific *paradigms* as characterizing the practice of science. These paradigms do not, unlike deductivism and inductivism, provide rules which the methods of research must slavishly follow, but provide only examples

> of good practice. . . . And scientists must themselves determine how the model is to be used. . . . Thus, scientists doing normal science do not merely have to agree upon what should serve as the basis of their work; they also have to agree upon how it should serve that purpose in every particular case. They are obliged to employ a paradigm much as a judge employs an accepted judicial decision.
>
> (B. Barnes 1991: 88)

Science develops according to the culture that scientists inhabit and this, not the rules of deduction and induction, determines their practices and choices of theories. If an example of counter-evidence is found to falsify a theory, then it will be the competence of the individual researcher which is called into question, not the theory. Scientists do not attempt to falsify a theory as such: 'Instead, they attempt to extend and exploit it in a variety of ways' (Kuhn 1972: 91). However, unlike other commentators who see no logic to the practice of science (Feyerabend 1978), Kuhn views science as a conservative endeavour which is challenged only by what he calls 'scientific revolutions'. At this point, a new paradigm replaces the old. This does not result from mounting empirical evidence which refutes the old paradigm but, for example, is due to younger scientists entering the field and bringing with them a new set of ideas and problems upon which they too can research and make their names. A misalignment then occurs between practices and assumptions; a process that leads to what Pierre Bourdieu (1993) refers to as 'heresy'. Despite the change of personnel, the conclusions of the discipline would, once again, not reflect some 'objective reality' independent of the minds of scientists, but would depend on 'the scientist's theoretical preferences rather than the empirical evidence' (Papineau 1978: 36).

We have travelled from the problems of inductivism and its atheoretical stance, through deductivism with its concentration on rules to which no science can, or arguably should, live up to, to arrive at the idea of Kuhn's paradigms which are argued to reflect the actual practices of science. To express it another way we have moved from the idea that there is an object world which science describes in a neutral manner, via an examination of the means of description that is employed in relation to that world, to a focus upon the means of description themselves without reference to an object world. The social and physical worlds are then seen to be constructed according to these descriptions and so it is the social practice of science itself that becomes of primary interest.

At this point in our discussions a recognition of the role of social elements in the production of science allows different ideas to develop and go off at what are complete tangents to each other. The idealism of ethnomethodology permits it to focus upon the inter-subjective construction of the object world, while postmodernists argue that science is nothing more than rhetoric or, to express it another way, as the 'real' cannot be represented, then the process of representation itself should be examined. An absence of a basis upon which to justify these insights then leads to charges of relativism (Latour 1988). Parallels are also found with Jacques Derrida's deconstructionist project whereby:

> Methodology can be read as rhetoric, encoding certain assumptions and values about the social world. Deconstruction refuses to view methodology simply as a set of technical procedures with which to manipulate data. Rather, methodology can be opened up to readers intrigued by its deep assumptions and its empirical findings but otherwise daunted by its densely technical and figural findings.
> (Agger 1991: 29–30)

These complicated debates have a productive potential in that they prompt a continual reflection upon the relationship between theory and research and the manner and means under which its practice takes place. Therefore, in the next section I wish to examine the ways in which different researchers and theorists have attempted to tackle the problems raised in the above discussions.

Situating social theory and research

There are several issues which Kuhn's concept of the practice of science raises for us as social researchers. In particular, the attempt to separate *what* we do, from *how* we do it, as considered by both inductivism and deductivism, is problematic. The ways in which we conduct our research is inevitably affected by the social context in which it takes place. This raises several issues for social research. First, within our disciplines (as noted in Chapter 1) there are different ways of viewing how we gain knowledge of social phenomena in the first instance. Therefore, our disciplines are characterized not by one single paradigm, but by divisions with regards to the aims and methods of social research. These, however, do not simply reflect schisms within the disciplines themselves, but the subject matter with which we are concerned: social life itself is characterized by divisions and is not a unified phenomenon. Second, all sciences, not just social sciences, are directly influenced and affected by interests which exist 'externally' to the discipline: for example, the values and interests of sponsors of research or the ways of working within the discipline itself which may exclude, for instance, the reception of feminist ideas.

At the same time, we are able, to some extent, to sever ourselves from particular interests at particular points in time. As a result, feminist critiques exist alongside, but not within, mainstream research practices. Third, paradigms are not closed systems of thought hermetically sealed off from one another and this gives us an advantage. There is a constant process in the practice of social science which enables us to compare one paradigm with another and to see the strengths and weaknesses of each. A process of clarification and mediation of theories within the practice of social research is then able to occur. As Anthony Giddens, from whose discussions the above characterizations are drawn, notes:

> The process of learning a paradigm or language-game as the expression of a form of life is also a process of learning what a paradigm is not: that is to say, learning to mediate it with other, rejected, alternatives, by contrast to which the claims of the paradigm in question are clarified.
>
> (Giddens 1976: 144)

Social researchers do not then have to content themselves with one paradigm as Kuhn would suggest. Social sciences are dynamic disciplines within which, depending upon the position of the researcher within an academic field, other paradigms can be considered. This enables an understanding and explanation of empirical inquiries and adds to the challenging of assumptions about social life as an important part of research practice. It is this 'openness' to engage in reflection upon which our basis as a discipline depends. A community of researchers should then be 'able, willing, and committed to engage in argumentation' (Bernstein 1976: 111). After all, the very objects that social science are concerned with analysing are so often themselves the subjects of power struggles over who may control the rules, relations and resources that constitute them in the first instance.

Apart from this ability to penetrate that which is taken for granted, there are differences which exist between the natural and social sciences. First, we are constantly dealing with social phenomena which people have already endowed with meaning before we arrive on the social scenes with our notebooks, questionnaires or interview schedules. Our work, therefore, involves the interpretation of social settings, events or processes by taking account of the meanings which people have already given to those settings or processes. That noted, a simple separation between the social and the natural is itself the subject of reasoned dispute. Our environments, for instance, produce risks which we take account of in our daily lives (see Beck 1992; Luhmann 1993; Lash *et al.* 1996). In this way our understandings, once again, become a precondition of the production of the research itself. Second, the results and practices of social research also feed back into social life. People, unlike molecules, engage in the interpretation of its findings and are co-participants in its process. Again, caution in terms of a simple separation between nature and culture should be exercised in this respect.

Given this 'feedback' of research into social life, researchers have to make connections between the language which is used in social theory and the methods of interpretation which people already use in attributing meaning to their social environment. Social theory, in other words, must take account of people's everyday understandings. Anthony Giddens (1984) refers to this process as the 'double hermeneutic'. He even suggests that it would not be unusual to find a coroner who has read Durkheim's classic study on suicide (Giddens 1990: 42). This acknowledges that there is a constant slippage between the language which we use as researchers to understand and explain social life and the meanings which people already employ to get on with the business of everyday life. Given this relationship, the issue is now raised as to whether we can have a theory of social life which does not take full account of people's experiences and understandings in everyday life. In order to assist in seeing the importance of this process for the relationship between theory and research, I wish to examine the ingenious ways in which social theorists and researchers have attempted to address these issues.

We have already seen (in Chapter 1) how standpoint feminism regarded people's experiences as a starting but not finishing point for research. Theory is then required to situate the experiences of women within a wider context and the production of knowledge is regarded as a social activity. It follows that if a certain type of knowledge predominates in a society, this is not necessarily because it is scientific, but due to the power that certain groups have to define what is right or wrong, or true and false. Theorizing about this state of affairs must take place within a democratic and participatory situation, otherwise it will become, like the practice of science itself, another way of regarding the experiences of particular people as faulty. The production of theory and research then become 'critical projects' which go hand in hand in challenging oppression in society – whether on gender, race, ethnic, class or other lines. This brings us round to a discussion of the relationship between critical theory and an understanding of everyday life.

Critical theory has a long tradition in the work of the Frankfurt School with the works of Adorno, Horkheimer and Marcuse who were influenced by Marx and Freud (see May 1996). It does not assume, unlike positivism, that the differences between facts and values can be sustained. It is also in opposition to the idea that the world cannot be changed. The interests of the researcher towards this end are not then bracketed by a concentration on 'fact-gathering' or neutrality, nor the development of hypotheses to be tested. Instead:

A critical social theory frames its research program and its conceptual framework with an eye to the aims and activities of those oppositional social movements with which it has a partisan, though not uncritical, identification. The questions it asks and the models it designs are informed by that identification and interest ... if struggles contesting the subordination of women figured among the most significant of a given age, then a critical theory for that time would aim, among other things, to shed light on the character and bases of such subordination.

(Fraser 1989: 113)

Critical theory approaches the question of the relationship between people's everyday meanings and the generation of social theory by not assuming that there is a truth that we can reach as researchers by simply concentrating on the techniques of social research (as with positivism and empiricism). Further, it would not regard research results feeding back into social life as a 'problem' for researchers. On the contrary, in the works of Karl Marx, the adequacy of social theory was not its ability to discover social facts as such, but its value 'in informing actions, and in particular, political actions' (Johnson *et al.* 1990: 144). The Italian social theorist Antonio Gramsci (1891–1937) produced a social theory which was 'designed primarily to analyze capitalist relations in order to point out the strategic lessons for the socialist movement' (Hall 1988: 57). In the works of the contemporary German critical theorist Jürgen Habermas (1973; 1989), theory is considered by its ability to diagnose the ills of society and form part of the process of understanding and explanation that has implications for political action.

Habermas is critical of the separation of so-called facts from people's experiences which is common to what he terms the empirical-analytic rather than critical-emancipatory sciences (Habermas 1989). The potential for change exists in the creation of what he calls 'ideal-speech situations' (Habermas 1984; 1987). In such situations, people would discuss matters in a rational way, free from the constraints and power relations which impose weights upon them in society, and reach a consensus about the social world. Research based on critical theory would then be measured by its ability to reveal the relations of domination which exist in society:

At the heart of critical social research is the idea that knowledge is structured by existing sets of social relations. The aim of a critical methodology is to provide knowledge which engages the prevailing social structures. These social structures are seen by critical social researchers, in one way or another, as oppressive structures.

(Harvey 1990: 2)

Aspects of critical theory have been considerably modified in recent years with the advent of postempiricism, postmodernism and poststructuralism (Laclau and Mouffe 1985; A. Heller and Fehér 1988; Fraser 1989; Agger

1991; Morrow with Brown 1994; Calhoun 1995). Despite this, critical theory might be argued to be claiming to know the 'wishes and struggles of the age' regardless of whether people are conscious of this or not. Its theories would not then represent the everyday understandings which people have of their social environments and we would still be left with a gap between social theory and people's interpretations of social life. Perhaps, therefore, we should abandon the idea of attempting to invent a theory which aims to transcend or supplant people's everyday understandings.

With this in mind we now turn to the 'interpretative paradigm' of social theory and social research and an underlying drift away from realism, towards idealism. This was most clearly represented by the works of the German theorist Max Weber (1949) for whom subjective meanings used by people in social interaction are a starting-point for the objective analysis of society. However, a gap still remains between everyday subjective meanings and the use of objective theories to explain the social world. Thus, while influenced by Weber, some theorists have argued that the theoretical constructs of research should simply reflect the same everyday constructs which people use to interpret social life. In this way, there would not be a gap between social theory and the data generated on social relations. The topic of investigation for researchers would then be the common-sense methods that people use in making sense of their social environments.

This was the argument of the social theorist Alfred Schutz (1899–1959) and his criteria of the 'postulate of adequacy' for social theory. This simply means that our theoretical constructs of the social world must be compatible 'with the constructs of everyday life' (Schutz 1979: 35). Our research would then focus on people's subjective experiences and, in the words of Stanley and Wise (1990), not treat these as 'faulty' in terms of the theoreticians' categories. The focus would be on how people 'make up' the social world by sharing meanings and how they 'get on' with each other (inter-subjectivity). However, we are not then able according to Schutz, in contrast to Weber, to theorize beyond this world of common-sense understandings about social life towards the realm of causal explanation. In other words, the gap is closed by regarding any attempt to explain the social world beyond people's everyday understandings as unfounded.

Unlike critical theory, which emphasizes the way in which we are constrained by society, this method of theorizing examines how we create the social world through an inter-subjective process. We could take this even further to make a link between data and social theory in two ways. First, we should not even presuppose, as Schutz does, that there are shared meanings in the social world through which people interact with each other. Second, we should cease to try and uncover meanings behind appearances and instead take those appearances at face value. As a result, all social interactions should be treated as skilled performances by people and, it is argued, our presuppositions about social life would then be open to full scrutiny. We do not, therefore, seek to find 'motives' behind people's actions. Our topic of inquiry is the way in which people view society and render it comprehensible to each other using a 'documentary method of interpretation' (Garfinkel 1967). Common sense itself is a topic of research. We assume little about social life and dispel the idea that we can have access to an objective world beyond people's interpretations. Our research results are now assumed to be fully grounded in people's everyday understandings.

This particular form of closing the gap between theory and data has, its exponents would argue, a very different aim in mind to conventional research and theorizing (Sharrock and Watson 1988). Despite this, we are back to the same issue raised by critical theory and, in particular, the work of Antonio Gramsci (1971). Gramsci argued that common sense resulted from the operation of political and economic power within society. If we study the operation of common sense then we are studying the product of these relations. Critical theorists, on the other hand, would argue that we should be interested in the process through which they are constituted so they might be challenged and changed. In addition, researchers influenced by ethnomethodology often write as if unfettered by the cultures that are the objects of their inquiry, thereby replicating the error of empiricism. For this reason, these forms of theorizing are criticized as being not only empiricist, but also conservative.

Another way of characterizing the differences between the above approaches is that between micro and macro theory. Micro theory is more concerned with understanding face-to-face interactions between people in everyday life whereas macro theory is concerned with the behaviour of collections of people and the analysis of social systems or structures. How these two strands of theory might be synthesized has been addressed by researchers and theorists (see Knorr-Cetina and Cicourel 1981; N. Fielding and J. Fielding 1986; Hage 1994; Archer 1995). There are also those who have advocated middle-range theories (Merton 1957) which should situate themselves between grand theory and empiricism. Research would then be left with a series of testable hypotheses on particular aspects of people's behaviours. Once again, however, underlying this is the notion that there are facts independent of theory. Finally, there is the strategy of retroduction which is associated with realism. Retroduction refers to the process of building models of the mechanisms and structures which generate empirical phenomena through using a process of description, explanation and redescription (see Blaikie 1993: ch. 6).

In examining the relationship between social theory and social research, we have moved from critical theory to an interest in the practical usage of common sense. In an innovative way, rather than try to seek knowledge about society through theory and research, some researchers have examined, historically, how knowledge in society is produced and intimately connected with social power. We do not then seek to find a truth about society simply beyond people's conceptions of it, or simply in people's everyday practices, but how truth is formed in a relationship between knowledge and power in social practices (see Foucault 1980; Barrett 1991). This method of 'interpretive analytics' (Dreyfus and Rabinow 1982) has been applied to areas such as the operation of punishment and discipline within society (Foucault 1977) and the social construction of 'madness' (Foucault 1971).

Summary

The basis of theory has been examined in several ways: first, in terms of its needing to be based solely in fact (inductivism); second, by its being subject to empirical falsification (deductivism); third, by its reflecting the dominant trends of the discipline – as not being based upon rules of method, but the preferences of its scientists (Kuhn's paradigms); fourth, by its ability to diagnose and inform change (critical theory) and finally, by being grounded in the same constructs as people use in interpreting their social environments in everyday life (Schutz and Garfinkel).

Each of the above has been subjected to examination in terms of its relationship to research. While these are complicated discussions, a simple distinction between social facts and social values is often maintained. It is commonly thought that if values enter the research process, this renders its findings void. However, it has also been argued that values should enter our theories as a condition of research which is capable of critically evaluating how knowledge is produced and why some groups, more than others, are able to perpetuate their beliefs within society. The adequacy of such a theory focuses not only on the ability to understand and explain social life, but also the potential to change it.

How does this leave us as researchers? We are left, it seems, with an ambiguity over the question of the relationship between theoretical construction, empirical work and values. The practice of science, natural or social, is not simply a choice between facts and theory as there is, in the words of one commentator on methodology, 'no longer a reliable difference between theory construction and empirical work' (Baldamus 1984: 292). Further, social life itself is diverse and complicated and perhaps, therefore, not amenable to understanding through the use of a single theoretical paradigm.

These issues should not deter us. On the contrary, they provide food for conceptual thought by producing new ideas about the process of validating our inquiries and the concept of objectivity itself. Instead of seeing these as a problem, perhaps we should be subjecting our own values and practices and those of others to critical scrutiny in the pursuance of social science? As Charles Taylor notes:

> There is nothing to stop us making the greatest attempts to avoid bias and achieve objectivity. Of course, it is hard, almost impossible,

and precisely because our values are also at stake. But it helps, rather than hinders, the cause to be aware of this.

(C. Taylor 1994: 569)

In considering this question, how values enter the research process and affect the product of research is of central concern. To understand the ways in which this occurs and its effects on the research process requires, as noted at the beginning, a reflexivity on the part of researchers or, to express it another way, a consideration of the practice of research, our place within it and the construction of our fields of inquiry themselves. This is assisted by the constant interaction that exists between different interpretations of social life and the data which we collect on it. It also necessitates a further understanding of the issues involved in research practice: in particular, the relationship between values, ethics and social research. It is to these subjects that I now turn.

Questions for your reflection

1 Is research practice inevitably deductive or inductive, or does it involve elements of each process?

2 What are the aims of critical theory? How might these be justified according to the canons of scientific inquiry?

3 Alfred Schutz spoke of the 'postulate of adequacy' for social theory. However, Giddens speaks of a 'double hermeneutic'. What is meant by these terms and how do they relate to the process and practice of social research?

4 How important do you consider social theory is for the production of social research and for what reasons?

Suggested further reading

Bryant, C. G. (1995) *Practical Sociology: Post-empiricism and the Reconstruction of Theory and Application*. Cambridge: Polity.

Fielding, N. (ed.) (1988b) *Actions and Structure: Research Methods and Social Theory*. London: Sage.

May, T. (1996) *Situating Social Theory*. Buckingham: Open University Press.

Morrow, R. A. with Brown, D. D. (1994) *Critical Theory and Methodology*. London: Sage.

CHAPTER 3 Values and ethics in the research process

Values and social research
    What are value judgements?
    Values in the research process
    The connection between values and research
Ethics and their relation to social research
    What are ethics?
    Relations between ethics and social research
Summary
Questions for your reflection
Suggested further reading

So far I have sought to stimulate what might be termed a 'problem con-sciousness'. This has been done in the belief that there are no easy answers to the issues encountered in the practice of social research, but to be aware of the assumptions and limitations of our work, as well as its strengths, enables us to reflect upon them in a productive fashion and take appropriate action. With this in mind, this chapter examines the nature of value judgements, how values enter the research process and the different perspectives which exist on their influence in the production of social data. In the second section, the place of ethics in social research is considered. Given the values and interests that so often guide the research process, frequently unanticipated, ethics are a central part of maintaining the integrity, honesty and legitimacy of research practice.

Values and social research

A great deal of writing in the social and natural sciences has been devoted to the relationship between values and scientific practice. The purpose of this section is not to review this literature, but to assist in understanding this relationship in three ways. First, by understanding what is meant by value judgements. Second, through a consideration of the ways in which values enter the research process, and third, by examining the arguments which exist on the relationship between values and research.

What are value judgements?

In our everyday conversations and judgements, we make statements of two kinds: *positive* and *normative*. One idea of science prides itself on the ability to separate statements of what does happen (positive) and statements of what scientists would like to happen (normative):

> Positive statements are about what is, was or will be; they assert alleged facts about the universe in which we live. Normative statements are about what ought to be. They depend on judgements about what is good or bad, and they are thus inextricably bound up with our philosophical, cultural and religious positions.
>
> (Lipsky 1982: 5)

According to such a distinction science should strive to make judgements free from values. While this appears to separate questions about 'what are' the facts from 'what ought to be' the case, this is rendered doubtful by their constant interaction and the absence of a clear separation between beliefs within society and ideas within science. For instance, some religious groups in the nineteenth century believed that the world was only a few thousand years old. Subsequent geological advances demonstrated that some rocks were a million years old and others considerably older. In the face of such findings these religious groups had several choices. First, they could deny the validity of the scientific findings. Second, they could modify their convictions to account for such findings. Indeed, one writer on the relationship between theology and philosophy sees this as an important part of the intellectual development of those who are firmly committed to a set of beliefs (McPherson 1974). Finally, a situation of ambivalence might hold in which beliefs remain unmodified and evidence is accepted. In this instance a 'positive' scientific finding has apparently countered a religiously held belief. Yet positive scientific findings can be accommodated within belief systems. The 'Big Bang' theory of the origin of the universe, for instance, can be incorporated by arguing that God was responsible for the initial occurrence.

These examples demonstrate that the social or natural world is not as clear cut as a strict separation between fact and value, or positive and normative statements, would suggest. On the contrary, there is a constant interaction between scientific practice and societal beliefs which affects research practice, as well as those beliefs themselves. Scientists, for example, debate among themselves the concept and effects of global warming and the relationship between the amount of sugar a person consumes and the health of that person's teeth – to say nothing of the origins of the universe!

In the social sciences we routinely deal with phenomena which people are already busily interpreting and endowing with meanings and values. This makes our task as researchers a different one from that of the natural scientist. Nevertheless, we should not over-extend this argument as some have done. The natural environment is not only a contested arena, for instance, in relation to conservation, but also a simple separation of the social and natural worlds is often a difficult, if not impossible task.

We now need to ask what exactly are value judgements? To answer this question I shall use some examples (from Emmet 1981). In the first example, two people are asked to say which is the longer of two sticks by looking at and touching them (using their senses). We can then measure them with instruments to apparently solve any debate over which is the longer. This is said to be a matter of fact. However, is it as simple as that? Say the sticks were made of metal. At one temperature one may be longer than another (they have different coefficients of linear expansion). Which can we then say is the longer? Similarly, I place one in water and the other on a table. Which is then the longer? If I ask someone to tell me by look-ing at them, the way in which the light is reflected back to the person's eyes will be distorted by the medium. Which is the longer now depends on their temperature, their coefficients of expansion, the accuracy of the measuring instruments and the conditions under which they are observed. We might then be able to say which is the longer by adding these 'clauses' to our conclusions.

Take another example. Someone asks you which of two runners is the 'better'. As a researcher who seeks clarification before accepting defi-nitions as self-evident, you ask what the questioner means by 'better'. Such questions take the form of 'it depends what you mean by X'. You may know that runner A is better than runner B over 400 metres, but runner B is better than runner A over 1,500 metres. So you need clarifi-cation before you can answer because you are being asked to make a *comparative assessment* between the runners. There is not a 'correct' answer, because each is faster than the other at certain distances. Your answer will depend on which you prefer and why?

Finally, I have a chair and ask two people to sit in it and express an opinion on its comfort. One person says it is comfortable; the other says it is the most uncomfortable chair she has ever sat in! These people are expressing an opinion which they hold about the comfort of a chair. It is not a matter of fact capable of being verified, but a matter of personal taste. In between so-called matters of fact and matters of taste, we have a whole realm of judgements – simply called value judgements with which we, as social researchers, are constantly dealing. We make such judge-ments when we rate one thing against another, for example, teachers rating one essay as better than another.

Many people find the idea of value judgements uncomfortable – why can't they be factual? As a methodological problematic, this would require a strict separation of the language of observation from a theor-etical description of that being observed – a characteristic of logical posi-tivism that is, in practice, impossible to maintain (see M. Williams and May 1996: ch. 2). Instead of this route we might say that values are a fundamental part of the human condition and we should pose the question in a different way and thus seek a different answer. We should not seek the impossible – the elimination of value judgements – but ask the more important question: what types of values are the judgements based upon and how do these affect the judgements themselves?

Value judgements are dependent on beliefs and experiences in everyday life. They also concern what we would like our experience to be. This may arise from a bad experience in circumstances which we thought would be more pleasant. For instance, we attend a political meeting or join an organization and find that everyone is not as friendly as we hoped they would be. We went with an expectation of there being, say, participatory dialogue within a supportive atmosphere aimed at the achievement of understanding and appropriate action. However, this was not met by our experiences. Nevertheless, we might come away with an idea about how that meeting or organization should run along more co-operative, efficient and pleasant lines. Thus, we are not seeking to eliminate values because they inform and relate to the very reasons why we hold our beliefs, as well as the things to which we aspire. That said, we might seek to change the values which guided the way in which the meeting was conducted or the organization run. We would then need to understand the ways in which values entered this process; to say nothing of the nature and dynamics of power relations.

Values in the research process

The majority of large-scale social research projects in the UK are sponsored by governments, or other organizations or agencies. It might reasonably be suggested that they have a vested interest in any results. This is not to suggest that this necessarily invalidates the conclusions because the work is 'interested' as opposed to 'disinterested' (often assumed to be a characteristic of scientific activity). This is a mistake that people often make in the link between 'interest' and the pursuit of 'truth'. As Pierre Bourdieu notes of sociologists:

> If the sociologist manages to produce any truth, he does so not *despite* the interest he has in producing that truth but *because* he has an interest in doing so – which is the exact opposite of the usual somewhat fatuous discourse about 'neutrality'.
> (Bourdieu 1993: 11, original emphasis)

It is important to be aware of the issues which surround the production of a piece of work and the place and influence of values within it. As a matter of routine the following questions can be asked of any piece of research: who funded it? With what intention in mind? How was it conducted and by whom? What were the problems associated with its design and execution and how were the results interpreted and used? This enables an understanding of the context in which research takes place and the influences upon it, as well as countering the tendency to see the production and design of research as a technical issue uncontaminated by political and ethical questions. All research, implicitly or explicitly, contains issues of this sort. This is not to render the research invalid but, on the contrary, a recognition of such issues heightens our awareness of the research process itself and thereby sharpens our insights. Table 1 therefore illustrates the stages in which values enter the research process.

Table I Values in the research process

(1) Interests leading to research

(2) Aims, objectives and design of research project

(3) Data collection process

(4) Interpretation of the data

(5) The use made of the research findings

As we are all aware, different groups within society have different interests and frequently behave in ways to further those interests. An ability to define a problem or issue according to values will, in its turn, affect all stages of the research process but, in the first instance, its design and aim.

Consider this definition of social policy research as the

> *process of conducting research on, or analysis of, a fundamental social problem in order to provide policymakers with pragmatic, action-orientated recommendations for alleviating the problem.*
> (Majchrzak 1984: 12, original emphasis)

In such instances, social researchers should be cautious in accepting that a problem exists for which there must be a solution. How a problem is defined will depend on several factors, all of which either influence values, or enable some groups' values to predominate over others. Three factors, in particular, are significant: culture, history and social power. First, different cultures have different values. Because the values of different groups vary, what may be a problem to one group is not a problem to another. Heterosexual marriage is a value which has found its way into law in the UK. However, the idea that this is the only acceptable form of two people living together is challenged not only by other cultures, but also by groups within our own society. The Lele tribe of East Africa practise polyandry (one women may marry two or more men), while in the UK the phenomenon of heterosexism is increasingly challenged by lesbian and gay groups who wish to possess the right to live in a way accepted as legitimate. Quite simply, to be different is not necessarily to be deviant. Thus, values not only between but also within societies differ and research cannot assume that societies are characterized by something called 'value-consensus'.

Second, history changes and with it the way we perceive social problems. As time moves on so attitudes towards events and groups can alter. What is considered wrong or deviant at one point in time can be considered normal at another time: for example, the suffragette movement was considered subversive in the earlier part of the twentieth century. While attitudes to women's liberation still, in the main, range from support to suspicion and hostility, it is clear that the position of women in society has altered to some extent – particularly in the case of voting rights. As a result, social research needs to be aware of the changing conditions which define social problems.

Finally, social power is not evenly distributed between groups. The definition that there exists a problem will often depend on the relative power that the people who define the social problem have over those who are defined: for instance, those with access to the media may possess more power in the construction of social problems than those with limited access. Further, it may be easier to gain access to social groups who cannot mobilize their resources to prevent or control access, than groups who are more powerful. Given these factors, rather than simply accepting the definition, it is equally valid to examine the process through which a phenomenon became defined as a problem in terms of the power of social groups. In this way the idea that there exists a problem (product) is abandoned in favour of researching how it became constructed as one (process). This is a subtle but profound difference in research technique whereby social values themselves are subject to critical scrutiny.

The call for 'relevant' research is frequently heard, despite an ambiguity over what this actually means (Eldridge 1986). It is usually taken as that which serves the ends of particular interests. In such cases, the social researcher should ask the questions 'relevant for whom and why'? These interests may be constantly fed information by a whole army of social scientists. It is these social scientists that Bourdieu describes as social engineers, 'whose function is to supply recipes to the leaders of private companies and government departments' (1993: 13). Nevertheless, even if researchers are given a free rein to design research in any way they decide, or to undertake a research project into any social area they wish, it does not follow that it is then immune from values. Further, we should remember that while the production of research findings may be employed as a means of persuading people to pursue particular ends, there are other, often more effective, methods available. Indeed, while the anti-foundationalist philosopher Richard Rorty sees the role of social science as an 'interpreter' of different cultures, he does not regard science as being able to arbitrate in disputes over reality itself. In such cases the resort to an assertion of interests in the pursuance of a working consensus is the only solution (Rorty 1992).

In considering the values that inform the decisions of researchers in the course of their practice, feminists argue that the androcentric values of male researchers affects all aspects of their research practice from design, through data collection to interpretation and application. Similarly, a racist attitude can affect the way in which research is conducted, while social researchers may be heterosexist in their methods and interpretation, believing and perpetuating, for example, that a 'normal' and 'legitimate' family is one man and one woman who are married with children. In this instance, the invoking of normality is a value term. As noted, the use of such a term assumes that people living together who do not meet these criteria are then 'deviant' or 'abnormal'.

In the process of data collection, there are decisions to be made over the strengths and weaknesses of particular methods in relation to the aims and objectives of the research project. The decision as to which method to use may be based upon the researcher's own preferences, as opposed to applicability for the task at hand. Additionally, within the data collection process itself, there are a number of ethical and political decisions to be made. Researchers may wish to concentrate on one group of people rather than another, reflecting their own bias towards that group. More practically, they may concentrate on one group because it is easier to study that group (a frequent criticism of social research is its concentration on less powerful groups. As such, we know relatively little about 'elite' groups who may possess the power to prevent research being conducted in the first place).

The anticipation of the needs of a sponsor throughout the research process can also lead to the selection of data and the interpretation of those aspects of the research findings which 'prove' the sponsors' prejudices. It may be argued that this is becoming more of an issue as academics and contract researchers are under increasing pressures to publish and acquire research monies from funding agencies who follow particular agendas. This is a problem of *selectivity*. In being selective, a number of interesting findings can be dismissed which could aid understanding and explanation. In addition, researchers may not only anticipate the needs of the sponsors, but also interpret what they consider 'society at large' would find acceptable. Take, for example, a researcher who is examining crime statistics. Society at large is concerned about youth crime judging, that is, by all the media attention and police resources which have been devoted to this issue. However, in the process of undertaking the investigations the researcher discovers that a large percentage of violence takes place against women and children in domestic situations. Evidence of this type would clearly question the values of not only the researcher, but also society in general who exhibit a reluctance to intervene in what is taken to be the sanctity and security associated with 'normal' family life.

In research design, data collection and interpretation the researcher will, depending on the circumstances, influence the conduct of the research. This is not necessarily a disadvantage, bearing in mind the arguments of standpoint feminists that women's experiences are fundamental for the production of less distorted knowledge. It does mean that from the first stage (interests leading to research), through the second stage (aims, objectives and design of research project), right through to the fourth stage (interpretation of findings) the researcher must be aware of the place of values in the research process. What is more difficult to control and account for are the wider influences of values and how they affect research. This becomes a particular problem when the results reach a wider audience (the use made of research findings).

In this last stage political circumstances can take over regardless of the good will or intentions of the researcher. The research results may then be used for purposes for which they were not intended (known as the 'unintended consequences' of social action). For instance, during the Vietnam War, social scientists asked the people in rural areas of Indo-China questions which were designed to elicit or discover their moral and political allegiances. Despite the researchers being told that it was for scientific purposes, the information was allegedly used by the military to select bombing targets (J. A. Barnes 1979: 17). This brings us round to the section on ethics and a discussion of means and ends in social research. Before this, however, I wish to conclude this part of the chapter by examining perspectives on the relationship between values and research.

The connection between values and research

For those who adhere to the idea of 'value neutrality' throughout the research process, there are insurmountable problems in mounting a defence for this position. Most scientists would not, if asked, attempt to maintain this in the face of overwhelming arguments to the contrary. However, there are those who would adhere to the *values* of science and objectivity.

Ernest Nagel (1961) was aware of the arguments that social science cannot be value-free, but critics of their value presuppositions failed to take account of different types of value judgements. Nagel thus made a distinction between two types of value judgements: *characterizing* and *appraising* (Nagel 1961: 492–5). When scientists make a characterizing value judgement they are expressing an estimate of the degree to which something is present, such as dissent among protesters against road building through the countryside or attitudes to the use of cars and lorries and their effects on global warming. On the other hand, appraising value judgements express approval or disapproval of some moral or social ideal: for example, the disapproval of mainstream political parties of the aims of the Campaign for Nuclear Disarmament (CND).

In drawing this distinction, Nagel notes how the two are often indistinguishable. We make statements which contain both characterizing and appraising value judgements. Nevertheless, he argues that their separation is a practical task and not an insoluble one. If we succeed in separating the two, then we are left with characterizing judgements as a routine part of both the social and natural sciences. The possibility of a value-free social science (in terms of appraising judgements) is therefore a technical matter and not a theoretical impossibility.

Max Weber (1949), unlike Nagel, argued that the subject matter of the social sciences is fundamentally different from the natural sciences. In trying to understand people, we are obviously dealing with specifically human characteristics and these include 'meaning' and also phenomena such as 'spirituality'. However, despite our goal being an understanding of the subjective meanings that people attribute to their world, alongside that of explanation, Weber does share Nagel's belief that social science can be objective. It is, he argued, logically impossible for the social sciences to establish in a scientific manner the truth of ideals which people believe in – the normative or 'what ought to be' statements. What social science allows for is the determination of the suitability of a given range of means for the attainment of specified ends. In other words, if people desire a particular goal, then social science can assist them in finding the best way to achieve that goal. Social science cannot, however, tell people that they should accept a given end as a value, or tell them what they ought to believe in. In this way, the role of the social scientist is to demonstrate the pros and cons of different means and perhaps the social, economic and political costs involved, but not tell people what they should desire as ends. That, as Weber argues, is for the 'contemplation of sages and philosophers about the meaning of the universe' (Weber, in Gerth and Mills 1948: 152). The issue for a social scientist, as Weber puts it, is the absolute separation between two problems in the conduct of their research:

> first, the statement of empirical facts (including facts established by him about the 'evaluative' behaviour of the empirical human beings whom he is studying); and secondly, his own practical value position, that is, his judgement and, in this sense, 'evaluation' of these facts (including possible 'value-judgements' made by empirical human being, which themselves have become an object of investigation) as satisfactory or unsatisfactory.
>
> (Weber 1949: 78)

Why does Weber believe this? Quite simply, absolute values are a matter of faith and not of scientific knowledge. As social scientists we may be sufficiently committed to choose a particular area of study and so make a value judgement, yet from this point on, our work can be objective. Thus, values enter into research only in the problem selection stage. In a similar vein, in his discussion of social theory and social policy, Robert Pinker (1971) argues that social theory should be based upon what the members of society actually believe, not what the theorist tells them they ought to believe. Beyond this, the researcher may seek 'to inform or change public opinion, and to help create consciousness of problems where this consciousness is absent' (Pinker 1971: 131). The overt nature of the role of values in social research is therefore recognized in this formulation, but values must not determine the final product: 'the first function of scientific theory is ... to help us distinguish correct from incorrect knowledge' (Pinker 1971: 130).

Weber, Nagel and Pinker all share, to one extent or another, a belief in the possibility of fact-gathering, while recognizing the crucial role which values play in the research process (noting that objectivity is a value position). What is at issue is the place, role and type of values in social research. According to critics of these positions, social research is not a neutral medium for generating information on social realities (Gouldner 1962). Instead it is

> an activity recognized by many as not just unveiling the facts but as constructing them, and the researcher plays a major role in this. Thus enters the question of values in research activities as well, and a fuller discussion of what is good – that is, what values should guide the researcher in her studies and interventions – is required.
>
> (Ravn 1991: 112)

Once we accept that values enter the process of research at all stages, then it can be argued that the above accounts of Weber, Nagel and Pinker are based on certain versions of objectivity that variants of feminism and critical theory have rejected. Values do not simply affect *some* aspects of research, but *all* aspects. Furthermore, the idea of objectivity as detachment was criticized in Chapter 1 as being based upon a limited idea of science through its separation of reason and emotion. Instead of the attempt to separate the researcher from the researched, there are those who argue for the taking of sides in the research process (Becker 1967).

Others, influenced by feminist-based research, argue for 'dialogic retrospection' which is defined as: 'an open and active exchange between the researcher and participant in a partnership of co-research' (Humm 1995: 63). This formulation of active partnership is said to recognize that feelings and experiences are a routine part of the research process. In order to address this issue, rather than attempt to distinguish correct from incorrect knowledge (Pinker) or subjective realities from objective analysis (Weber), research must be a co-operative endeavour in which the researchers and participants share information and experiences. 'Correct' knowledge does not then come from detachment based on a limited concept of reason, as we saw in Chapter 1. Further, it is important to note that in questioning the relationship between research and objectivity as 'detachment', it does not follow that research cannot produce accurate knowledge.

For Habermas (1990), the strive towards what he calls 'objectivism' comes from bracketing the hermeneutic, or interpretative dimension, of the research process thus failing to see the historical influences upon our consciousness. If the social sciences are concerned with the explication of meaning then, by necessity, the interpretation of that meaning by the researcher must be included within the objects of its inquiries. It is at this point that a great deal of confusion arises concerning value-freedom. Because a researcher must explicate the meaning of an event, then values are clearly part of that process. For postmodernists, those values are specific to a given community and thus relative, thereby negating the scientific desire to generalize from specific instances. However, it does not follow that the means through which we interpret events are not themselves open to rational inquiry (Habermas 1992). To this extent, Weber's argument that ultimate values are beyond rational justification and therefore the province of the social sciences, is mistaken.

Those thinkers who argue for value-freedom, in whatever form, are viewed as inheriting a mythical distinction between reason and emotion so characteristic of the scientific claims which feminists seek to debunk. The consequences are that the researcher is expected to perform a role which no individual could possibly perform. To translate this into a feminist methodology, the research process should become:

> a dialogue between the researcher and researched, an effort to explore and clarify the topic under discussion, to clarify and expand understanding; both are assumed to be individuals who reflect upon their experience and who can communicate those reflections. This is inherent in the situation; neither the subjectivity of the researcher nor the subjectivity of the researched can be eliminated in the process.
>
> (Acker *et al.* 1991: 140)

In this criticism, experiences and encounters are recognized as part of the research process. Most feminist researchers do not seek their elimination, but their understanding; they do not seek to detach themselves from research, but instead seek to understand their place and experiences within social research as a central part of its process and product. This focus places researchers and their experiences at the centre of research which also enables a greater understanding of the social world. As one feminist researcher has put it:

> In my research diary (which was hard to distinguish from a personal diary since I was concerned to record my experiences and inter-actions within the prison, rather than so called 'objective obser-vations'), I noted a number of points which were relevant to the influence of (my) gender, age and race.
>
> (Gelsthorpe 1990: 95)

The place of commitment towards the improvement of women's position within society and the goals of a rational science, in some assumed detachment from the social world, are argued to be incompatible and impossible to sustain (Ramazanoglu 1992). Research which is explicitly and consistently feminist in orientation is conducted for the purpose of overcoming women's oppression. Values thus explicitly inform the design, process and product of research.

To separate the means and ends of research, in the manner Weber suggests, could not be sustained by the commitments of a feminist or critical research programme. Research which assumes 'facts' can be collected on the social world simply reflects and perpetuates unequal power relations which already exist within society. Weber's position would preclude the researcher from making any analysis and critique of the ends which any society, organization or group, pursues. Richard Titmuss, who placed values such as social justice at the forefront of his work on social policy, recognized this:

> There is no escape from values in welfare systems. . . . Not only is 'policy' all about values but those who discuss problems of policy have their own values (some would call them prejudices). But, whatever they are called, it is obvious that the social sciences – and particularly economics and sociology – are not, nor can ever be, 'value-free'.
>
> (Titmuss 1974: 132)

The above view does not lead to an 'anything goes' view of research. Certain standards are still needed in the conduct of research, particularly if the idea of a 'discipline' is to be maintained. Martyn Hammersley, in a neo-Weberian defence of value-neutrality, argues that:

> the most effective, though never fully successful, means of achieving objectivity in the process of inquiry is through the institutionalisation of research communities specialising in the production of knowledge (which is not to say that this is either a necessary or sufficient condition).
>
> (Hammersley 1995: 116)

Now the ways in which a community of researchers is constructed and conducts itself is of the upmost importance. This is an 'internalist' question regarding the ethics of a research community. At the same time, researchers, whatever their perspective, are routinely faced with choices about what is right or wrong in the conduct of their research on a given subject. This is the 'externalist' question of the relationship between researchers and the subjects of their research. It is with these latter questions that writings on the ethics of social research are mostly concerned.

Ethics and their relation to social research

Continuing with the theme of reflexivity in the research process, this section is divided into two parts. The first part asks the question 'what are ethics'? The second section then looks at the actual place of ethics in social research by considering the relationship between means and ends and the main ethical issues raised in the research process.

What are ethics?

How may we define the term ethics? To the layperson:

> the word 'ethics' often suggests a set of standards by which a par-
> ticular group or community decides to regulate its behaviour – to dis-
> tinguish what is legitimate or acceptable in pursuit of their aims from
> what is not. Hence we talk of 'business ethics' or 'medical ethics'.
>> (Flew 1984: 112)

In so far as researchers critically reflect upon their own views or those of
others, or consider the justification for their actions in comparison to
others, they enter the realm of philosophical ethics. Such considerations
are known as '2nd Order' questions: they are questions 'about things',
rather than simply taking them at face value.

A definition of ethical problems as they apply to social research is given
by John Barnes. He defines ethical decisions in research as those which

> arise when we try to decide between one course of action and
> another not in terms of expediency or efficiency but by reference to
> standards of what is morally right or wrong.
>> (J. A. Barnes 1979: 16)

Barnes is making a distinction here and basing ethical decisions upon
principles rather than *expediency*. This is an important point. Ethical
decisions are not being defined in terms of what is advantageous to the
researcher or the project upon which they are working. They are concerned with what is right or just, in the interests of not only the project,
its sponsors or workers, but also others who are the participants in the
research.

At the same time the particular interests that govern a research project
can influence those decisions that subsequently take place. Knowledge is
not simply a politically neutral product as would be maintained by positivism and empiricism. Ethical decisions will therefore depend upon the
values of the researchers and their communities and will inform the
negotiations which take place between the researcher, sponsors, research
participants and those who control access to the information which the
researcher seeks ('gatekeepers'). The amount of control the researcher
can exercise over the research process will also influence the exercise of
ethical decisions themselves.

For the above reasons the relationship between ethics and social
research is a complicated one. While the development of a code of ethics
for social research is a laudable aim, many argue that it must also recognize those factors which influence the conduct of research. Thus, Warwick and Pettigrew attempt a set of guidelines, but still note that there
are

> sources of ethical difficulties beyond the confines of social science
> itself – the sponsors of research and the mass media of

communication. Repeatedly, our discussion has shown how these influences contribute to ethical problems in policy research.

(Warwick and Pettigrew 1983: 368)

Given such a state of affairs, there are two ways in which approaches to ethics and social research have proceeded. These two approaches may not accurately reflect all ethical decisions which are made, but they are useful 'heuristic' devices (which means helping to study or discover, as in Weber's 'ideal types'). These approaches are known as *deontology* and *consequentialism*.

Deontological approaches to morality are associated with the work of Immanuel Kant (1724–1804). Quite simply, ethical judgements in social research would, from this point of view, follow a set of principles which guide the conduct of research itself. Research ethics take on a universal form and are intended to be followed regardless of the place and circumstances in which the researcher finds themselves. One such doctrine is that of 'informed consent'. This refers to a freely given agreement on the part of the researched to become a subject of the research process. However, this is not only based on a complete understanding of the aims and processes of the research itself, but also may assume to encompass any consequences that may follow from its publication in the public domain. A researcher might, and in many cases ought, to take all possible steps to protect the identity of any person in the anticipation of it being used for purposes other than those intended. Yet no individual can reasonable guarantee this outcome, while the actions they observe or accounts they receive may themselves transgress laws, morals or ethical codes.

With these scenarios in mind, consequentialism is not so concerned with following a set of inviolate rules, but with the situation in which researchers find themselves and with the consequences of their acts. According to this view, a set of doctrinal rules for the conduct of social research does not take account of its context. Thus, the British Sociological Association code of ethics states: 'Guarantees of confidentiality and anonymity given to research participants must be honoured, *unless there are clear and overriding reasons to do otherwise*' (1993: 3, emphasis added).

An argument might also be made that adherence to deontological ethical codes would entail undue restrictions on the researcher's activities and creativity. In this sense, actions may be justified if it prevents harm or offence to a person. The dilemmas that the researcher encounters are therefore not so different from those which we all face in everyday life:

The only difference is normally one of degree. That is, in 'research' settings most social scientists rarely have very intimate friends. If we had intimates in the settings, we would not be likely to think of the settings as a 'research' one. Since they are not intimates, we are under less social obligations to keep secrets about them. And we can

normally deal with almost all our problems of privacy by maintaining the anonymity of the people we write about.

(Douglas 1979: 29)

That said, Douglas does not rule out those who believe in professional
ethics, simply those who believe that ethical rules of research must be
applied rigorously in all settings. In particular, he notes that the development of professional ethics provides something of a safeguard against
encroachments on freedom of speech and research (Douglas 1979: 32).

Overall, rigid and inflexible sets of ethical rules for social research
(deontology) could leave us with undesirable consequences. Further, we
might conclude that 'the only safe way to avoid violating principles of
professional ethics is to refrain from doing social research altogether'
(Bronfenbreener, quoted in J. A. Barnes 1979: preface).

On the other hand, a loose and flexible system involving 'anything
goes' so easily opens the research door to the unscrupulous. As a result,
there are those who feel that both sides have their merits and weaknesses
(Plummer 1990: 141). If research is to be viewed as a credible endeavour,
then perhaps the relations which are established with all those party to
the research must utilize some ethical basis which provides guidelines for,
but not simply constraints on, the researcher?

With a huge growth in information technology and the potential for a
routine invasion of people's privacy, it becomes more likely that they may
refuse to co-operate with research. The formulation and adherence to a
set of ethical guidelines then enables the researcher to continually reflect
on the expectations which they make of people and their relationships
with those party to the research. This, as Douglas suggests, not only helps
to prevent social research becoming a mouthpiece of powerful vested
interests, but also assists in maintaining public co-operation and trust in
social research (Bulmer 1979b). Here, the 'internalist' concept of ethics
comes into play. The ways in which a centre or department concerned
with the production of social research conducts itself and discusses its
ideas in an open and inquiring manner, is a fundamental part of the
research process itself.

Relations between ethics and social research

In comparing ethical issues in the social and natural sciences, John Barnes
(1979) notes that those in the natural sciences relate more to the application than to the gathering of information. However, the use of animals
for experimentation and the ethical issues surrounding nuclear energy
and genetic engineering, for example, make this distinction less tenable.
This difference, therefore, as Barnes speculated (1979: 17), is now much
less apparent, particularly as studies of natural science have made clear
the role of social factors in the data gathering process itself (see Law
1994).

I have deliberately raised the question of ethics and natural science research. When reading about ethics in social sciences, there is a tendency to believe that ethical issues are not so important in the conduct of natural, as opposed to social science research. In addition, the use of the term 'science' often carries with it a justification of using various means of collecting information in pursuance of 'truth'. There are also those for whom the end may be justified in terms of the furtherance of a political cause or the heightening of a particular issue in the public conscience. This relationship between the means and ends of research has provided the focus for much debate.

Max Weber refers to the 'ethic of ultimate ends'. Under the banner of scientific inquiry in the search of truth, some would argue that it is possible to justify their actions. However, whatever the merit of their ends:

> From no ethics in the world can it be concluded when and to what extent the ethically good purpose 'justifies' the ethically dangerous means and ramifications.
>
> (Weber, in Gerth and Mills 1948: 121)

The means, in other words, cannot justify the ends. Yet in our current climate research is highly dependent on government and agency funding. These bodies have a vested interest in the conduct and findings of research. They may even explicitly impose their own conditions on the research process or, more commonly, their political expectations may govern the decisions which can be made during the research: for example, research on poorer sections of the community for the purposes of determining their 'eligibility' for state support. Should such information be gathered at any cost to the dignity of the individuals concerned, in order to try and save the government of the day money? If the government of the day justifies its actions by reference to democracy and the 'wishes of the majority' would this be satisfactory? Researchers would then have to ask themselves a number of questions to ethically justify being part of such a project.

First, if we are talking about a majority wish, this would work in a 'direct democracy' where all people have a channel of communication to all political decisions made in their interest. This is clearly not the case in any country which claims to be a democracy. Second, even if the majority 'willed' it, as one of the greatest advocates of democracy Alexis de Tocqueville (1805–59) was only too aware, the exercise of the 'tyranny of the majority' may predominate. Minority rights may then be ignored and we do not have to look deep into history, or glance at modern times, to see the disastrous consequences of such a course of action. Third, the researchers might ask themselves what autonomy from the sponsors they would have in the project in order to exercise some discretion in the design, collection and analysis of data; to say nothing of anticipating how the results might be used.

If researchers ignored the ends for which their research is intended and there are those who do through invoking various justifications, they could still provide the means for dubious ends. Claims of ignorance or lack of control may be justified in some instances, but 'collusion' can occur whether the researchers intended it or not. For Weber, however, social science could provide only the means, but not tell people the ends to which it should be employed. Researchers may even advise on the best means to pursue given ends, but again may not comment, as a social scientist, on the ends themselves. This is problematic. As noted, Habermas would challenge, from a rational viewpoint, the values which govern the ends to which research is used. More generally, it might be argued that means are inextricably related to ends.

The relationship between means and ends in research is a problematic one to which there are no simple answers. It is further clouded by a number of factors. Most importantly, there is the extent to which a scientific community organizes itself in a manner that promotes free and rational inquiry and recognizes and works against and not with, underlying power relations. I have in mind, for example, relations between younger and older members, women and men, black and white, and those on permanent and temporary contracts. Without this awareness in place, dubious practices are likely to flourish.

We are still left with a question: 'should the production of knowledge be pursued at any cost?' If so, we can then justify our means in terms of our ends. There is no simple answer to this. Once research reaches the public domain, as Warwick and Pettigrew (1983) noted, the control that the researcher can exercise over it changes. With a growth in information technology and the use to which research findings can be put, in the face of mass communication researchers find their power limited. However, this is not simply a one-way relationship. A wide dissemination of information can also work to undermine vested interests, as the use of coded information on the Internet for those fighting totalitarian regimes has made clear. Therefore, researchers can make tactical decisions in the process of research which have an ethical content and consequences. In this balance between people's privacy and the generation of knowledge, one of the classic debates centred around a research project undertaken by Laud Humphreys (1970). Although this work is dated, it is also often misunderstood and illustrates these dilemmas very clearly.

Humphreys conducted his doctoral dissertation as a covert participant observer (observation conducted without the knowledge of those being observed). He focused upon a number of homosexual acts in what were known as 'tearooms' (public rest-rooms). He became a familiar part of the social scene. This was assisted by his pastoral experiences in a part of Chicago known as 'queen parish', by making the 'rounds of ten gay bars then operating in the metropolitan area' and by attending 'private gatherings and the annual ball' (Humphreys 1970: 25). As a result, he was then able to adopt the role of 'watch-queen', the function of which was to act as a look-out, but who was also recognized as deriving pleasure from watching homosexual encounters. In this role, which he termed the 'sociologist as voyeur', Humphreys was able to record the events he witnessed.

During the period of his observations, Humphreys made a note of 134 licence plate numbers of the cars belonging to the men. By pretending to be a market researcher and making use of friendly contacts in the police force, he collected their names and addresses. Approximately one year later, after changing his appearance and now being employed on a social health survey of men, he sought the permission of the project director to add 100 of those original names to the health survey. He did this in order to collect further data on the participants. Most of the men in his study were married and not overt members of the gay community – often considering themselves neither bisexual or homosexual. He then called on their homes, under the guise of the health survey, to conduct his additional research. Their names were kept in a safe deposit box, no means of identification appeared on the questionnaires and the interview cards were destroyed after completion of the schedule (Humphreys 1970: 42).

Reactions to the publication of Humphreys' study were variable. As he notes in a postscript to the book: 'several have suggested to me that I should have avoided this research subject altogether' (1970: 168). He was accused of deceit, the invasion of privacy and increasing the likelihood of the sample's detection by the police force. One account suggests that some faculty members at Washington University were so outraged 'that they demanded (unsuccessfully) that Humphreys' doctoral degree be revoked' (Kimmel 1988: 23). On the other hand:

> The research was applauded by members of the gay community and some social scientists for shedding light on a little-known segment of our society, and for dispelling stereotypes and myths.
>
> (Kimmel 1988: 23)

In this sense, the means could be said to justify the end. Humphreys brought into the public domain an understanding of an issue which American society had done so much to repress. To his critics, however, the means can never justify the ends:

> Social research involving deception and manipulation ultimately helps produce a society of cynics, liars and manipulators, and undermines the trust which is essential to a just social order.
>
> (Warwick 1982: 58)

For those who have used such methods, they may be justified according to the nature of the research materials which they produce in relation to the power that one group may hold over another. Rosenhan's (1982) research involved eight sane people gaining admission as 'pseudopatients' to mental hospitals. This followed their display of certain 'symptoms'.

This process may be argued to have gained information on psychiatric diagnoses not available by other means. It became apparent that, despite the 'science' of psychiatry, 'we cannot distinguish the sane from the insane in psychiatric hospitals' (Rosenhan 1982: 36). As he notes, this was a general criticism of the psychiatric system and was not aimed at the individuals who treated these pseudopatients. Indeed, he notes that these staff were committed and cared for their patients (Rosenhan 1982: 37). This research thereby constituted

> a striking example of how knowledge as enlightenment may be obtained by the benign use of deception and where the use of deception on obtaining information increases rather than decreases its credibility.
>
> (J. A. Barnes 1979: 125)

Similarly, Nigel Fielding's (1981) reflection on his work on the National Front saw him adopt the role of interpreter between the inner workings of this organization and society in general. His hope was that the end result assisted people outside of the organization to 'understand its appeal' and that in a more political vein, this enabled the National Front's opponents 'to persuade those susceptible to membership that the answers to our problems do not lie in racist politics' (N. Fielding 1982: 104).

The relationship between means and ends in social research and the ethical decisions, power and disposition of the researchers themselves, are clearly difficult issues. Any debate tends to focus upon the use of covert participant observation because it seems to raise the central issues of knowledge production and its relationship to privacy. Yet in an information society where so much data is routinely stored on individuals (Poster 1990), invasions of privacy are more likely to become a routine part of our lives. This does not give social research licence to conduct itself without due consideration to privacy. It does, however, widen the scope of ethics and social research to incorporate surveys (Bulmer 1979a), as opposed to exclusively focusing upon covert participant observation. It also focuses our attention on the relationship between the production of research and the use to which it is subsequently put.

Summary

From our discussions on values and ethics, it is evident that the idea of research free from values is problematic. Indeed, value-freedom is itself a value position! Social research takes place within a context in which many of its rules of procedures are taken for granted. These 'background assumptions' (Gouldner 1971), upon which research decisions and analysis are based, should be open to scrutiny. Without this in place, social research can so easily reflect the prejudices of society in general, or a research community in particular. At the same time, it is worth remembering that social life, while illuminated by social research, does not ultimately depend upon it. Decisions are constantly made which directly affect our lives and which are not based upon systematic research. As one commentator puts it: 'Life cannot wait for social research to catch up with it' (Shipman 1988: 67).

As feminist and radical critics have pointed out, simply 'knowing about' the issues of values and ethics is not a sufficient basis upon which to conduct research; they need to form part of research practice itself. Values and experiences are not something to be bracketed away as if ashamed by their entry into the process. On the contrary, many now argue that an examination of the basis of values and their relationship to decisions and stages in research is required in order to provide justifications for systematic and valid social research. The aim is not their elimination, for this is impossible. Instead, these criticisms acknowledge that research takes place within a context where certain interests and values often predominate to the exclusion of others. 'Objective' research is not then achieved by uncritically accepting these as self-evident. This standpoint may well result in the perpetuation of discriminatory practices. At the same time, social researchers may have to acknowledge that their individual power may be limited in acting on this state of affairs. Despite their best efforts, they cannot guarantee to control the use to which research might be put, nor to exercise full control over the process.

Social researchers need to recognize that there are limits to counteracting and apologizing for the wider societies of which we are all a part. This recognition, however, does not license acquiescence, nor relieve a research community from a responsibility for drawing up and conforming to a set of ethical guidelines. The development and application of research ethics is required not only to maintain public confidence and to try and project individuals and groups from the illegitimate use of research findings, but also to ensure its status as a science.

Questions for your reflection

1 In what ways do values enter into social research?

2 Can values be justified?

3 Does an acknowledgement of the role of values in social research necessarily diminish its status as a science?

4 You have been awarded £50,000 by a large sponsor of social research to conduct research into the characteristics of young people who commit crime. You are told that the results of your research will be used by the police, social and probation services in 'tackling' offending. What value and ethical dilemmas do you face in conducting this research?

Suggested further reading

Bulmer, M. (ed.) (1979a) *Censuses, Surveys and Privacy*. London: Macmillan.

Hammersley, M. (1995) *The Politics of Social Research*. London: Sage.

Homan, R. (1991) *The Ethics of Social Research*. London: Longman.

Kimmel, A. (1988) *Ethics and Values in Applied Social Research*. London: Sage.

PART II Methods of social research

CHAPTER **4** **Official statistics: topic and resource**

Sources of official statistics
The social construction of crime statistics
Official statistics: the debates
Summary
Questions for your reflection
Suggested further reading

The information that is available on the demographic characteristics of the population, their opinions, attitudes, values and lifestyles, is considerable. The volume of material collected on a routine basis by the government and its agencies provides a rich source of data for the social researcher. In the first section of this chapter, I shall examine the common types of official statistics that researchers may utilize. However, there is a temptation to use such data without due consideration being paid to their weaknesses, as well as their strengths. Official statistics, like social research itself, may employ unexamined assumptions about social life which, if one is not cautious, may be inherited and reproduced in studies. Given this, we should view them not simply as 'social facts', but also as social and political constructions which may be based upon the interests of those who commissioned the research in the first instance. As such, the researcher needs to understand how they were constructed and for what purpose. In order to assist in this process, the second section of this chapter will consider the construction of crime statistics. A third section will then outline various perspectives on the use of official statistics for the purpose of conducting social research.

Sources of official statistics

The term 'official statistics' normally refers to data collected by the state and its agencies. In 1837 the General Register Office was established, with registration of deaths placed on the political agenda. During the 1840s regular statistical reports began on subjects such as births, deaths and crimes.

In contemporary times official statistics cover the economy, crime, employment, education and health – to name but a few. This heading would also include the ten-year Census of the population, which began in 1801 with government concerns over the growth of the population exceeding its available resources, as well as the Family Expenditure Survey, which began in the 1950s for constructing the Retail Price Index as a cost of living indicator, but has also been used as an estimate for the number of people living in poverty (see McGregor and Borooah 1992). Included also are the General Household Survey (GHS) and British Social Attitudes Surveys (BSAS). The former began in the 1960s and the latter in 1983, both with the intention of being used for secondary analysis (see Kent 1981; A. Dale *et al.* 1988).

Secondary analysis is defined as

> any further analysis of an existing data set which present interpretations, conclusion of knowledge additional to, or different from, those presented in the first report on the inquiry as a whole and its main results.
>
> (Hakim 1982: 1)

Official statistics, such as the BSAS and GHS, represent an extensive source of data on changing attitudes to particular social issues and the composition and incomes of households which are then available for analysis. However, while the General Household Survey represents a rich data set, the topics included 'are those accepted as of significance to officialdom' (A. Dale *et al.* 1988: 18). For this reason, as we shall see in the third section of this chapter, there is a debate over the use of such surveys.

This is not an exhaustive list of official statistics. For instance, we could add the Central Office of Information which produces an *Official Handbook* covering such topics as the environment, economic and social and cultural affairs. Compiled with the assistance of some 250 organizations, including government departments, its intention is to provide: 'a factual overview of Government policy and developments in Britain' (Central Office of Information 1994: foreword). In Europe, Eurostat produces *Europe in Figures* which covers some eighteen areas including the labour market, standards of living, money and finance and services such as transport and tourism. Its task is to

> provide today's Europeans with information in developments in Community policies based on uniform definitions and data-collection methods to enable them to make informed choices and decisions.
>
> (Eurostat 1992: foreword)

These sources gives some idea of the enormous volume and range of data which are produced or sponsored by the state, government and its agencies that may also be accessible via the Internet. To these we could add what are referred to as ad hoc or one-off surveys conducted by the

Office of Population Censuses and Surveys (OPCS). A. Dale *et al.* (1988) note, for example, 'Smoking Attitudes and Behaviour', 1984 Women and Employment (WES) and Family Formation surveys. Such studies

> usually relate to a specific topic that is of current policy interest. They are commissioned not just for the purposes of providing back- ground data but also with the aim of increasing understanding within the area of concern.
>
> (A. Dale et al. 1988: 9)

These statistics enable us to understand the dynamics of society – perhaps along race, class, age and gender lines – as well as charting trends within society (hence the title for one of the most detailed government statistical publications, *Social Trends*). This information provides government and social policy formulators with data upon which to base their decisions, as the Eurostat foreword indicated, as well as the means to forecast and evaluate the impact of new social policy provisions (see Berridge and Thom 1996). In short, enormous amounts of information are collected, stored and used about individuals in society. This information is also used by market researchers who, for commercial reasons, are interested in the tastes, habits and opinions of the population.

Both the production of official statistics and their secondary analysis are not unproblematic enterprises. It is at this point that the different theoretical schools of thought and their approaches to research become apparent. Each of these considers the use of official statistics in a differ- ent way. Therefore, it is helpful to frame this discussion by using an example and for this purpose I have chosen crime statistics. In so doing the reader should be aware that these are commonly criticized for their limitations and some of the discussion should not be uncritically applied to other areas of statistical compilation. However, it does demonstrate the process through which official statistics are produced and how that affects the final product. As we shall see in the third section, there are those who believe the product is useful for social research and those who reject their utility and concentrate only upon the process of their con- struction.

The social construction of crime statistics

Criminal Statistics are published for England and Wales each year. They provide policy-makers and researchers with an indicator of the types of crimes being committed and the extent to which crime is increasing or decreasing according to the implementation and impact of criminal jus- tice policies. In addition, there are the *Prison Statistics, Probation Statis- tics* and *Judicial Statistics*.

It is not uncommon for us to read in newspapers of a 'new crime wave'. This contributes to a fear of crime which alters the habits of society's vulnerable groups: for example, elderly people locking their doors, not going out at night and avoiding certain areas. Researchers have also shown that women's fear of crime, in particular, is real enough and should not be dismissed as simply 'false' (Stanko 1990). That noted, can we be sure that these statistics are an accurate picture of the extent and nature of crime in this country? If not, then the decisions of policy-makers and media presentations of crime, based upon this information, will be limited and in some instances entirely wrong. In order to understand this question we need to examine the ways in which an initial act becomes officially defined as criminal.

To have confidence in using official statistics on crime, we must be sure that they fulfil the criteria of *validity* and *reliability*:

> Research is valid when the conclusions are true. It is reliable when the findings are repeatable. Reliability and validity are requirements for both the design and the measurement of research. At the level of research design, we examine the conclusions and ask whether they are true and repeatable. At the level of measurement, we examine the scores of observations and ask whether they are accurate and repeatable.
>
> (Kidder 1981: 7)

The following conditions must hold in order to sustain the validity and reliability of official statistics on crime. First, a similar incident or act of breaking the law must be categorized in the same way by those responsible for compiling the crime statistics. We must assume, therefore, that there is little room for discretion to enter the recording of such information and if it should, it is exercised in a manner that produces the same final classification. If this is not the case, then similar incidents will be categorized in different ways. Second, our statistics must be mutually exclusive so that two different occurrences cannot be categorized in the same way. If two different incidents can be categorized in the same way, then our statistics cannot be reliable: that is, accurate and repeatable. Third, it follows that the categorization of criminal acts must be exhaustive: that is, all criminal acts committed are categorized under a particular heading and included in the official statistics. For instance, all burglaries committed on a daily basis are recorded by the police. To consider how official statistics on crime measure up to these criteria, I shall examine the process through which a criminal act becomes a crime statistic.

First, an act is defined as being criminal. At this point there are two important aspects to bear in mind. For an act to be 'criminal' it must be defined as such by the criminal law (and we make a distinction between criminal and civil law). In addition, someone, aside from the perpetrator, must know that a criminal act took place, otherwise, quite simply, it will not be detected except in cases of self-confession, or the perpetrator is caught for another act and asks for others to be 'taken into consideration' (TICs). Even at this first stage we face two issues in the compilation of crime statistics: the *definition* of an act as criminal and the *detection* of that act.

While the idea of 'definition' may seem non-problematic, it is important to remember that what is criminal in one society may not be in another, while the definition of criminal varies across time. As with the discussion on social problems in Chapter 3, the idea of what is criminal changes in societies with history, culture and the power that particular groups have to frame social definitions. In other words, the idea of a 'criminal' is not a static definition, but changes with time: it is a *diachronic*, not *synchronic* concept.

The issue of detection is also problematic. The decision to report a crime by a member of the public will depend on a number of factors. These include a sense of obligation that a crime ought to be reported, or that the crime was of a serious nature, or that by reporting the crime it lessens the risk to others. Further, the individual may benefit through the possibility of recovering their property, reducing their risk of further incidences of victimization, or that it is a requirement of an insurance company. Finally, they may do so because they wish an offender to be caught and punished accordingly (Mirrlees-Black *et al.* 1996: 24). At the same time we are often faced with the spectre of the 'anonymous attacker' on our streets. Of course, such events occur. However, it is not necessarily the public arena where women, for example, may be threatened:

> While initial concerns about sexual danger focused on the malevolence of faceless men, familiar and familial men in women's lives – intimates, acquaintances, authorities and service providers, pose the greatest threat to women's physical and sexual safety.
>
> (Stanko 1990: 175)

Given this, will a woman who is the victim of domestic violence perpetrated by her partner necessarily report it to the police according to the criteria listed above? As the authors of the *British Crime Survey* Report note: 'there is some doubt as to how accurately the BCS measures domestic violence' (Mirrlees-Black *et al.* 1996: 30). Studies have shown that women tend to conceal such experiences from the police, as well as from researchers (Stanko 1990). The detection of the crime of domestic violence depends upon the possibility of the victim reporting it without fear of repercussions – physical, emotional and material. In addition, it depends upon police practices and their willingness to see an incident as a legitimate part of their normal duties. As Jill Radford concludes from her research on violence against women:

> routine harassment and assault, such as being followed, flashed at or verbally abused are such regular experiences for women and so readily dismissed as 'trivial' or discounted on the grounds that 'nothing actually happened' that few women even consider them as worth reporting to the police. Yet, it is clear from the accounts we heard

that these attacks are as much a form of terrorism as those acknowledged by the patriarchy as 'criminal'.

(Radford 1990: 35)

Although very different in form, crimes at work are often not reported for
fear of losing jobs, or companies not wishing to attract adverse publicity,
or simply that there is a lack of confidence in the capabilities of official
agencies to tackle the crime effectively (Croall 1992). For these reasons,
crime statistics tend to reflect so-called street crimes which are visible,
rather than white-collar and domestic crimes which are difficult to detect
and take place within conventional working environments or domestic
spheres.

In terms of the types of offences that official statistics reflect, *Criminal
Statistics* comprise the following offences recorded by the police. First,
most indictable offences (defined as those triable by a judge and jury at
Crown Court). Second, some summary offences which mean those
offences which, if reaching the trial stage, are triable at a magistrates
court, and third, 'either way' offences. These final categories, as the name
implies, may be tried in either court. Overall, this range is frequently
assumed to reflect more 'serious' offences recorded by the police. However:

> many minor offences are included; all thefts are included, even
> though the property stolen may be some sweets or a bottle of milk
> from a doorstep. By contrast, no statistics are provided on the inci-
> dence of most summary *offences*, although some information is
> given about *persons processed* for such offences in the statistics
> about offenders.
>
> (Coleman and Moynihan 1996: 27, original emphasis)

Matters of detection, definition and police practices thus affect the production of crime statistics. In turning our attention to these issues, we
have examined the initial process through which a crime statistic is produced. The compilation of official statistics on crime are now dependent
upon two criteria which directly influence their validity and reliability.
First, a set of *discretionary procedures*, for example, the decision of individuals to report an incident to the police and the decision of police
officers to record an incident and take the matter seriously. Second, *insti-
tutional practices*, which include the policies of the police force and the
government in tackling certain offences. In practice, these two are very
difficult to separate. Thus, what a police officer decides to do will depend
not only on the circumstances of the incident, but also on the organizational policies which the officer is instructed to follow and the culture of
the police organization itself. It is this latter aspect that may come to predominate in the performance of duties. The process of socialization of
new recruits leads them to focus upon 'not what the job is for, but how
it is and ought to be done' (N. Fielding 1988a: 50). Examining police

cultures and their corresponding interpretive procedures therefore tells us more about how statistics are compiled, than taking official crime statistics at face value.

In focusing upon the organizational culture of the police we are beginning to see that 'criminal facts' do not simply speak for themselves, but possibly tell us more about organizational practices and power relations within society. If an incident occurs where the police are faced with a case of violence in the home and their organizational and discretionary definitions of domestic violence are not capable of categorizing this, we cannot then say it did not happen! In addition, even if the police do act in such circumstances, the courts may categorize such incidents as 'trivial' in comparison to other crimes – despite the severity of the offence (Edwards 1990). Quite simply, if a crime act does not enter the statistics then, officially at least, it did not occur. For these reasons official statistics on crime are criticized by researchers for revealing little about violence against women, in particular (Kelly and Radford 1987), and more generally, for their sexist nature (Oakley and Oakley 1979; Ginn and Duggard 1994).

Officially, the procedures and ideas through which an act becomes a crime statistic looks like the stages shown in Table 2.

Table 2 The stages in the process of compiling official statistics – the official version

The law is democratically arrived at and applied equally to all people at all times

A criminal act takes place and the law is broken

The crime is known to a member of the public who reports it to the police

The police react and all similar incidents are treated in a similar way without prejudice

The offender is detected, apprehended and charged with the offence

The offender is, without prejudice, subject to sanctions by the criminal courts

The initial act becomes a crime statistic

If we move away from the formal definition in Table 2 to one which reflects the situations we have described so far, we end up not with 'facts' about crime, but the result of a series of decisions and practices which do not produce either valid or reliable outcomes. The process then becomes more like Table 3.

It appears that we cannot assume that the law applies equally to all incidents as this depends upon the initial detection of the act and the way

Table 3 The stages in the process of compiling official statistics – an alternative version

---

The law changes over time. Further, it does not apply equally to all people at all times

➡

A crime is committed, but is it reported?

➡

If reported, will the decisions of the police apply to all similar incidents in the same way?

➡

The crime may be reported, but not recorded

➡

If recorded, not all offences are included in the statistics

➡

If recorded, the perpetrator may not be apprehended by the police

➡

If detected, not all people are treated in the same way by officials in the criminal justice system, even when they have committed similar crimes

➡

Official statistics are compiled which are neither valid nor reliable

---

in which the matter is dealt with by the police. Holding aside the question as to whether the law is biased in the first instance, it was noted that this will depend on whether the incident is reported and what action is taken as a result. From surveys conducted by interviewing a random sample of the general public, estimates show that, over time, between 36 and just under 49 per cent of crimes committed on a daily basis are reported to the police (Hough and Mayhew 1983; Mirrlees-Black *et al.* 1996). Thus, according to these estimates, between six in ten, or one in every two crimes committed on a daily basis, never even reach the attention of the police as gatekeepers of the official crime statistics.

The key elements in the alternative process as constructed in Table 3 are *interpretation*, *discretion* and differential *application* and *enforcement*. Between the construction of the law, someone breaking that law and being sanctioned for the original act, there stands the interpretation of the victim, police and other officials in the criminal justice system. Will all officials act in a similar way so we can say that they are both valid (a true picture) and reliable (always recorded in the same way)? If different people record the same incident in different ways and people are treated differently for the same crime, then how can the statistics be valid? As we have seen, the decision to report a crime in the first instance, the decision to pursue a particular case and how its outcome will be determined are not neutral products applying to all people at all times. As a final example to clarify these issues, I shall consider the link between crime statistics and race.

Afro-Caribbean groups form approximately 1.5 per cent of the total population in the UK. In the British prison population as a whole, they form nearly 12 per cent (Penal Affairs Consortium 1996). In other words, many more people from this group end up in jail in comparison with their percentage in the general population. An immediate conclusion seems to indicate that black people are more criminal than white people. After all, statistics seem to demonstrate this clearly. However, let us look at the criminal justice process to see if this is an 'objective' indicator of criminality, or the result of discriminatory decision-making.

We start, once again, with the decision to report a crime. The police are reliant upon the general population to report crimes to them. Yet evidence shows that if an assailant is thought to be black, white people are more likely to report an offence to the police than if the same offence were committed by a white person (Carr-Hill and Drew 1988). Further, when it comes to the police detecting crime themselves, research conducted at two London police stations found that young black males, aged 16 to 24, were ten times more likely to be stopped by the police under stop and search powers (C. Willis 1983). Further, even if arrested for the same offence, white juveniles are significantly more likely to receive a caution than their black counterparts (Crow 1987). If then processed through the criminal courts, black people are also liable to be dealt with in a different way by the courts (Shallice and Gordon 1990). Evidence also suggests that black people are sent to prison more often than their white counterparts (Voakes and Fowler 1989). Of course, this might be accounted for in the differences in the offences committed. However, even where the severity of offences is controlled for, studies have found significant differences in the custody rate for black offenders over their white counterparts (Hood 1992). As John Solomos puts it:

> There is widespread evidence that the criminal justice system is now one of the key mechanisms by which ideas about racial differences in British society are reproduced.
>
> (Solomos 1993: 133)

What exactly is going on here? Is it a neutral process of reporting, detecting and processing criminals regardless of their race? Research into the actual process of criminal justice appears to show that statistics which link race and crime are not neutral, but the product of a series of discriminatory decisions. It is for these reasons that so many black people end up in prisons. The creation of racial stereotypes within the criminal justice system has an indirect impact on attitudes and actions which, in turn, construct the crime statistics. For this reason, a consortium representing some 31 organizations associated with criminal justice has pointed to the need for programmes of action which aim 'to combat discrimination in the criminal justice process' (Penal Affairs Consortium 1996: 8). At the same time, it is important to bear in mind that issues of race, while of clear significance in the interpretation of these findings, also interact with other variables: for example, those of class, age, gender and belief systems.

We have seen the problems associated with the construction of criminal statistics. From the decision to report a crime, through the police decision to pursue an investigation, to the courts' decision to sanction offenders – if they are caught – a number of different practices leads to a variable outcome. For these reasons, we should treat official statistics on crime with considerable caution. Nevertheless, these issues are not so clear cut and as we shall see in the next section, there exists a debate on the use of official statistics as a resource for conducting social research.

Official statistics: the debates

We have considered the means by which one of the most contentious of official statistics are compiled. However, in order to enable the reader to consider the issues surrounding their use, it is important to bear in mind two points. First, what *type* of official statistics are we talking about? Second, what is the *aim* of the research which is either compiling or examining these statistics? Official statistics will vary in terms of not only their accuracy – statistics of birth rates compared, for example, with crime statistics – but also the way in which they are compiled. Thus, these considerations will affect our judgements about their utility for analysis. Further, what are the statistics being used for? You may wish to examine statistics on crime as an indicator of the incidence of drug-taking. On the other hand, perhaps the police are concentrating on drug-taking and while this will mean an increase in the statistics, you decide not to examine the accuracy of the statistics themselves, but use them as an indicator of police practices. The aim of this project would be very different from one wishing to 'objectively' discover the incidence of drug use in the population as distinct from interpretative procedures. Having made these points, attention will now be turned to the debates between schools of thought on official statistics.

For the sake of illustration, we can divide perspectives on official statistics into three broad schools of thought. First, the *realist* school, second, the *institutionalist* school and finally, the *radical* school of thought. What do these three terms mean? The realist school is not to be confused with realism as covered in Chapter 1. Broadly speaking this school is characterized as taking official statistics to be objective indicators of the phenomena to which they refer. As a result, they may be characterized as drawing their inspiration from positivism and empiricism.

The institutionalist school of thought rejects the idea that official statistics are objective indicators of the social conditions they seek to describe. Instead, they consider official statistics as neither valid nor reliable indicators of objective phenomena. For the institutionalists, official statistics will tell us more about an organization's behaviour or the discretionary actions of individuals within them, rather than the phenomenon itself. In the above example on drug use, the institutionalists would argue that statistics on drug use tell us more about an organization's priorities and the actions of its representatives, than about the amount of drugs which the population are taking at any one time. This is why people refer to the 'iceberg phenomenon' when it comes to crime statistics: that is, all we ever see is the tip of the iceberg and most crime is out of sight and undetected. This school of thought therefore parallels idealism, in terms of its emphasis upon the social construction of statistics, as discussed in Chapter 1.

Finally, there is the radical perspective. While agreeing with the institutionalists that such statistics represent an organization's priorities or are the product of discretionary practices, they would locate these within a wider theory of the dynamics and structure of society. For instance, the government compile social statistics on the health and income of the nation which itself could be argued to facilitate the order and regulation of the population (Foucault 1980; Squires 1990):

> The invention of programmes of government depended upon and demanded an 'avalanche of printed numbers', which rendered the population calculable by turning it into inscriptions that were durable and transportable, that could be accumulated in the offices of officials, that could be added, subtracted, compared, and contrasted. The term given to these practices of inscription was 'statistics'.
>
> (N. Rose 1991: 6)

From a perspective more informed by critical theory, to this group we could add the ways in which the police concentrate on and process more working-class crime because this group are relatively less powerful and their crimes more visible compared to middle-class groups (Hall *et al.* 1978). Thus, we should note that those whom I have placed in this school of thought might not necessarily 'read off' official statistics as indicative of underlying structures of power: for example, along the dimensions of race, class and gender. Michel Foucault's pluralist theory of power, for instance, does not lend itself to such a mode of analysis (see May 1996: ch. 9). Statistics are also analysed in terms of their effects as *products* as well as in terms of being *constructions*:

> because the definitions used are determined by organizations and are usually imposed upon the subjects of statistics irrespective of the meaningfulness of these categorizations to the subject.
>
> (Thomas 1996: 3.2)

What are the effects of this production and construction of official statistics in practice? Take the example of child abuse. Who are the people who sexually abuse children? They are typified to us are through the newspapers, television and other media in particular ways. So what is our *typical* offender? The impression is often of someone who lurks in an old raincoat near children's playgrounds and school playing fields; they are isolated and inadequate individuals whose inadequacies constitute a danger to children. The police, in their turn, police public areas, not the private homes of individuals. They seek those individuals who may fit this stereotype and act on it by using grounds of 'reasonable suspicion'. Some individuals are apprehended who reflect this stereotype and it appears that its 'truth' has been established. However, as one writer on child abuse has noted: 'The closer to home the abuse, the more ambivalent the legal and indeed the popular response' (Viinikka 1989: 132).

The accounts of incest survivors, coupled with the work of the feminist movement, have brought such issues more into the public arena. This has resulted in changes in the practices of the police and other agencies, such as social services. The question remains, however, as to whether this is but an act of trying to maintain the legitimacy of the family as a 'safe' institution. More critical accounts of this process suggest that the compilation of these statistics reflects the notion of an ideal family and that 'every man's home is his castle'. To this extent changes do not challenge underlying relations of patriarchy which relates to the power that men exercise over women and children (Radford and Stanko 1996).

From this point of view we can say that the more private and invisible from the gaze of agents of social control (including social services), the less the chance of detection of child abuse (the feminist criticism of the public/private dichotomy). Indeed, evidence suggests that such abuse is far more widespread than the statistics would have us believe (Driver 1989; Coleman and Moynihan 1996). Most child abuse takes place in families and is often not detected. Thus, it may not be the stranger in the old raincoat at the local park who constitutes a danger to children: the abuser may be a close relative, friend or acquaintance.

Given this state of affairs it is argued by critics of official statistics that they help to generate myths by reflecting power relations and ideologies within society – in this case the 'familial' ideology of the harmonious and secure institution of the family. Of course, this is not to suggest that an abuser may not be a 'stranger', simply that official definitions distort the idea of those who are mostly responsible for this offence, as well as its underlying causes (see Hester *et al.* 1996).

Earlier on I quoted a statistic saying that fewer than four out of ten crimes committed are reported to the police. If the official statistics are so inadequate, how did I know this? At regular intervals from 1981 to 1996 (see Hough and Mayhew 1983; 1985; Mirrlees-Black *et al.* 1996) the Home Office has undertaken random surveys of the population in England, Wales and Scotland (from 1993 Scotland had its own survey). By asking people questions about their experiences of crime, a picture was formed of the number of crimes committed in England and Wales, but which were not reported to the police for various reasons. The results of this self-report study have been used in comparison with official statistics as recorded by the police. It is then possible to compensate for deficiencies in validity and reliability using this data. Therefore, what is needed is the employment of more accurate methods in order to account, objectively, for certain patterns of behaviour in society.

The above point noted, the *British Crime Survey* (BCS) still has its limitations. For instance, going back to the example of domestic violence, if a woman is interviewed with a male partner present, will she admit to being a victim of domestic violence when the perpetrator is in such close proximity? As the authors of these reports note, some violent incidents, such as domestic violence and sexual violence, are issues that may be too sensitive for people to admit to interviewers (Mirrlees-Black *et al*. 1996: 27). On the other hand, the BCS is argued to correct for a lack of validity and reliability in police statistics. For instance, it allows researchers to note that over 98 per cent of car thefts are reported to the police (Hough and Mayhew 1985). They could then use official records upon which to base a sample of people to interview, bearing in mind this high rate of reporting (May 1986). However, if researchers wished to conduct a study on the incidence of thefts *from*, as opposed to thefts *of* cars, the actual incidence is approximately four times higher than that reported to the police (Mirrlees-Black *et al*. 1996: 43). Thus, realists would argue that official statistics do have their uses, depending on the types of data that are utilized.

While those who contributed to one volume on official statistics (Irvine *et al*. 1979) regarded them as in need of 'demolition' and 'demystification', institutionalists concentrate on the social practices through which they are constructed. Studies adopting this perspective include Max Atkinson (1978) on the social organization of suicide, Aaron Cicourel (1976) on juvenile justice and Gilbert Smith (1977) on the exercise of professional discretion in Scottish Children's Panels. Atkinson's work on the topic of suicide is particularly interesting because it charts his change of research focus from the influence of Durkheim (1952) to a focus influenced by the work of Garfinkel (1967).

This latter approach abandons the idea that suicide statistics represent facts about a certain type of behaviour (what has been termed the 'realist' position). Additionally, they are not simply regarded as indicative of wider power relations and structures in society (the radical position) and are examined as 'accomplishments'. In Atkinson's study, he focuses on the methods by which coroners formulate judgements and categorize deaths as suicide. This does not assume that there is a 'shared definition' which coroners employ which, as noted in the discussion on crime statistics, is problematic. As soon as the idea that officials do not simply share definitions from which their practices can be 'read off' is abandoned, the aim of the research changes. This avoids the problems that come from trying to reconcile the theoretical categories of the researcher with the organizational and legal definitions themselves.

Instead of assuming the prior existence of a definition – theoretical or legal – that could explain the decisions of coroners, Atkinson turned his attention to an investigation of the factors which surrounded the circumstances of the death in relation to the coroners' judgements of it as suicide: for example, the presence of suicide notes, previous threats of suicide, the mode, location and circumstances of the death and the biography of the deceased. He therefore examined the methods that coroners used in categorizing sudden death. We have now moved away from facts, to the method of their construction. As John Heritage notes, social research now considers:

> what counts as 'reasonable fact' in a casual conversation, in a courtroom, a scientific laboratory, a news interview, a police interrogation, a medical consultation or a social security office? What is the nature of the social organization within which these facts find support? To what vicissitudes, exigencies and considerations are the formulation of these facts responsive?
>
> (Heritage 1984: 178)

An examination of the process, not the product, is the institutionalist approach to official statistics. The methods that officials who are responsible for their compilation employ, become the topics of research. Unlike the radical approach, the analysis does not fit within a more general theory of social and political organization: for example, a Marxist approach to the processing of the working classes by the criminal justice system as symptomatic of wider capitalist relations (I. Taylor *et al.* 1973).

Summary

Social research is increasingly dominated by the government and its agencies (Bulmer 1986b). While social researchers do enjoy some latitude in the design and execution of such research, there has been increasing concern over the government's control of official information. The production of accurate information was questioned during 1989 by, among others, the former head of the Government Statistical Service and president of the Royal Statistical Society. The effect was to render official statistics increasingly problematic for the purposes of conducting research into a number of important issues. Take, for instance, the measurement of poverty. A series of reports by the Department of Social Security entitled *Households Below Average Income* did not even accept, nor employ, a meaningful definition of poverty (Townsend 1996). This shows, as a Government Statisticians' Collective have written, that

> statistics do not, in some mysterious way, emanate directly from the social conditions they appear to describe, but that between the two lie the assumptions, conceptions and priorities of the state and the social order, a large, complex and imperfectly functioning bureaucracy, tonnes of paper and computing machinery, and – last but not least – millions of hours of human grind.
>
> (Goverment Statisticans' Collective 1993: 163)

It is the last part of this quote that indicates that there may be something positive to gain from the use of official statistics. Martin Bulmer (1984c) notes that while they have their problems, they are still useful for research purposes. Contrary to some critics, he argues that official statistics produce interesting findings on contemporary society which, despite their shortcomings, have been used by radical and realist researchers alike. He also notes that the conceptual issues facing those who compile official statistics are not dissimilar to those faced by social researchers in general. Thus, despite differences in theoretical orientation, they still provide useful empirical data. After all, statisticians go to con- siderable lengths to reduce error: 'British data derived from birth and death registration, for instance, is probably among the highest-quality data currently available' (Bulmer 1984c: 140).

If researchers become more aware of how these errors occur, they can correct for shortfalls, but there is good reason to be concerned over their accuracy and potential for political manipulation. Researchers at the Unemployment Unit based in London, for example, still calculate the unemployment rate based on pre-1982 definitions. This strategy allows for accurate comparisons across time (the definition of unemployment has been altered over twenty times since 1980). In turn, this enables the Unit to consider how successful government policies have been in reduc- ing unemployment, rather than the government's success in manipulating the statistics. Ruth Levitas (1996) employs a similar method to reveal their shortcomings and more generally, statisticians have used official data in order to show how they are systematically biased in one way or another (Bhat *et al.* 1988).

To say that official statistics can be useful in the above ways is not to suggest that you cannot still 'lie with statistics' (Huff 1981). Due to their susceptibility to political manipulation, the debate will continue. The realist will look for more accurate techniques for generating such infor- mation; the radical will criticize and use such information as indicative of more immediate or wider power inequalities in society and the institu- tionalist will concentrate on the process of their production.

Each of these approaches, however, is not as incommensurable as is sometimes suggested. We should also note that official statistics do not simply exist independently of the actions of those who compile them, they also feed back into everyday practices. It is not simply the process (the institutionalists) or the product (the realists) which should be part of the research focus, but the ways in which the process affects the product and vice versa. After all, official statistics are formulated by the actions of individuals within organizational settings and by governmental policies. Yet they also generate a view of the world which feeds back into those practices. A circle is then formed, rather than the straight lines of examin- ing construction, or of uncritically utilizing the final product. From this point of view we investigate how people are 'made up' by statistics. In the process we could discover how a particular category is produced for their classification and its effects, *alongside* their emergence as a distinct group (Hacking 1986).

As described in the first section of this chapter, official statistics are mainly based upon the use of surveys which are a central method of social research. As a main aim of this book is to examine the place, use and analysis of particular methods in social research, the next chapter is devoted to this topic.

Questions for your reflection

1 List five different types of official statistics.

2 Bearing in mind your answer to the first question, why do you think they are produced and what are they are used for?

3 Are criminal statistics similar to, or different from, other forms of official statistics? In what ways?

4 Having considered the above arguments, what is your opinion on the use of official statistics?

Suggested further reading

Bulmer, M. (1984c) Why don't sociologists make more use of official statistics?, in M. Bulmer (ed.) *Sociological Research Methods*, 2nd edn. London: Macmillan.

Coleman, C. and Moynihan, J. (1996) *Understanding Crime Data: Haunted by the Dark Figure*. Buckingham: Open University Press.

Government Statisticians' Collective (1993) How official statistics are produced: views from the inside, originally published 1979, in M. Hammersley (ed.) *Social Research: Philosophy, Politics and Practice*. London: Sage.

Levitas, R. and Guy, W. (eds) (1996) *Interpreting Official Statistics*. London: Routledge.

CHAPTER 5 Social surveys: design to analysis

With Malcolm Williams

The logic of survey method
Sampling
   Probability samples
   Non-probability samples
Stages in constructing a survey
   Preliminary work
   Types of questionnaires
   Designing and testing questions
   Types of questions
   Coding
   Attitude scales
   Question wording
The analysis of questionnaires
   Levels of measurement
   Relationships between variables
Surveys in critical perspective
Summary
Questions for your reflection
Suggested further reading

This chapter provides an introduction to survey method and specifically offers practical guidance on how to conduct a survey. First, it looks at types of surveys. Second, it considers the logic of survey method and sampling. Third, it outlines the stages in questionnaire construction, including types of questionnaires, and finally, it considers the analysis, as well as methodological issues associated with this method.

The image of a person standing in a crowded shopping centre with a clipboard, stopping people, asking them questions and then ticking boxes, is a common one. While this is usually market-based research, the use of surveys is also a central part of social research as they provide a rapid and relatively inexpensive way of discovering the characteristics and beliefs of the population at large. Surveys are one of the most frequently used methods in social research and are used by government, academic researchers in universities and campaigning organizations alike. Nearly all surveys are characterized by the collection of data from large, or even very large, numbers of people. They can range from relatively small local surveys of just a couple of hundred people to large-scale national surveys of several thousand. Virtually all surveys aim to describe or explain the characteristics or opinions of a population through the use of a representative sample. A population can be anything from all of the inhabitants of a country such as France or the United States to the users of a local bus service.

The purpose of surveys is likewise varied. Large-scale government surveys, such as the British General Household Survey, collect a wide range of socio-economic data, on a regular basis. This allows a description not just of the changing characteristics of 'households', but of British social life in general. More local surveys may be used, for example, to find out the housing needs, or extent of disability in a locality. Campaigning organizations often use surveys to measure support for their cause, while academic researchers often use surveys to test aspects of sociological or political theory. Surveys have been characterized under four headings: factual, attitudinal, social psychological and explanatory (Ackroyd and Hughes 1983). First, factual surveys are one of the earliest types to be used systematically in Britain. They aim to gain information from individuals concerning their material situation rather than attitudes or opinions as such. The cost of these surveys is an important consideration: to interview everyone in a population would be prohibitively expensive. For this reason, the Census takes place only once every ten years and is not a sample, but a total *enumeration* of the population.

The second type of survey moves away from an interest in the material conditions of the population, towards the use of surveys for gaining data on attitudes, for example, what people think about life in general and events in particular. This constitutes a shift away from the so-called 'hard data' basis of factual surveys. The idea of public opinion is perhaps the key to this type of survey. For countries with democratic aspirations, it is important that they gauge the beliefs of their citizens. Often a policy is justified by 'what the public demands'. However, how do we know what the public demands? Attitude surveys can fulfil the function of providing this information.

Political opinion polls also fall into this category. These attempt to *predict* how people will vote. Therefore, there is an assumed correspondence between what people say they will do and what they will actually do (will someone who says she is going to vote Liberal Democrat actually do so on the day?). On *average*, the polls are said to be fairly accurate. This does not suggest that one individual poll is correct, but that if you calculate the average results of all the polls, they will predict the outcome. Occasionally this fails when, for example in 1992, opinion polls failed to predict the outcome of the British general election. Conversely in 1997 opinion pollsters accurately predicted the scale of the Labour victory.

One reason for the improved poll accuracy was that analysis of the 1992 poll predictions showed that Conservative voters were either more likely to refuse to answer opinion poll questions, or to give answers consistent with the way they actually voted. Once this bias was known, pollsters could 'weight' their polls accordingly. Nevertheless, attempts at accurate measurement of opinions do not address the argument that the polls themselves do not simply reflect, but also structure public opinion (C. Marsh 1979).

The results of using attitude surveys developed other interests among researchers, in particular, the relationship between attitudes and behaviour. In this sense, both the social psychological and explanatory surveys are more theoretically oriented. The measurement of attitudes became the subject of many an academic paper. The question is exactly how do you measure attitudes? Attention is also focused on the relationship between attitudes and behaviour: quite simply, does the possession of a certain attitude necessarily mean a person will then behave in a particular way? However, this change in focus was not so much an interest in attitudes themselves, but in attitudes as one characteristic of the 'personality' of an individual. By building up a profile of personality types – using attitude questions among other techniques – it is believed possible to explain a person's behaviour. These developments within social psychology led to a movement away from an interest in general statistical profiles of the population – as in factual and attitude surveys – to a concern with small group behaviour.

To some extent all surveys are explanatory. They ask questions about, say, voting behaviour and seek to explain how people's attitudes or intentions are linked to their background or other *explanatory variable*. However, explanatory surveys are specifically designed to test hypotheses which are derived from theories: for example, Durkheim's (1952) idea that suicide is inversely related to social integration.

The logic of survey method

Surveys have their origin in the positivistic tradition (described in Chapter 1), though to describe surveys nowadays as 'positivist' is an over-simplification. Nevertheless survey research employs a methodology that has logical similarities to that used by physical scientists. While some surveys explicitly set out to test theories and some aim to construct theories, all begin with at least some kind of theory.

Good survey research follows a common process in the testing and development of a theory (even though in the latter case, because theory is being developed, the researcher may begin only with a 'hunch') whereby a hypothesis or hypotheses will be formed. A *hypothesis* is conjecture which is deduced from a theory, which if found to be true will support the theory. Conversely if found to be false will falsify all or part of the theory. The question of confirmation and falsification of theories is complex and controversial (see M. Williams and May 1996: ch. 2), but usually researchers seek statistical evidence for a theory rather than 'proof'. It is often said that surveys aim to show causal relationships: for example, what 'causes' people to migrate from one part of a country to another? Might it be low wages, unemployment, or the desire for career advancement? For the most part, however, surveys can show only the strength of statistical association between *variables* – literally any attribute or characteristic that can vary. For instance, if we were interested in the relationship between the variables of migration and unemployment, we might hypothesize that it is more *probable* that an unemployed person will migrate than an employed person.

Because surveys measure facts, attitudes or behaviour through questions, it is important that hypotheses can be *operationalized* into *measures*. This means that they must be turned into questions that respondents (the people who answer the questions) can understand and are able to answer. The answers must then be capable of categorization and quantification. Having collected and analysed the data the researcher is then in a position to decide whether the hypotheses have been confirmed or falsified and what this means for the theory. While it is possible a single survey will wholly 'confirm' or 'falsify' a theory, this is unlikely and the usual outcome is the amendment of the theory in light of the new findings. This, in turn, generates the material for new hypotheses and new surveys.

Parallels with the methodology of the physical sciences do not end there. Survey research is also predicated on a rigorous approach that aims to remove as much bias from the research process as possible and produce results that are replicable by following the same methods. This, it is claimed, can be achieved in a number of ways.

First, there is *standardization*. This refers to the conditions under which a survey is conducted, but specifically how a questionnaire is designed, administered and analysed. This

> covers the whole process of exactly specifying the questions to be asked, the manner of asking them, how the replies are to be scored etc. A standardized interview is one that has been constructed in this rigorous way, has been tried out, and is ready for use in the population to be studied.
>
> (McMiller and Wilson 1984)

The theory is that if all respondents are asked the same questions in the same manner and if they express a difference in opinion in reply to those questions, these variations result from a 'true' difference of opinion, rather than as a result of how the question was asked or the context of the interview. Thus questionnaires concentrate upon the replies of respondents within a *structured* interviewing situation (see Chapter 6). Their responses and characteristics are then quantified and aggregated with others in the survey sample, in order to examine patterns or relationships between them by employing the techniques of statistical analysis.

Second, there is *replicability*. It should be possible for other researchers to replicate the survey using the same type of sampling, questionnaire, etc. A replication of a survey producing the same results with different groups at different times will increase confidence in the first findings. This also relates to both *reliability* and *validity*. A survey should aim to be both reliable, whereby we obtain the same result from the same measurement on different occasions, and valid, whereby it measures what it is intended to measure:

> In fact, it is not the measure that is valid or invalid but the use to which the measure is put. We might use educational level to measure social status. The issue is not whether we have measured education properly but whether this is a suitable measure of social status.
>
> (de Vaus 1991:54–5)

Finally, there is *representativeness*. As it is the intention to make generalizing claims about a population it is important not only that the sample is representative of the population, but also that the findings are statistically significant, i.e. whether they are larger or smaller than would be expected by chance alone. This topic is considered in a little more detail below. First, however, let us turn to the important topic of sampling.

Sampling

Surveys, through the use of questionnaires, measure some characteristic or opinion of its respondents. Depending upon its aims, the procedures it adopts and the number of people who are interviewed, generalization can then take place from the sample of people interviewed to the population as a whole. A survey may therefore be defined as:

> A method of gathering information from a number of individuals, a 'sample', in order to learn something about the larger population from which the sample is drawn. Thus, a sample of voters is surveyed in advance of an election to determine how the public perceived the candidates and the issues. A manufacturer makes a survey of the potential market before introducing a new product.
>
> (Ferber *et al.* 1980: 3)

It is very important that the sample characteristics will be the same as those of the population. For this reason the way sampling is done is central to survey design. There are many types of samples but all samples are either probability samples (often called random samples) or non-probability samples. Strictly speaking only probability (or random) samples allow a statistical generalization from sample to population. However, for reasons described below, it is not always possible to use such a sample.

Probability samples

Probability samples are so called because it is possible to express the mathematical probability of sample characteristics being reproduced in the population. An important principle is that each person in the population of interest has an equal chance of being part of the sample. The population can be anything from the population of a country, or a town, to a doctor's list of patients. However, what is vital for a probability sample is that a complete (or as complete as possible) list of the population exists. This 'list' is called a *sampling frame* and from this a sample is randomly selected. Hence the other name for this type of sampling is 'random'. Random in this case does not refer to a haphazard selection of names, or addresses, but instead means mathematically random whereby each person/address etc., in the sampling frame is given a unique number starting at one and a mathematically random selection of the sample is then made. Usually this is done with the aid of a computer or specially produced random number tables.

A question often asked is how big should a sample be? The mathematical reasoning underlying the determination of the size of a sample is complex and beyond the scope of this discussion (see Moser and Kalton 1983: ch. 4). However, suffice to say that, in sampling, size is not necessarily the most important consideration! A large, poor quality sample, which does not reflect the population characteristics, will be less accurate than a smaller one that does. The *ratio* of sample size to population will depend on the level of statistical 'error' that is acceptable versus the resources available. While tables of sample sizes for different populations are available (de Vaus 1991: 71–2) a rule of thumb is that the smaller the population the bigger the ratio of sample to population has to be. Larger populations permit smaller sampling ratios. One of the reasons for this is that when researchers analyse their data they need enough 'numbers' to work with. In small samples of under 100, 1 per cent will be less than a person!

Many probability samples are what is known as 'simple random sampling', but often it is not possible to simply select a sample from a sampling frame. The reasons for this are varied (de Vaus 1991: 64–70), but commonly resources, or the need to be sure our sample is as accurate as possible, leads us to modify the 'simple' design. For example, suppose our sampling frame was a list of all voters in a particular county or state – say 300,000 people – we would need to find a method that would obviate the need to randomly select from all of these people. In this case we might use *multistage cluster sampling* whereby our initial sampling frame might be districts, or electoral wards within the county. The sampling may be in several stages, but in each the random procedure remains the same. In a two-stage procedure we may select 20 out of 200 electoral wards and having obtained those, select voters from within those wards.

Sometimes the researchers' concern is that the group they are interested in is fully represented in the sample. In this case a *stratified random sample* may be used whereby a stratification according to characteristics such as age group, gender, type of housing, etc. is first made and then a random sample drawn from each of the stratified lists. This allows researchers to weight the sample – in other words over-represent a particular characteristic. In both these modifications of probability sampling some care is required to insure accurate representation (for a discussion of this procedure and its associated problems see Moser and Kalton 1983: 111–16). Lastly a probability sample that has a number of pitfalls, but is sometimes the only procedure practically available, is that of *systematic random sampling*. Here the researcher begins by selecting a random number as a start and then systematically samples every *n*th person/ household, etc. The most important difficulty here is that the very systematic nature of the sampling can build in sample bias. For example the way a sampling frame is constructed may mean every fifth person will have a particular common characteristic. Some years ago a certain London Borough conducted a survey of residents of several blocks of high-rise flats asking them about their attitudes toward their housing. The results showed that a frequent complaint was noisy lifts, but the problem had its origins in the sample selection of every fourth flat, which as a result of a common building design, happened to be the one closest to the lift! (This was, of course, a legitimate grievance.)

Non-probability samples

Probability sampling requires the existence of some sort of sampling frame, even if that sampling frame is just *n* number of flats in a particular location. Importantly the size of *n* must be known. This is not always the case or, if it is, then no sampling frame is readily available. In these cases the researcher must use a non-probability sample. Indeed and particularly in theory building, it is not always the case that generalization from sample to population is required. In other cases – particularly in market research – the statistical accuracy of probability sampling is less important than the criterion of 'fit for purpose'. The manufacturer of chocolate bars is interested only in finding out how many chocolate bars might be sold and to whom. If a cheaper sampling method delivers the results, that is considered 'good enough'.

A form of sampling often employed in market research is that of quota sampling. Here the general characteristics of a population are often known from data obtained from, for instance, the Census. The proportion of people in particular age groups, social classes, etc. is known beforehand and the sample will consist of a proportionate quota of people with these characteristics. This method is often used for street interviewing and while arguably representative if properly selected, often suffers from sample bias in so far as those who are easier to interview are selected, or those that more obviously display the desired characteristics. Thus the temptation for a researcher, required to interview 20 people between 25 and 45, is to pick those people who are more obviously in that age group thereby omitting those at the extremes of the age distribution.

Purposive sampling whereby a selection of those to be surveyed is made according to a known characteristic (such as being a politician, trade union leader, etc.) is often used in political polling. Numbers may often be small here and once again the 'fit for purpose' defence of the method may be deployed. Similarly newspapers or radio stations will often use availability samples asking people to phone in their views on a matter. Unsurprisingly, such surveys have found overwhelming numbers believing in close encounters of the third kind, or in one case overwhelmingly in favour of a return to judicial flogging! Organizations, such as pressure groups or charities, have obtained useful information through leaving questionnaires in strategic places (such as post offices or community centres) for members of the public to complete (Van Zijl 1993).

Finally, when a population is widely distributed or elusive, such as homeless people or intravenous drug users, snowball sampling may be the only way of obtaining survey data. In this approach initial contact may be made with a member of the population who will lead the researcher to other members of the same population (see Chapter 7). Here generalization is not really legitimate mainly because we have no idea of the size of the population, yet the method has often proven valuable as a means of learning about a population prior to using sophisticated counting techniques designed to estimate the size of a given population (Sudman *et al.* 1988).

Stages in constructing a survey

Moving away from the place of questionnaires in social research and methods of sampling, this section looks at some of the key issues in the construction of surveys.

Preliminary work

Having clearly identified the underlying theory or theories informing the potential research, there is a great deal of preliminary work to do before commencing the design of the questionnaire. First, it is crucial to have spent time reading around the topic of interest to see what theories other researchers have held and indeed what research has already been carried out. Only rarely does survey research begin with a blank sheet; most of the time researchers are building on past work. From a solid base of familiarity with the topic it is possible to develop testable hypotheses, but a crucial question is whether or not a survey is the best way to approach the research. Indeed in some cases research questions will require a *multi-method* approach utilizing more than one method – such as field research and surveys. In such cases it is necessary to identify which parts of the research can best be accomplished through a survey.

Having decided a survey is the best approach to the research question and identified testable hypotheses, decisions must be made about who the population are, how will they be sampled and what type of questionnaire should be used. If, for instance, you were interested in educational achievement and or opportunity, the population may not necessarily be those still in education, but instead those who have left. While the research question may be about the views held by, say, the US population as a whole it may be more meaningful to think in terms of different populations. Those who had left education would be in a position to take an overall and retrospective view of their experience. Conversely those still in education would offer insights on day-to-day experience. The current or past experience of education is what defines them as different populations. Sampling decisions are therefore bound up closely with the survey's target population. Furthermore, the unit of analysis – i.e. the person or thing being studied – may not be an individual, but may instead be a household (or indeed a political party, a school, etc.). In such a case the sample would consist of households and although individuals may actually respond to the questionnaire, the analyses produced will be those of the characteristics of the household rather than the specific individuals answering the questions.

Types of questionnaires

The type of population, the nature of the research question and resources available will determine the type of questionnaire to be used. Data collection in surveys is conducted mainly through three types of questionnaire: the mail or *self-completion* questionnaire; the *telephone* survey and the *face-to-face* interview schedule. Increasingly data are collected by the researcher keying responses directly into a computer allowing the administration of more sophisticated questionnaires in a simpler way (J. Martin and Manners 1995).

The mail or self-completion questionnaire offers a relatively cheap method of data collection over the personal interview. As their name implies, they are intended for the respondent to fill out themselves. As a result, once the questionnaire is sent out after the pilot work (see pp. 92–3) the researcher has little control over the completion of the survey. A covering letter explaining the purpose of the questionnaire stressing the need for co-operation and the anonymity of replies is therefore required. At the same time, they provide people with a medium for the anonymous expression of beliefs: for example, in researching an organization in times of rapid change where feelings ran high, this method provided an outlet for the anonymous expression of strongly held views (May 1991). That said, unless people have an incentive, either through an interest in the subject which the survey is covering or some other basis, then response rates are likely to be low and the figure of 40 per cent, or four out of every ten people sent a questionnaire, is not uncommon.

Interest in the survey will affect the response rate and this will depend on the nature of the target population. The return rates of a random sample of the general population might well be lower than a specific targeting of people with similar interests. It is possible that only some groups will reply and not others. The replies might then be systematically biased towards one part of the population. For instance, in one health survey, people appeared more healthy than was generally thought the case. An examination of replies found that there was a lower response rate in more deprived areas. As there is a relationship between health and income, this biased the results showing a more healthy population than was actually the case (Mawby 1991). This bias may be checked against the Census data, but as this occurs only once every ten years, the data may be up to nine years out of date.

Once the questionnaire is sent to people's addresses or distributed for self-completion, the researcher then has no understanding of the considerations which people make in answering a question. The layout, instructions and questions must therefore be simple, clear and unambiguous. That said, mail questionnaires are cheap to administer, but you usually need to send reminders to people to raise response rates. Stamped addressed envelopes are required and reminders may be sent two and four weeks after posting the initial questionnaire:

> A rule of thumb is that 300 to 400 envelopes and stamps and 160 questionnaires may be needed for every 100 people in the sample (200 envelopes – outward and return – being used in the first mail-out).
>
> (Hoinville and Jowell *et al.* 1987: 138)

We can now summarize the main strengths and weaknesses of mail questionnaires. First, they have a lower cost than face-to-face interviews. Second, if dealing with ethically or politically sensitive issues, their anonymity may be advantageous. Third, people can take their own time to fill in the questionnaire and consider their responses. Fourth, as interviews are not used this could lead to less bias that results from the way in which different interviewers ask the questions. Finally, it is possible to cover a wider geographical area at a lower cost. The disadvantages, on the other hand, include the need to keep questions relatively simple and straightforward as the researcher has no control over how people are interpreting the question once it has been mailed. Second, the possibility of probing beyond the answer that people give is absent. Third, there is no control over who answers the questionnaire; you may wish to target women in the household, but men fill it in instead. Fourth, the response rate may well be low and it is possible that you cannot check on the bias of the final sample.

Telephone surveys are a growing part of the researcher's methodological armoury. By the mid-1980s in the United States,

> telephone surveying had become commonplace, and in many instances it is the most preferred approach to surveying. It is a methodology that has achieved a respected status as a valid means of gathering information to aid effective decision making in both the public and private sectors. In fact, much more money is spent on telephone surveys by market researchers than by public opinion pollsters and academic researchers combined.
>
> (Lavrakas 1987: 10)

At one time, this method was considered to be highly problematic due to its inbuilt bias. If you used a telephone directory (your sampling frame) several problems arise. First, people will, for various reasons, opt to be ex-directory. Second, in phoning someone you may get the wrong person or the right person at the wrong time, thus causing problems in response. Third, in many countries there is an inbuilt class and gender bias in telephone directories. It is likely that it will be the males in the household whose names will be in the phone book. Further, the distribution of phones between classes is disproportionate with, in the UK, 98 per cent in the Professional Class having telephones, but only 73 per cent of those in the Unskilled Manual Class (Central Statistical Office 1990). A simple probability sample would therefore not fully represent those in all classes (the distributions are different in the USA). On the other hand, if the aim of the research is to target professional groups only, then biases may be of a different order, for example, along race and gender lines as particular groups of people are under-represented in these strata.

The advantages of telephone surveys, as with postal surveys, are that they are convenient and relatively cheap:

> Postal surveys and telephone interview surveys can both cost roughly half as much as surveys using personal interviews, but telephone surveys have the additional advantage of greater speed.
>
> (Hakim 1987: 59)

Further, response rates may be high as people might be less concerned about talking to someone on the phone, rather than opening a door to a caller. In addition, the monitoring of the work of telephone interviewers can be done from a central office where the dialling takes place. However, people may 'break-off' an interview more frequently, than in a face-to-face situation, and the information may not be so detailed, for instance, the interviewer's ability to describe the environment of the interviewee in terms of their housing, area, lifestyle and so on.

Whether the researcher administers the questionnaire, or whether a team of researchers do, the theory is still one of standardization. However, in the face-to-face interview schedule the interviewer is also able, if required, to record the context of the interview and the non-verbal gestures of the respondent. As a result, unlike the other methods, there is a visual-interactional component between interviewer and interviewee. This has both advantages and disadvantages. As Fowler notes:

> Because of the central role they play in data collection, interviewers have a great deal of potential for influencing the quality of data they collect. The management of interviewers is a difficult task, particularly in personal interviewer studies. Furthermore, the role of the interviewer is a somewhat neglected topic in many survey texts.
>
> (Fowler 1988: 107)

From this he considers three roles which the interviewer has to perform in the collection of data. First, to locate and secure the co-operation of the respondents. Second, to motivate and guide the respondent through the questionnaire and finally, to ask questions in a clear, standardized and concise way, to record the answers carefully in accordance with the survey instructions and maintain a rapport with the respondent (Fowler 1988: 107).

In comparison with the other two methods, this method yields a high response rate, at a high cost (depending on how many interviewers are used), with a higher control of the interview situation, but at a slower speed. The actual mechanics of this process will be elaborated upon in the next section noting that the design of the questionnaire will depend upon its aims, the audience to which it is directed and the amount of resources available for conducting the research.

Alongside the three main types of questionnaire there is a small, but increasing, use of Computer Assisted Telephone Interviewing (CATI) and Computer Assisted Personal Interviewing (CAPI). Instead of collecting data on paper, in both cases, researchers enter data directly on to computer. Depending on the responses given the computer application will route the interviewer automatically to the next question appropriate to the respondent. The method is said to have a number of advantages: no data entry from questionnaire to computer is required; complex questionnaires are more easily administered; customized questions can be used and the computer can check for a number of interviewer errors (Sainsbury *et al.* 1993). Against this, initial design work requires sophisticated computing skills and because each interviewer requires a computer, it is expensive. It is also worthy of note that these methods should be seen not as separate developments, but viewed in relation to face-to-face and telephone interviewing with many of their comparative advantages and disadvantages.

Designing and testing questions

The most important part of the actual design of questions is to construct them unambiguously and to be clear in your own mind what the question is for, who it is to be answered by and how you intend them to interpret it. You might think that the meaning of a question is clear enough, but it does not follow that the people answering the question will agree with your interpretation. This is why it is useful, if possible, to conduct some initial fieldwork based either on interviews and/or observation work with the sample. This assists the researcher in understanding the concerns of the people who are being questioned and how they might interpret particular questions.

This is the point where the *operationalization* of the hypotheses begins so it is important to establish clear definitions. Operationalization means to define a concept or variable so that it can be identified or measured (operated on) (Vogt 1993: 159). If, for example, you are interested in the question of homelessness you must be clear and consistent about what you mean by the term (M. Williams 1997). However, it is important not only that the definition of concepts in the hypotheses are clear, but also other concepts to be used in the construction of the questionnaire. A study on homelessness may require information from respondents on their housing prior to being homeless, whether they work, the state of their health, etc. These concepts need to be turned into clear indicators so that both researcher and respondent are clear about the meanings they have. The process of clarification and question construction is aided by drawing up a list of topics that can be clarified and then turned into questions.

Even if initial fieldwork is possible, the questionnaire still needs to be piloted on a subsample before it reaches the full sample. During this stage, after people have answered the questions, it is worth having a chat with them concerning their opinions on the order of the questions, the types of questions themselves and any difficulties they experienced in answering them. Following this, it is then possible to revise the layout, question wording and design to take account of any criticisms and problems. Therefore, piloting aims to see how the survey:

> works and whether changes are necessary before the start of the full-scale study. The pretest provides a means of catching and solving unforeseen problems in the administration of the questionnaire, such as the phrasing and sequence of questions or its length. It may also indicate the need for additional questions or the elimination of others.
>
> (Kidder 1981: 162)

Questions also need to be asked which the target population will not only understand, but also possess the knowledge to answer. Asking students, for example, about their experience of drug-taking during the Second World War is not likely to elicit a uniform response, for this question assumes that they would have lived during this period in history. Most, but not necessarily all answers, are likely to be blank. However, even if you interviewed those who lived through and remembered this period, you would also be presupposing that the sample were either aware of drug-taking or engaged in it themselves. While this appears to be an extreme example, it is still possible to build in presuppositions in the design of questions which are less apparent, but which still have a direct effect upon the answer.

Types of questions

Classification questions are the 'personal' section of the questionnaire and are often referred to as demographic or face sheet information such as age, income, housing, etc. The problem is that if you ask these questions at the beginning of the questionnaire, it may put people off. If you ask at the end after eliciting their opinions and the person then refuses to answer, this may jeopardize your chances of analysing the answers according to what are known as these *explanatory variables*: for example, age may in itself be strongly associated with certain views held by people. Quota samples mostly use these questions at the beginning of the questionnaire, otherwise it may be a waste of time if the person is not in the quota group the interviewer wishes to target.

The use of classification questions needs a word of explanation to the respondents otherwise they may fail to see the need of them. You might need to stress how opinions need to be related to the kinds of people answering the questionnaire. For instance, you might be interviewing a student population and ask which course they are registered for. A general word of explanation for such questions not only adds to the chances of a good response, but also assists with the important aim of communicating the need for research and enhancing its participatory, rather than parasitic nature.

Most surveys concern themselves with either facts or opinions. With *factual questions*, as opposed to opinions, more latitude can be given to the interviewer to probe, explain and possibly even vary the question wording in a way which would bias an opinion question. These would be designed to elicit, for example, the newspapers which people read. However, while apparently easy to ask, without careful design, ambiguity can still arise. For instance, asking people how many newspapers they have bought in the last week appears simple. However, you are not only relying on their memory, but also assuming that they read newspapers. You have also used the word 'bought'. Again, this appears simple, but according to the golden rule of question design, is there a correspondence between the intention behind the question and the way in which the person will interpret it? As Oppenheim notes: 'Does this include buying for others? Does it include buying on account? Does it include things paid for by and bought on behalf of someone else?' (1973: 53). Good pilot work and an understanding of the frames of reference of the sample can help correct such ambiguities.

With *opinion questions*, wording alternations can easily elicit different answers. According to the principle of standardization, each respondent must reply as a result of unambiguous questions and not as the result of poor question wording, the way in which the question is asked, or as a result of the context of an interview. On this latter point, administering a face-to-face questionnaire to a person in front of a group of friends may well elicit a different answer from when the person is interviewed alone. Unlike questions of fact, the interviewer can only repeat the question and not elaborate upon it as this would bias the answer.

There is also the decision where and when to use *open* or *closed questions*. Open questions give respondents a greater freedom to answer the question because they answer in a way that suits their interpretation. The interviewer then records as much as possible of the answer, which is analysed after the interview. While closed questions limit the number of possible answers to be given, their analysis is quicker and cheaper. Many questionnaires will use at least some open-ended questions, but if it is found that many, if not most, of the questions are of this type it may be worth rethinking about whether a survey, as opposed to in-depth or semi-structured approaches, is the best way to approach the research question.

In summary, the advantages of closed questions are that they are cheaper to use and analyse relative to open questions and they also permit comparability between people's answers. However, they also compartmentalize people into fixed replies (often considered an advantage) and they are problematic if people have not thought about the question which is asked. One report, comparing the two, suggests that open questions are a useful follow-up to closed questions (e.g. 'You answered X earlier – could you tell me why you thought that?') and

> When situations are changing very quickly . . . open questions may prove the better form. Finally, as survey responses are increasingly used as a basis for historical research, open responses have the value of enabling researchers to explore raw data and to devise new coding categories.
>
> (Social and Community Planning Research 1981: 7)

Coding

Most questionnaires are pre-coded to allow the classification of responses into analysable and meaningful categories; it is

> the way in which we allocate a numeric code to each category of a variable. This coding process is the first step in preparing data for computer analysis. It constitutes the first step in mapping our observations into data.
>
> (D. Rose and Sullivan 1996: 38)

For instance, you have a question which has five possible answers; these would then be given a number from 1 to 5 (perhaps using 9 for a missing answer and 6 for a 'don't know' reply) and a column on the right-hand side of the page is used for recording the answer given (see the example in Figure 1, p. 97). Pre-coding of this nature makes the questionnaire much easier to analyse. However, in deciding to use such questions careful pilot work is required and the answers should fulfil two criteria: they should be not only *mutually exclusive* but also *exhaustive*. In other words, it should not be possible for someone's answer to fall into two of the categories used (exclusive) and all possible answers should be encompassed by the categories chosen (exhaustive): for example, if you are asking people about the type of housing they live in (house, flat, rented or owner-occupier, etc.), the categories used should cover all possible replies from the sample and no reply should be able to be categorized by any more than one answer. Each questionnaire should be given a unique identification number also (note the box for this purpose in the top right-hand corner of Figure 1).

Attitude scales

Within question design attitude scales play an important role. They consist of a set of statements which the researcher has designed and the respondent is then asked to agree or disagree with the pre-coded answers. It is then possible to test a series of attitudes around a particular topic and not to rely upon one question as an indicator:

> Since so much depends on the way the issue is put into words, a single item or single question is often unreliable and, because it usually approaches an attitude from one particular direction only, may give rather one-sided results. Thus, agreement with the statement 'Divorce should be made easier' can hardly, by itself, be a reliable index of a broader attitude, such as the respondent's radicalism . . . agreement may, in any case, be due to personal circumstances; but by having many items we can reduce the effects of one-sided responses.
> (Oppenheim 1973: 120)

Figure 1 is an example of what is known as a *Likert* scale, which places people's answers on an attitude continuum. Statements are devised to measure a particular aspect in which the researcher is interested; the respondent is normally invited to agree strongly, agree, neither agree nor disagree, disagree or disagree strongly with these statements. Figure 1, however, was designed to measure the extent to which probation officers believed that different groups influenced the policy changes they were experiencing. Its design followed an examination of the organization's history, a preliminary interviewing of officers and observations of their work, during which time considerable disquiet was expressed at the lack of consultation over organizational changes.

Despite the length of the final mail questionnaire, by spending some time learning about the issues in which the officers were interested, explaining the purpose of the research and ensuring the confidentiality of

Figure I An example of questions using a scaling method.

□□□
(1−3)

The following questions concern your beliefs and opinions on
various aspects of probation work. Please consider your answer
to each question before <u>placing a circle around the answer that most
approximates your opinion.</u> (The numbers are for coding purposes
only)

Please Note: <u>Where the term 'Probation Management' is used this
refers to members of the Chief Officer's Management Team</u>

Question I
How influential do you believe the following are in the forming of
Treen Probation Service policies?

	Very influential	Influential	Not very influential	Not influential	
The Treen Probation Ctte	I	2	3	4	(4)
The Home Office	I	2	3	4	(5)
The Government	I	2	3	4	(6)
Public Opinion	I	2	3	4	(7)
Probation Management	I	2	3	4	(8)
Treen Magistrates	I	2	3	4	(9)
NAPO	I	2	3	4	(10)
Assoc. of Chief Officers of Probation	I	2	3	4	(11)
Senior Probation Off.	I	2	3	4	(12)
Maingrade Officers	I	2	3	4	(13)
Ancillaries	I	2	3	4	(14)

replies, the response rate was 70 per cent (May 1991). Note that the
researcher was interested in the concept of influence and then had to
devise questions that were indicators of this, bearing in mind the frames
of reference of the target population. The number of groups who could
have influenced this process were also identified in order that the
questions covered all possible responses (exhaustive). Note also that the

questions are pre-coded (from 1 to 4) and the introduction to the question resolving any potential ambiguities over interpretation of the categories.

Other scaling methods include the Osgood Semantic Differential scale, Guttman scale, Thurstone scale and Factorial scales (see Henerson *et al.* 1987; Fowler 1995).

The Semantic Differential scale was developed as a quantitative measure of meaning on subjective dimensions. In this technique, people are asked to tick a box between pairs of opposite adjectives. This yields rating scales, for example, between good/bad; fast/slow; mild/strong; cool/hot, and so on. Of course, their use will depend upon the aims of the research. However, this is said not only to provide matters of opinion, but also to rate the images which people have of particular topics or items; one example of the use of this method is to evaluate people's images of a product in market research.

Question wording

Having decided upon the nature and types of questions to be used, the process of actual question wording is of central importance:

> In reality, questioning people is more like trying to catch a particularly elusive fish, by hopefully casting different kinds of bait at different depths, without knowing what goes on beneath the surface!
>
> (Oppenheim 1973: 49)

Eleven points are listed below which you should consider when writing your questions. These points are not intended to be exhaustive and you are recommended to consult some more specific texts before proceeding (see Oppenheim 1973; Fowler and Mangione 1990; de Vaus 1991; Schuman and Presser 1996).

1 Ensure that questions are not too general or insufficiently specific. 'What do you think of the Prime Minister?' is vague. Instead it would be better to break the question down (perhaps) to create attitude scales on various aspects of the Prime Minister's performance or personality.
2 Use the simplest language possible to convey the meaning of the question, bearing in mind the intended audience.
3 Avoid using prejudicial language. Apparently straightforward questions can be, unwittingly, sexist or racist in their assumptions. This is illustrated by Margrit Eichler (1988) who takes the following two questions from an interview schedule in which a person is asked to either agree or disagree:

It is generally better to have a man at the head of a department composed of both men and women employees.

It is acceptable for women to hold important political offices in state and national governments.

Both of these questions assume a male norm against which women are measured. Indeed, it is not possible to express a preference for a female head of department – just to agree or disagree with the statement. On the other hand, the questions could be phrased as:

What do you think is generally better: to have a woman or a man at the head of a department that is composed of both men and women employees?

What do you think is generally better: to have women or men hold important elected political offices in state and national government?

(Eichler 1988: 43–4)

Answers might then range around the preference which the person answering the question has for women and men in such posts.

4 Avoid ambiguity, that is, using words with several different meanings, double negatives, or 'two questions in one', for example, 'How long have you been unemployed and in receipt of benefit?'
5 Eliminate vague words as they encourage vague answers.
6 Avoid leading questions such as 'You don't think that . . . do you?' People replying will either react negatively to your presumption or answer in accordance with what they believe to be your wishes when the aim is to discover their opinions.
7 Ensure that respondents have the necessary knowledge to answer the question (as noted above in the example of student knowledge of drug-taking in the Second World War).
8 Do not presume that respondents follow the patterns of behaviour you wish to know about. If you are interested in how many cigarettes people smoke a day don't ask this straight away. You could begin with a *filter* question (no pun intended!) 'Do you smoke cigarettes?' If the answer is 'Yes', you could then ask 'And how many cigarettes do you smoke per day?'
9 Avoid hypothetical questions, which elicit hypothetical answers. People may simply shrug their shoulders and say 'Who knows?'
10 Exercise some caution in the use of personal questions for both ethical and practical reasons. Insensitive use can lead to a termination of the interview or a refusal to answer the rest of the questionnaire. De Vaus (1991: 84–5) offers an example of ways of avoiding the direct (and insensitive!) question: 'Have you murdered your wife?'

- The casual approach: 'Do you happen to have murdered your wife?'
- The numbered card approach: 'Will you please read off the number on this card which corresponds with what became of your wife?'

Table 4 An outline of stages in questionnaire construction

What is the theoretical starting-point of the research? What is known already? What research has been done? What can your proposed research contribute and therefore what are its aims?

➡

What information is required to fulfil these aims?

➡

Undertake exploratory initial fieldwork

What type of questionnaire will be used and how will the sample be derived?

➡

Consider the most appropriate questions to ask, which will depend upon the aims of the research, the target population and the time and resources at your disposal

➡

Construct a first draft taking into account that pre-coded questions are easier to analyse and the order of questions is the best social-psychological sequence

➡

Pilot the questionnaire and elicit the opinions of a subsample. Gain critical but supportive comments from those familiar with the design and analysis of questionnaires

➡

Edit the questionnaire to check on form, content and sequence of questions. Make sure the questionnaire is neatly typed and all instructions and coding are clear and filter questions, if any, are understandable

➡

Administer the questionnaire noting the dynamics of the interviews and comments of the interviewers (if used)

➡

Analyse the questionnaire drawing upon statistical techniques

---

- The everybody approach: 'As you know many people have been killing their wives these days. Do you happen to have killed yours?'
- The other people approach: 'Do you know any people who have murdered their wives?' Pause for reply and then ask 'How about yourself'?

11 Recognize the problem of recall. An element of caution is required in the use of memory questions. Quite simply, people may not remember the information which is required, or it may not have had the significance in their lives which you presuppose. Once again, good pilot work can correct for these problems.

Finally, the order of your questions needs to be well planned and the questionnaire well laid out and neatly typed or word-processed; instructions on its completion to either the respondent (mail questionnaire) or interviewer (face-to-face) should be clear, unambiguous and easy to follow. The purpose of the questionnaire should normally be explained at the outset so that people feel involved with what you are doing. The opening question should also put people at their ease. Beginning a questionnaire with personal information concerning a person's sexual orientation is not a good start. This may seem like an obvious point, but prejudice and insensitivity can operate in less obvious ways. The questions themselves should be interesting and not simply personal; they should also relate to each other. One method is to start with broader questions and then move to more specific ones. Therefore, the order of the questionnaire is not the best *logical* sequence, but the best *social-psychological* sequence.

In summarizing this section, Table 4 is designed to assist you in considering and remembering the procedures in questionnaire construction.

In this process we move from the conceptual aims and hypotheses informing the survey through to its operationalization in a questionnaire, to the results. These can then be analysed to see whether the original theoretical propositions require modifying or new information has come to light. Thus, to go back to the discussion in Chapter 2, this process is a combination of both inductive and deductive techniques of social research.

The analysis of questionnaires

Having obtained data from completed questionnaires it is necessary to analyse them. This section is a brief introduction to the process of data analysis. A number of excellent texts are available to assist you in this (C. Marsh 1988; Bryman and Cramer 1990; D. Rose and Sullivan 1996), as well as texts on how to present data (Sprent 1988) and how not to (Huff 1981). Nowadays virtually all analysis of survey data is conducted through the use of computer, utilizing either a personal computer or a mainframe version of SPSS (Statistical Package for the Social Sciences). Thus in order to successfully analyse questionnaire results some familiarity with a statistical analysis package is indispensable (see Bryman and Cramer 1990; Kinnear and Gray 1994; D. Rose and Sullivan 1996).

Levels of measurement

The methods of analysis depend upon the data produced. In order to use some statistical methods legitimately it is necessary that data are of a certain type. Broadly speaking there are three levels of measurement applicable to the social sciences: *nominal, ordinal* and *interval* (see Wright 1997).

Nominal variables are simply those which are identified by names such as 'religious affiliation'. Ordinal variables *rank* the differences in replies. For example, answers to the degree of difficulty of a particular undergraduate course or the agree–disagree continuum of the Likert scale. Ordinal scales, however, cannot specify that the differences between each of the scores will be identical (agree and agree strongly is the same as the difference between disagree and disagree strongly). For this purpose, measurement at an interval scale is required. Examples of true interval scales would be number of children in a family, or age in years. Nevertheless, in the former example an interval scale could be replicated by asking respondents how strongly they feel (for example) about a topic on a scale of 1 to 10 where 10 represents the strongest expression of feeling.

In the social sciences most variables are of an ordinal form and for that reason statistical techniques which require an interval level of measurement are frequently invalid (Blalock 1984: 20). In order to overcome these limitations researchers have devised sophisticated statistical analysis techniques specifically for social research (see Gilbert 1981; 1993). With these issues in mind, this section is only a brief introduction to analysing the relationship between two variables; other, more sophisticated techniques are available that allow the analysis of relationships between several variables (see Bishop *et al.* 1975; Dobson 1990; Gilbert 1993).

Relationships between variables

One of the characteristics of questionnaires discussed earlier involved the relationships between variables, the example used being that between age and conservatism. The aim of questionnaire analysis is to examine patterns among replies to questions and explore the relationships between variables that the questions represent. This takes the form of seeing to what extent one variable is influenced by another. Variables are described as *dependent* or *independent*. A dependent variable is 'explained' by reference to the influence of the independent variable. In the example given the dependent variable would be conservatism because the extent to which a person is 'conservative' might be explained by the person's age. Alternatively a conservative outlook might be explained or associated with a different independent variable such as social class – it is possible that people of different socio-economic groups have a different outlook on life. To return to an example used in Chapter 2, there could be a relationship between class and voting behaviour, *independent* of age. A younger person who is a member of a profession may be more conservative than an older person who is a manual worker. In this instance it may not be age, but class, which influences a particular outlook on life. In order to analyse this relationship, the questionnaire would have to contain replies to questions on the respondent's age, occupation and voting behaviour.

The process of specifying the exact relationship between variables is achieved by *elaboration* (see Rosenberg 1968; 1984; Moser and Kalton 1983). An independent variable (class) is then deemed to have an effect on a dependent variable (conservatism) in what is known as a *bivariate* relationship. In the above example, the results of age might be cross-tabulated with voting behaviour to produce a bivariate relationship. When the respondent's occupation is introduced into the equation, the relationship might become even stronger. It is then the task of the researcher, sitting at the computer terminal, to discover exactly what variables are influential and in what manner. How is this decided?

There are two tests which can be used for this purpose: first, tests of significance and second, tests of association. One test of significance is known as chi-square (χ^2). For this to be reliable 'the data must consist of randomly selected, independently measured cases' (Erickson and Nosanchuk 1992: 251) and the number of people in each category must not be too small as this measure is sensitive to fluctuations in sample size.

The result of such a computation gives a particular value for chi-square which is then checked by using a table of chi-square values. If the test of a relationship between a person's occupation and his or her voting behaviour is significant at a 1 per cent level, this means that there is only a 1 in 100 possibility that this happened because of chance; we can therefore say that we are 99 per cent confident in this result. A test of significance, however, tells us only of the probability that the relationship between two variables happened because of chance and how legitimate it then is to generalize to the population (one of the aims of a sample-based questionnaire). It does not tell you what the *strength* of the relationship between the observed variables in your sample is. For this purpose, a measure of association is used which computes a value depending upon the strength of the association: common measures are 'phi' and 'Cramer's V'. Both produce results which vary between 0 and 1 depending on the strength of the association (see D. Rose and Sullivan 1996: ch. 7).

Together, tests of significance (to see to what extent it is legitimate to generalize from the sample to the population) and association (which tells you how strongly the sample variables are related) allow you to infer that one variable is related to another after testing the relationship by introducing third variables (e.g. age and voting behaviour and then introducing occupation in our above example).

Should you decide to use a questionnaire for your own research, you are now aware of the basic ideas that underlie survey analysis and the techniques which are employed for this purpose. Yet more sophisticated methods also exist to analyse questionnaires, bearing in mind the earlier comments on levels of measurement.

Surveys in critical perspective

It remains to consider the criticisms of the survey method. In reading this, it might appear like climbing down from the heady heights of statistical analysis, but this is just the point. In this chapter we have moved from a conceptual consideration of surveys to a hands-on approach to the construction and analysis of questionnaires. The survey method and particularly the statistical representation of the social world are not without problems or critics. Statistics are only a tool and when it comes to a critique of survey research, its opponents are not impressed by numbers, whether they be percentages, proportions, means or chi-square values.

Let us recap on some of the characteristics of questionnaires: the idea of causality; the concern with measurement versus understanding; the concept of standardization and the testing of hypotheses. Each of these has been addressed, albeit indirectly, in the earlier chapters. A common criticism of survey method is that it attempts to show causal relations between variables, a strategy which is simply not applicable to the realm of human action which is rule-following, not 'caused'. Age or occupation, for example, does not simply *cause* opinions. Two variables may be associated, but this *correlation* does not mean that one variable causes a change in another. To say that there is a correlation between age and conservatism does not mean that age *causes* conservatism. While causality (i.e. the claim that A occurs only when B does) is attributed to phenomena only after 'looking at variation in that variable across cases and looking for other characteristics which are systematically linked with it' (de Vaus 1991: 5) in most cases researchers do no more than show the strength of association between variables. In any case, causal claims would not be legitimate in considering only two variables in isolation, but this does not rule out the possibility of measuring association.

An associated criticism is that survey method rules out the possibility of understanding the process by which people come to adopt particular values or behaviours. This criticism seems entirely legitimate if survey research is conducted without a thorough grounding in theory. Unfortunately, such surveys are not uncommon and are often favoured by governments in the production of official statistics (see Chapter 4). Yet surveys are often used as part of a multi-method approach wherein qualitative methods precede and/or follow a survey, thus permitting the development of an understanding of agents' perspectives, social process and context.

That researchers have presuppositions, such as the relationship between age and voting behaviour, leads them to ask particular questions is a common criticism. Because these restrict the way in which people can answer, it becomes inevitable that the theories are 'proven'. By the very design of questionnaires, it has already been decided what are the important questions to ask. It is then said that this deductive method fails precisely because the theorists' presuppositions have guided the research. The survey researcher might reply it is also inductive because the results of the answers generate relationships between variables which either lead to new ideas, as in the use of bivariate analysis, or refute the theories themselves. How can this be so? By using the concept of standardization, people do not have the opportunity to challenge ideas on their own terms. Furthermore, the myriad of differences in people's attitudes and the *meanings* which they confer on events can hardly be accommodated by compartmentalizing them into fixed categories (closed questions) at one point in time (the actual completion of the questionnaire).

Differences are accommodated in questionnaires by the 'fixing' of complex answers within a series of simple categories. Yet not only is this a simplification of a complex social world, but also it takes no account of change in opinions across time. To correct for this, some surveys are *longitudinal*. Of these, a *panel study* takes a group or cohort of people and interviews them across time: for example, groups of children born at a particular time are then interviewed at five-yearly points in their life cycles to see how their attitudes, opinions, values and so on change over time (de Vaus 1991: 38). Yet these are expensive and thus not a common form of research, while it still remains the case that if the researcher is relying on only a questionnaire method of research, people's opinions are represented by a fixed number of categories.

The above problems are thought to be overcome by an attention to design, measurement and good pilot work. However, this can simply become an empiricist concern with measurement. The central issue in social research for the critics of questionnaires is a hermeneutic one: how can researchers legitimately understand the ways in which people interpret the world around them and act within their social universe? How can survey researchers guarantee that their questions will be interpreted by the respondent in the manner in which they intended when there is no opportunity for a participatory dialogue in order to reach understanding? As we have noted:

> A bland choice of 'level of satisfaction', where 1 = very dissatisfied and 5 = very satisfied, leaves the interpretation of 'satisfied' open to the respondent. The irony here is an assumed congruence of meaning between what the designer intended and the ways in which it is interpreted by the respondents. From this point of view, one could say that all quantitative research assumes an ethnographic dimension to its design where the latter is characterized as being concerned with meaning construction in everyday life.
> (M. Williams and May 1996: 140–1)

A response to this issue, as we have seen, is to argue for meaning equivalence between design intent and interviewee interpretation. Even if meaning equivalence can be upheld, as some research suggests it can by deriving the categories used in the questions from prior fieldwork (Social and Community Planning Research 1981), this still leaves survey research with another problem: attitudes and actions are two different things, or what people say they do is very different from what they actually do.

The problematic relationship between attitudes and actions was considered by Richard Lapiere as long ago as 1934 and it remains relevant in the late 1990s. Having surveyed hotel proprietors with the aim of obtaining 'comparative data on the degree of French and English antipathy towards dark-skinned peoples' (1934: 230), he found a widespread prejudice against letting rooms to those who fell into this category. However, he then had the opportunity to travel with a 'young Chinese student and his wife' (1934: 231). In a hotel with a reputation for its prejudiced attitude he noted the receptionist's 'raised eyebrow', but they were admitted without hesitation:

> Two months later I passed that way again, phoned the hotel and asked if they would accommodate 'an important Chinese gentleman'. The answer was an unequivocal 'No'.
>
> (Lapiere 1934: 231–2)

From this point on, despite the widespread prejudice uncovered by the questionnaire, there was only a single incident in a total of 251 in which they were refused accommodation. As he concludes:

> If social attitudes are to be conceptualized as partially integrated habit sets which will become operative under specific circumstances and lead to a particular pattern of adjustment they must, in the main, be derived from a study of human beings in actual social situations.
>
> (Lapiere 1934: 237)

Lapiere neatly encapsulates the difference between attitudes and actions and the problem of tapping what people 'mean' when answering questionnaires. However, his concluding comments also appear to be a recommendation for good pilot work. For this reason, there are those who would argue that questionnaires can tap meanings if adequately designed and piloted and that the divide which is often thought to exist between quantitative and qualitative research, actually 'impoverishes' the aim of understanding and explaining human relations (McLaughlin 1991).

Cathie Marsh (1982) argued that questionnaires can adequately deal with meaning. While she acknowledged that ambiguous questions must be avoided, people will answer in a different way depending upon the meanings they attribute to a question. Other questions built into the questionnaire can enable the researcher to capture the reasons for this variation, as she noted in discussing the work of G. Brown and Harris (1978). Broadly speaking, Brown and Harris studied a series of life events, to which women reacted, which then produced such feelings of hopelessness they induced clinical depression. The dimensions of this study thus included both the understanding of these reactions *and* these events as 'causal' factors leading to depression. As Marsh then noted:

> The first involves asking the actor for her reasons directly, or to supply information about the central values in her life around which we may assume she is orientating her life. The second involves collecting a sufficiently complete picture of the context in which an actor finds herself that a team of outsiders may read off the meaningful dimension . . . the mistake is to think that it is only action that is human and understandable – reactions are too.
>
> (C. Marsh 1982: 124)

G. Brown (1984) was also to show how it was possible to capture both the meanings which actors attributed to an event and explain those in causal terms. As quantitative researchers have argued (Husbands 1981; C. Marsh 1984), the use of questionnaires in these various ways distances them from a positivist legacy upon which critics tend to focus.

In the quest to compartmentalize surveys within a positivist orientation and to produce a dichotomy between qualitative and quantitative methods of social research, their broad appeal can be easily overlooked. For instance, Ken Young (1981) argues that the outcome of policy is governed by two issues: first, the degree of control an organization exercises over its discretionary officials, and second, the extent to which the officials and policy-makers' definitions of the situation inhabit common ground (K. Young 1981: 45). By the study of what he calls 'assumptive worlds', or 'definitions of the life situation' (K. Young 1977: 4), it is possible to begin to understand the 'subjective factors' and 'situational determinants' that different actors, at different levels of an organization, have and experience. These 'assumptive worlds' can be tapped through the use of questionnaires.

Within the tradition of critical theory, Karl Marx made use of questionnaires in his research on the dynamics of capitalism (see Harvey 1990: 39–49). Further, another group of researchers, who included the German critical theorist Theodor Adorno, produced a study entitled *The Authoritarian Personality* (1950). In this study, they built up profiles of 'personality types'. People scoring highly on their tests were viewed as possessing a type of personality which is prone towards stereotypical and anti-democratic beliefs: in particular, disciplinarian and rigid patterns of behaviour based upon childhood upbringing. Feminist critics of positivism, often persuaded by more qualitative forms of research, have also employed statistical and survey analysis. Some research of this type has challenged the androcentric nature of behavioural research (Shibley Hyde 1990); attempted to overcome the tendency of surveys to compartmentalize or 'fracture' women's experiences (H. Graham 1984); tapped cultural norms on family obligations (Finch 1987) and shown how statistics are useful, but often used to intimidate people:

> They are only numbers: they are constructed, as words are in an ethnography; and they reflect their construction *even if outsiders do not know enough about the context of their production to recognise this*. Equally it is important not to be frightened by statistics, to let them intimidate you, or naïvely believe that 'statistics = bad'. Counting is an everyday action basic to many activities. Statistics need to be demystified.
>
> (Pugh 1990: 110, original emphasis)

Summary

Despite this broad appeal, a debate still remains over the place and applicability of questionnaires in social research. There are those researchers who would not, under any circumstances, countenance their use. There are those who would slavishly apply its methods without due regard to its weaknesses, and then hide behind a mask of elaborate statistical analysis. There are also those who know of the weaknesses of particular methods of research and make a judgement of which method to use based upon this information and the aims of their research. They may even decide to use multi-method approaches in their research. The results of survey research may then 'be used to direct the researchers to individuals as instances for depth observation' (Fielding and Fielding 1986: 84). Nevertheless, while a combination of quantitative and qualitative approaches, perhaps in a multi-method approach, may resolve some of the above difficulties it is not automatically a resolution of all methodological difficulties, nor does it avoid the issues covered in the first three chapters.

An important skill in becoming a researcher, as noted, is the ability to weigh up the practical value and methodological limitations of particular methods in social research. Towards this end, the next three chapters are devoted to interviewing, participant observation and documentary research.

Questions for your reflection

1 List the stages that should be considered in designing a survey. What are the problems which you envisage at each stage and what should the researcher be aware of during these?

2 What is the importance of conducting pilot studies? What role would other methods of research play in the design and analysis of questionnaires?

3 'Questionnaires measure only attitudes; they tell us nothing about the way that people behave'. Is this a valid criticism of surveys as a method of research?

4 If you were asked to devise a questionnaire which examined the relationship between race and crime, what ethical, political and theoretical questions might this raise for you as a social researcher?

Suggested further reading

de Vaus, D. (1991) *Surveys in Social Research*. London: UCL Press.

Fowler, F. (1995) *Improving Survey Questions: Design and Evaluation.* London: Sage.

Marsh, C. (1982) *The Survey Method*. London: George Allen and Unwin.

Rose, D. and Sullivan, O. (1996) *Introducing Data Analysis for Social Scientists*, 2nd edn. Buckingham: Open University Press.

CHAPTER 6 Interviewing: methods and process

Interviews in social research
    Structured interview
    Semi-structured interview
    Unstructured or focused interview
    Group interview
Conducting interviews in social research
    Common prescriptions for interviewing practice
    The practice of focused interviews
    Feminist approaches to the process of interviewing
The analysis of interviews
Issues in interviewing
Summary
Questions for your reflection
Suggested further reading

The aim of this chapter is to provide an overview of interviewing in social research. For this purpose it is divided into four sections. First, a consideration of the various forms of interviewing which are employed in social research. Second, an account of the ways in which interviews are conducted and the issues which inform this process. Third, an overview of the main ways in which the resultant data may be analysed. Finally, an examination of the critiques of interviewing in social research.

Interviews in social research

The methods of maintaining and generating conversations with people on a specific topic or range of topics, and the interpretations which social researchers make of the resultant data, constitute the fundamentals of interviews and interviewing. Interviews yield rich insights into people's experiences, opinions, aspirations, attitudes and feelings. In order to achieve this, however, social researchers need to understand the dynamics of interviewing, sharpen their own use of the method and understand the different methods of conducting interviews and analysing the data, together with an awareness of their strengths and limitations.

Broadly speaking, there are four types of interviews used in social research. While these characterizations appear to strictly demarcate one method from another, a research project may not simply be one of the following, but a mixture of two or more types. They are the structured interview, the semi-structured interview, the unstructured or focused interview and the group interview. In moving from the structured interview to the unstructured interview, we shift from a situation in which the researcher attempts to control the interview through predetermining questions and thus 'teach' the respondent to reply in accordance with the interview-schedule (standardization), to a situation in which the respondent is encouraged to answer a question in her or his own terms. With this in mind, we can characterize interviews along a quantitative–qualitative dimension, varying from the formal standardized example (surveys), to an unstructured situation of qualitative depth which allows the respondent to answer without feeling constrained by preformulated questions with a limited range of answers. I shall expand on each of these types in turn.

Structured interview

The use of structured interviews is associated with survey research. This is probably the technique which most people are familiar with. While the other techniques, particularly focused interviews, may directly involve the researcher as a subject and co-participant in the data collection process, this method relies upon the use of a questionnaire as the data collection instrument. The theory behind this method is that each person is asked the same question in the same way so that any differences between answers are held to be real ones and not the result of the interview situation itself. Given this, the role of the interviewer is to direct the respondent according to the sequence of questions on the interview schedule and if clarification is sought, then little or no variability in such elaborations should be apparent. The neutrality of the interviewer's role is emphasized in this manner. The rules for conducting such interviews are, therefore, standardization of explanations, leaving little room for deviation from the schedule; eliciting only the responses of the person with whom the interview is being conducted; not prompting or providing a personal view; not interpreting meanings and simply repeating the questions and finally, not improvising (adapted from Fontana and Frey 1994).

The method is said to permit *comparability* between responses. It relies upon a uniform *structure*, while a calculated number of people are interviewed so that they are representative of the population for the purposes of generalization. Resultant data are then aggregated and examined for patterns of responses among the target population via statistical analysis. For instance, an interest in the relationship between class and educational attainment would necessitate the eliciting of data on both class position and educational qualifications. Its success is dependent upon good pilot work and the training of interviewers in order that the range of possible responses are covered by the interview schedule and the replies result from questions which are asked in a uniform and non-directive manner. This also depends upon the interviewer being similar to the target group, who, in turn, need to share a similar culture in order that the interpretation of the questions and the dynamics of the interview do not vary to any significant extent. Given this:

> Where languages are too diverse, where common values are too few, where the fear of talking to strangers is too great, there the interview based on a standardised questionnaire calling for a few standardised answers may not be applicable. Those who venture into such situations may have to invent new modes of interviewing.
> (Benney and Hughes 1984: 216)

This method of interviewing is increasingly popular in telephone interviews for marketing purposes. Here a supervisor can walk around a room of interviewers listening to conversations and checking the extent to which the schedule is adhered to by those charged with its administration.

Semi-structured interview

In between the focused and structured methods sits one which utilizes techniques from both. Questions are normally specified, but the interviewer is more free to probe beyond the answers in a manner which would appear prejudicial to the aims of standardization and comparability. Information about age, sex, occupation, type of household and so on, can be asked in a standardized format. Qualitative information about the topic can then be recorded by the interviewer who can seek both *clarification* and *elaboration* on the answers given. This enables the interviewer to have more latitude to *probe* beyond the answers and thus enter into a dialogue with the interviewee. As Nigel Fielding notes in using the semi-structured method when researching police socialization: 'They were semi-structured by a thematic guide with probes and invitations to expand on issues raised' (Fielding 1988a: 212). In this case the meaning of the statements contained within the interview data were analysed in terms of the cultural resources available to police recruits. The data then enabled an understanding of 'the conventions and devices recruits use when asked to offer accounts of action and belief' (Fielding 1988a: 212).

These types of interviews are said to allow people to answer more on their own terms than the standardized interview permits, but still provide a greater structure for comparability over that of the focused interview. If a researcher has a specific focus for their interviews within a range of other methods employed in their study, the semi-structured interview may be useful (for example, see Newton 1996). As with all of the interviewing methods, the interviewer should not only be aware of the content of the interview, but also be able to record the nature of the interview and the way in which they asked the questions. However, in comparison with the structured method, the context of the interview is an important aspect of the process. In its literal sense, to which all but the most crude behaviourists would subscribe, the standardized method can only be assumed to elicit information untainted by the context of the interview. Given the greater degree of latitude offered to the interviewer in the semi-structured method and a need to understand the context and content of the interview, although trained interviewers may be used, researchers often conduct interviews of this type themselves.

Unstructured or focused interview

The central difference of this form of interviewing from both the structured and semi-structured interview is its open-ended character. This is said to provide it with an ability to challenge the preconceptions of the researcher, as well as enable the interviewee to answer questions within their own frame of reference. Some might regard this as a licence for the interviewee to simply talk about an issue in any way they chose. Nevertheless, this apparent disadvantage is turned into an advantage:

> a phenomenon like rambling can be viewed as providing information because it reveals something about the interviewee's concerns. Unstructured interviewing in qualitative research, then, departs from survey interviewing not only in terms of format, but also in terms of its concern for the perspective of those being interviewed.
>
> (Bryman 1988a: 47)

Sometimes called the 'informal', 'unstandardized' or 'unstructured' interview, this method achieves a different focus for the following reasons. First, it provides qualitative depth by allowing interviewees to talk about the subject in terms of their own frames of reference. By this I mean drawing upon ideas and meanings with which they are familiar. This allows the meanings that individuals attribute to events and relationships to be understood on their own terms. Second, it thereby provides a greater understanding of the subject's point of view.

This technique includes what are known as life-history, biographical and oral history interviews. In relation to life-history interviews writers have noted the importance of preserving a 'feel' of the exchange between interviewer and interviewee in their resultant transcripts (Simeoni and Diani 1995). Thus, in asking women about their experiences, as opposed to assuming that they are already known, this approach is said to challenge

> the 'truths' of official accounts and cast doubt upon established theories. Interviews with women can explore private realms such as reproduction, child rearing, and sexuality to tell us what women actually did instead of what experts thought they did or should have

done. Interviews can also tell us how women felt about what they did and can interpret the personal meaning and value of particular activities.

(K. Anderson et al. 1990: 95)

We are now squarely at the qualitative end of the research spectrum. Structured interviews are thought to allow very little room for people to express their own opinions in a manner of their choosing. They must fit into boxes or categories which the researcher has predetermined.

The focused interview obviously involves the researcher having an aim in mind when conducting the interview, but the person being interviewed is more free to talk about the topic. Thus *flexibility* and the discovery of *meaning*, rather than standardization, or a concern to compare through constraining replies by a set interview schedule, characterize this method. With flexibility in mind, Ray Pahl (1995) preferred the term 'restructured interviews' in his study on anxiety and stress among the 'rich and successful'. Not only were transcripts sent to interviewees for their comments and amendments after the interviews, but the purpose for which the data was collected was altered both during and after the interviews were conducted (Pahl 1995: 197–201).

Group interview

Group interviews constitute a valuable tool of investigation, allowing researchers to focus upon group norms and dynamics around issues which they wish to investigate. The extent of control of the group discussion will determine the nature of the data produced by this method. In the words of one text on this subject:

> The contemporary focus group interview generally involves 8 to 12 individuals who discuss a particular topic under the direction of a moderator who promotes interaction and assures that the discussion remains on the topic of interest. . . . A typical group session will last one and a half to two and a half hours.
>
> (Stewart and Shamdasani 1990: 10)

A balance must therefore be struck between the group being too small for interactive study or too large thus preventing all group members from participating in the discussion. However, as with all research guidelines, this will depend on what is possible in circumstances over which the researcher may have no control, as well as the aims of the investigation and the resources available.

Group interviews have been used in studies of steel workers who had experienced changes in working practices (Banks 1957); the effects of long-term imprisonment (Cohen and Taylor 1972); innovations and conflicts within organizations (Steyaert and Bouwen 1994) and in a rich fusion with autobiographical accounts, women's experiences of mental health (A. Butler 1994). In Banks's study, steel workers were interviewed both individually and as a group. While a degree of consistency was found between the data yielded by both methods, the group responses tended to take account of the situations of others present and there was a greater tendency to express grievances with the management.

It appeared to be possible to gain different results from using group and individual interviews. However, it does not follow that one result is 'true' and another 'false'. Group and individual interviews may produce *different* perspectives on the *same* issues. This comparison demonstrated that interaction within groups (such as on the factory floor) affects us all in terms of our actions and opinions. As most of our lives are spent interacting with others, it comes as no surprise that our actions and opinions are modified according to the social situation in which we find ourselves. For this reason, group interviews can provide a valuable insight into both social relations in general and the examination of processes and social dynamics in particular. At the same time, caution should be exercised in attributing the opinions of such a group to a whole population, particularly given the current trend for using this method among market researchers and political parties.

Conducting interviews in social research

The first section covered four methods of interviewing which have different ideas and methods underlying their practice. For this reason and by way of an introduction to the process of conducting interviews, I shall concentrate in this section on the main points which you might consider if adopting one or more of these techniques. However, the actual use of these pointers will clearly depend upon the interview method being employed. This part of the chapter is also demarcated as texts on social research tend to adopt a particular perspective when it comes to the interviewing process. The first part will consider common prescriptions for interviewing which are mainly, but not exclusively, applicable to structured and semi-structured forms. The second part will then move on to consider the process of conducting focused or unstructured interviews. As will become evident, feminist-inspired researchers, in particular, have criticized certain accounts of the interviewing process as both impractical and undesirable. Given this, the third part of this section will outline the main issues to consider when conducting feminist-based interviewing.

Common prescriptions for interviewing practice

Commonly, a tension is thought to exist between subjectivity and objectivity in the interviewing process. On the one hand, interviews are said by many to elicit knowledge free of prejudice or bias; on the other, a self-conscious awareness must be maintained in order to let the interview 'flow':

There is a tension in the biographical interview between, on the one hand, the need of the interviewer to establish and maintain a rapport and a trusting relationship in which the interviewee will disclose significant personal information and, on the other, the practical demands and constraints of any research enquiry . . . what transpires is inevitably something of a balancing act.

(Gearing and Dant 1990: 152)

The interviewer and interviewee therefore need to establish an intersubjective understanding. At the same time, the pursuit of objectivity requires a 'distance' in order to judge the situation. We seem to have two polar opposites – full engagement to detached analysis:

The problem is clear. The more the interviewer attempts to sustain a relationship with the subject . . . the more he feels the interview is 'successful'. The more standardized the interviewers are in their relation with the subject, the more reliable the data presumably become.

(Cicourel 1964: 77)

In order to achieve this 'balance', several issues arise in texts on interviewing which need to be considered by the researcher. First, there is the question of the interviewer's role: what effect is the interviewer having on the interviewee and hence the type of material collected? Is the interviewer's role during the interview one of impartial scientist or friend and how does this affect the interview? Related to this are discussions on the characteristics of interviewers: what is their age, sex, race and accent? This is an important issue which directly affects the type of information elicited. For instance, a study was conducted in Tennessee among black respondents using white interviewers. The idea was to consider the attitudes of black people and the extent to which they were satisfied with their social, political and economic lives. When interviewed by white interviewers, the people's attitudes were classified as expressing a 'high' level of satisfaction. However, when interviewed by black interviewers, attitudes changed and a more radical opinion was expressed.

Before conducting interviews it is important to consider a match of characteristics, on the basis not only of race, but also of age, sex and accent. This helps to guard against the substitution of the interviewer's words for the respondents. Thus, texts speak of 'blending-in'. Quite simply, it may not be appropriate for a grey-suited person more familiar with the deviants of the financial world to interview Hell's Angels about their beliefs and actions. Nevertheless, this observation should be tempered by reference to the purpose, expectations, content and context of the research process.

Following the work of Cannell and Kahn, Claus Moser and Graham Kalton (1983) suggest that there are three necessary conditions for the successful completion of interviews. Although specifically discussing survey interviews, they raise issues which are worthy of more general consideration. The first necessary condition is that of *accessibility*. This refers to whether or not the person answering the questions has access to the information which the interviewer seeks. This may seem a simple point yet, as noted when discussing questionnaires in particular, there may well exist a gap between the understanding of the interviewer and the interviewee. Of course, depending upon the interviewing method used, the interviewer may possess the flexibility to clarify the questions.

A lack of information may result for several reasons. For instance, the person once knew the answer, but has now forgotten; for the person to disclose certain types of information involves undue emotional stress; a certain type of answer or method of answering is expected which the person is not familiar with (the frames of reference are discrepant) or, quite simply, people may refuse to answer for personal, political or ethical reasons, or a combination of any of these. In such situations the interviewer must make a judgement whether or not to continue the line of questioning, or the interview itself.

The second necessary condition is *cognition*, or an understanding by the person being interviewed of what is required of him or her in the role of interviewee. Interviews are social encounters and not simply passive means of gaining information. As with all social encounters they are rule-guided and the parties bring with them expectations of their content and the role they may adopt as a result. It is important, therefore, that interviewees not only know the information that is required, but also understand what is expected of them. Without this, the person being interviewed may feel uncomfortable and this affects the resultant data. For these reasons, clarification is not only a practical, but also an ethical and theoretical consideration. Once again, this will depend on the type of interview being used. In a structured situation, the nature of the answer is guided by the interview schedule. On the other hand, the focused interview rests its strength upon eliciting answers which are, as far as possible, in the person's own words and frame of reference.

Third, and related to the above is the issue of *motivation*. The interviewer must make the subjects feel that their participation and answers are valued, for their co-operation is fundamental to the conduct of the research. This means maintaining interest during the interview (Moser and Kalton 1983: 271–2). Once these matters are considered and acted upon, during the course of the interview there are certain techniques for asking questions. First, a distinction is made between 'directive' questions, which require a Yes or No answer, and 'non-directive' questions, which allow more latitude for the response. Thus, an interviewer may ask for a reply to be framed in a particular way, or the interviewer may be less directive and ask, for example, 'Could you tell me a little more about that?' Another recommended method is to repeat what the person has said, but with a rising inflexion in the voice. For instance, if the answer is, 'I enjoyed meeting them', the interviewer then says, 'You say you enjoyed meeting them. . . ?' This is said to gain important elaborations of a person's statement.

In everyday life we sometimes find ourselves in conversations where a person is either hostile to the line of questioning or becomes embarrassed for one reason or another. The interview is no exception to this. Of course it may be wrong to pursue the line of questioning, but one method of preventing embarrassment or hostility is to ask by way of generalization. Instead of posing a direct question: 'What do you think about X?' You might ask: 'Many people consider that . . . do you have an opinion on this?' This use of probes is widely recommended. Probing is defined as 'encouraging the respondent to give an answer, or to clarify or amplify an answer' (Hoinville and Jowell *et al.* 1987: 101). These vary from so-called neutral probes in standardized situations, to more open types in unstructured interviews.

An ability to probe is reduced as the interview becomes more structured, for any variations in probing can reduce comparability. However, a change in the emphasis of a question, or a similar question posed in a different way, can not only provoke further thought on the subject, but also offers a catalyst enabling the interviewee to make links to other answers already given. This allows elaboration by a method of using information subsequently gained during the interview and applying it to a later stage in the conversation. There are some parallels here with the idea of 'retrospective–prospective interpretation' (Garfinkel 1967). Along these lines, it is also possible to ask people about *future* possibilities in relation to *past* experiences. This enables the interviewer to gain an idea of how people think about issues or come to terms with events in their lives, allowing them to build up a picture of the event or issue so that it is not 'compartmentalized', but related to other factors that are considered important.

Another technique commonly urged is probing for comparable and codeable answers. This falls more in to the structured and semi-structured methods. In interviewing people they may make similar responses to those previously interviewed. As a result of this knowledge, you may decide to pursue the line of questioning in order to understand the extent to which the answers are similar and may therefore be coded in the same way.

Without due consideration to interviewees as persons in their own right, they can easily be left with the impression that the researcher is doing them a favour – a bizarre twist of circumstances! Practically speaking, if people feel valued then their participation is likely to be enhanced – as well as their attitudes towards future involvement in social research. One idea which can help researchers is to imagine themselves in the same position in similar circumstances. Would they be prepared to co-operate and answer their own questions? In order to assist this process attention is given to the issue of *rapport*. This refers to the development of a mutual trust 'that allows for the free flow of information' (Spradley 1979: 78).

This brings us round to a discussion of focused interviews and the establishment of rapport utilizing this method.

The practice of focused interviews

The establishment of rapport in focused interviews is of paramount importance given that the method itself is designed to elicit understanding of the interviewee's perspectives. Initial contacts with, for example, managers, may elicit official responses reflecting how the organization ought to appear in terms of the rhetoric of its own image. We need to remember, therefore, that language is more than an act of speaking, it is also an act of representation. In this case, if researchers wish to move beyond official representation, to find out how things actually are, then they will have to seek the trust of the individuals being interviewed – assuming their willingness to enter into such a dialogue. As Whyte puts it in considering the build-up of first contacts:

> The interviewer deliberately keeps the conversation away from evaluative topics and tries to get the informants to make descriptive statements. We may begin asking informants just what their jobs entail, what they do at what time, and how their jobs fit into the whole production process.
>
> (Whyte 1984: 104)

Spradley (1979) views the establishment of this rapport as a four-stage process. First, there is the initial apprehension that both the interviewer and interviewee have of the process. This is perfectly understandable if the parties are strangers and the interviewer should not feel it is a personal weakness on their part. To overcome this, both parties must begin to talk to each other which is assisted, as Whyte notes, by the use of *descriptive questions*. These include, for instance, the amount of time that a person takes to perform a task in which the interviewer is interested. These could take the form of 'grand tour' questions such as asking someone to give an account of an average day at work, whether in the home or elsewhere. This could be reduced to 'mini-tour' questions by asking someone what is done in a particular role, for example, what tasks are actually involved in the performance of a given role. It is also possible to ask people about particular things that have happened to them. Spradley uses the example of an interviewee saying that someone gave him a 'hard time'. He then asked what he meant by this. More generally, you could ask people what experiences they particularly remember surrounding the topic in which you are interested or, finally, asking people what terms they use for particular places or things. In Spradley's example he learns that a jail is called a 'bucket' and this enabled him to ask questions around that topic using the language of the interviewee.

The use of such questions also helps in the second stage of establishing rapport: *exploration*. Here each party to the interview begins to discover what each is like and how the interview will proceed and for what reason. Again, this is assisted by asking descriptive questions which leads to the third stage of *co-operation* where each party to the interview 'knows what to expect of one another' (Spradley 1979: 82). The final stage could take many weeks to arrive at and will depend upon the time at the disposal of the researcher and respondent. This stage is called *participation*:

> a new dimension is added to the relationship, one in which the informant recognizes and accepts the role of teaching the ethnographer. When this happens there is a heightened sense of cooperation and full participation in the research. Informants begin to take a more assertive role. They bring new information to the attention of the ethnographer and help in discovering patterns in their culture.
>
> (Spradley 1979: 83)

The focused interview is a process of building up trust and co-operation. It utilizes not only descriptive questions, but also what Spradley calls *structural questions* (1979: 120). These enable the interviewer to explore areas of a person's life and experiences in greater depth; they can also be used to explore and disconfirm particular ideas the researcher has. These 'verification' questions might take the form of asking what types of people the interviewee tends to socialize with. However, there is a need to be aware of the sensitivity of some issues and how to phrase such inquiries.

As with all research, interviews do not simply begin when the first question is asked. Preparation by reading and initial exploratory work, understanding the situation into which you are going, clarifying any ambiguities which people might have of the research and eliciting their co-operation and being sensitive to ethical, political and theoretical considerations in the process, form a central part of its practice. It may be the case that the people whom the researcher wishes to interview are not amenable to direct approaches or are difficult to trace. In terms of the former, two researchers on biker gangs noted how 'Bikers would not humor many questions and they did not condone uninvited comments' (Hopper and Moore 1990: 369). As for the latter, in these circumstances, the technique of *snowball sampling* may be employed:

> This approach involves using a small group of informants who are asked to put the researcher in touch with their friends who are subsequently interviewed, then asking them about their friends and interviewing them until a chain of informants has been selected.
>
> (Burgess 1990: 55)

This form of non-probability sampling is very useful in gaining access to certain groups. However, researchers also have to be aware that they inherit the decisions of each individual as to whom is the next suitable interviewee. This may not present a problem, but it may lead the researcher to collect data that reflect a particular perspective and thereby omit the voices and opinions of others who are not part of a network of friends and acquaintances. To this extent one has to guard against the tendency to succumb to what Pahl (1995: 198) has termed Methods are Resembling Saloon Bar Sociology (MARSBARS)!

Another method of assisting in the process of rapport and recall is called 'sequential interviewing'. This may be applicable to all methods of interviewing, but is of particular interest to those which permit a greater flexibility for the person to answer in his or her own terms; it involves interviewing people about events in the way they might, or have, unfolded. By using this chronological format it enables people to reflect on or project their experiences in terms of the event(s) which are of interest. If an unstructured format is used, its flexibility allows people to return to a point previously made and elaborate upon it. Further, as the account of the event unfolds, it also enables the interviewer to ask about a previously stated belief in terms of the information gained. This method of 'reflecting back' allows interviewers to confirm their interpretations and to seek elaborations upon the person's account. It also allows interviewees not only to elaborate, but also to correct and/or modify their accounts.

The chronological method of interviewing is associated with the idea of a person's 'career'. Originating in the work of the Chicago School of social research (see Bulmer 1984a; Kurtz 1984), this does not mean changes in a person's occupational status, but the transformations people undergo in adopting particular roles as the result of new experiences. Erving Goffman spoke of the value of this idea in terms of its 'two-sidedness':

> One side is linked to internal matters held dearly and closely, such as image of self and felt identity; the other side concerns official position, jural relations, and style of life, and is part of a publicly accessible institutional complex.
>
> (Goffman 1968: 119)

While Goffman is making a point regarding the use of observation of people's actions to check their accounts of those actions through interviews, this method has been used by Howard Becker (1963) in his classic study of marijuana users.

Becker examined, through the use of 50 interviews, the process by which people learnt to become marijuana users. According to Becker people built up an identity as a user of this drug. The simple fact of smoking the drug, in itself, was not enough. People had to develop the habits, techniques and patterns of behaviour of others before they were able to fully enjoy its effects. The novice was therefore

> curious about the experience, ignorant of what it may turn out to be, and afraid it may be more than he has bargained for. The steps outlined below, if he undergoes them all and maintains the attitudes

developed in them, leave him willing and able to use the drug for pleasure when the opportunity presents itself.

(Becker 1963: 46)

The stages through which people had to pass were then mapped in his account by using extracts from the interview data collected. These illustrated how each stage was an important part of learning to become a marijuana user. They were 'learning the technique', 'learning to perceive the effects' and 'learning to enjoy the effects'. Through this method Becker was able to chart a person's socialization into a subculture from their initial willingness to try a drug, to a first experience of it, to learning the techniques to get a 'high' and finally, learning to enjoy what was likely, at first, to be an unpleasant experience (dizziness, thirst, tingling of the scalp and misjudgement of time and distance). By adopting the concept of a career in the interviewing process, Becker ends up with a fascinating insight into what many people regard as deviant behaviour.

We are now firmly at the qualitative end of the interviewing spectrum where life history and biographical interviews rest. Both types seek qualitative depth. Typically, they are detailed conversations which attempt to gain a fuller insight into a person's biography. Clifford Shaw's (1930) work uses a life-history method which relates the story of a teenage boy who was in prison for Jack Rolling (a similar type of offence to the mugging of drunks). Shaw focuses on the early childhood of Stanley (the Jack Roller) and the death of his mother. After this period, he ran away from home and spent time in various institutions, before finally living on the streets and becoming a Jack Roller. The data upon which his life story was based took six years to collect. The flexibility of this method enabled Shaw to return to Stanley from time to time when he was asked to expand on his accounts. Shaw was then able to build up a picture of his life and the circumstances which led to his actions.

Feminist approaches to the process of interviewing

Ann Oakley (1979) interviewed women about their experiences of the transition into motherhood. The research itself involved conducting 233 interviews which generated a total of 545 hours and 26 minutes of tape-recorded data (Oakley 1979: 309). The women whom she interviewed were at a critical stage in their lives and wished to know the answers to questions, or simply be comforted in the ordeal ahead of them. As a result, she was asked a total of 878 questions, 76 per cent of which were requests for information on medical procedures, physiology and baby care, etc. The remainder of the questions were divided into 'personal' and 'advice' questions and those concerning the research process itself. Personal questions included being asked of her own experiences of motherhood and childbirth (see Oakley 1984).

In the face of these requests, how could she entertain the prescriptions of textbook interviewing? For example, it is supposed to be a one-way process of gaining answers from people, but not answering their questions. Disengagement in the interviewing process is not, therefore,

> a realistic description of what occurs, but an idealized and wishful set of statements and prescriptions which we construct after the event and around our account of this. In other words what we present is a 'doctored' account.
>
> (Stanley and Wise 1993: 155)

In the process the experiential aspects of the interviewing process are subsumed by theoretical categories which are used, retrospectively, to interpret the data. This is not to suggest that reconstruction is not necessary (Stanley and Wise 1993: 155), but that the experiential should not be bracketed in the name of disengagement. With this in mind, Ann Oakley (1990) lists three reasons why disengagement cannot work. First, it was not reasonable to adopt this exploitative relationship with the women she interviewed. As a feminist faced with questions such as 'Does an epidural ever paralyse women?' An answer such as 'That's a hard one, I have never thought of that' (Oakley 1990: 48) is in line with textbook prescriptions, but hardly satisfactory. Second, given that one aim of feminist research (as noted in Chapter 1), is to counter the public–private divide by giving a voice to women's issues and experiences, she

> regarded sociological research as an essential way of giving the subjective position of women not only greater visibility in sociology, but, more importantly, in society, than it has traditionally had.
>
> (Oakley 1990: 48)

Third, the idea of not answering questions posed by the interviewee was not conducive to the traditional aim of establishing rapport. A refusal to answer, or an evasive answer, is not a genuine reciprocation of information. To expect someone to reveal important and personal information without entering into a dialogue is untenable. For these reasons, *engagement*, not disengagement, is a valued aspect of the feminist research process.

This critique is taken a stage further. Disengagement is seen to reflect a 'masculine paradigm' of research (Oakley 1990) whose implications require researchers to examine their own assumptions and perspectives (Stanko 1994). The idea of 'controlling' the social distance or familiarity between interviewer and interviewee, or controlling for the dangers of 'over-rapport' as some texts put it, is a contradiction in terms:

> I think that a female interviewer who is interviewing women and who is aware of the way in which women are treated and the position of women, is going to be aware of this contradiction between

what the textbooks say interviewing is all about and how a feminist feels she should treat other women.

(Oakley, in Mullan 1987: 194)

Establishing 'rapport', being 'disengaged' and conducting the interview in a hierarchical relationship between the parties are all rejected in both theory and practice.

In contrast to the need to establish rapport in her study of clergy wives, Janet Finch was 'startled by the readiness with which women talked to me' (1984: 72). This was not simply the result of using an in-depth interviewing technique, but that a woman interviewing other women is 'conducive to the easy flow of information' (Finch 1984: 74). She attributes this to three factors. First, women are more used to intrusions into their private lives through visits from doctors, social workers, health visitors, etc. and are therefore less likely than men to find questions about their lives unusual. Second, in the setting of their own homes, the interviewer becomes more like a 'friendly guest' than an 'official inquisitor'. Third, the structural position of women in society and their 'consignment to the privatised, domestic sphere . . . makes it particularly likely that they will welcome the opportunity to talk to a sympathetic listener' (Finch 1984: 74).

Other considerations in feminist-based interviewing are interactions between men and women and the ways in which everyday conversations are structured, thus affecting any dialogue involving the two sexes. Are everyday conversations between men and women a genuine and mutual exchange of views without social power operating in such a way as to bias the exchange in the male's favour? According to the results of one study, men tend to dominate conversations. Pamela Fishman concludes how men and women differ in the way they maintain interactions:

> The women seemed to try more often, and succeeded less often than the men. The men tried less often and seldom failed in their attempts. Both men and women regarded topics introduced by women as tentative; many of these were quickly dropped. In contrast, topics introduced by the men were treated as topics to be pursued; they were seldom rejected. The women worked harder than the men in interaction because they had less certainty of success. They did much of the necessary work of interaction, starting conversations and then working to maintain them.

> (Fishman 1990: 233–4)

In other words, if we take for granted the 'normal' manner of conversation in our work with other researchers and those who are part of our research, the chances are that it will exclude many women from equal participation, a particularly important point if conducting group interviews which contain both men and women. Therefore, once again, the reflexive examination of research practices becomes a fundamental part of the interviewing process.

Reflexive examination of the gendered nature of interviewing reveals both differences and similarities. Maureen Padfield and Ian Procter (1996) interviewed young women about their aspirations and originally sought to control for the interviewer's gender by 'standardizing' the interviews. When it came to the sensitive topic of abortion, they found a consistency of responses in relation to the question asked. However, in relation to voluntary elaborations on the topic through reference to personal experiences, differences did emerge between the two interviewers: 'in Mo's interviews this was revealed, whilst in Ian's it was not' (Padfield and Procter 1996: 364). Yet other sensitive information in relation to relationships and attempted rapes, for example, were revealed to Ian Procter. Therefore, while it is possible for inappropriate aspects of masculinity to be bracketed to some extent, differences still emerged. This shows the need to attend to not only the gender of the interviewer, but also the ways in which the interviewees' ideas of gender serve to structure their accounts.

The analysis of interviews

In this section I shall outline the ways in which interview data can be analysed, as opposed to the actual mechanics of analysis. However, these are only some of the ways analysis may be performed. During the course of the discussion I shall therefore refer to works on data analysis in order that you are aware of alternative sources should you wish to pursue this topic further. As the use of analysis for questions using structured interviewing has already been covered in Chapter 5, I shall concentrate on other methods.

Benney and Hughes (1984) note two conventions which characterize interviews: *equality* and *comparability*. The former operates to the advantage of the respondent in so far as it aims at participatory dialogue in the interviewee's own terms – as some exponents of the focused techniques would advocate. At the same time, there is a lack of structure in such interviews. This makes the task of comparison between interviews more difficult because the responses to particular questions, except in the case of some semi-structured forms, will not be uniform. For some researchers, the structured and to some extent also the semi-structured format, are preferred because of the greater ease of comparative analysis. However, interviews have different *aims* and the convenience of analysis should not be a reason for choosing one rather than another.

The first point to consider is the use of a tape recorder or notes on the interview. While attractive, recording has advantages and disadvantages. These fall under three headings: interaction, transcription and interpretation. At an interactional level, some people may find the tape recorder inhibiting and not wish their conversations to be recorded. Transcription itself is also a long process – a one-hour tape can take eight or nine hours to transcribe fully, depending upon your typing ability. Nevertheless, tape recording can assist interpretation as it allows the interviewer to concentrate on the conversation and record the non-verbal gestures of the interviewee during the interview, rather than spending time looking down at his or her notes and writing what is said. Further, once the conversation is started, many people can forget the tape is on (including the interviewer when the tape shuts off noisily in the middle because the recording time was not long enough!). Plus, editing the tapes according to theoretical categories in which the analyst is interested, assists in the comparative analysis of interview responses. Finally, tape recording guards against interviewers substituting their own words for those of the person being interviewed, but it can also make the analyst complacent as it is frequently believed that once the data are collected most of the work is done.

Following the interview, the work is only just starting. Not only does the writing up of notes or transcription of tapes have to take place, but so does the analysis. As Paul Atkinson notes, once they have collected their data researchers expect

> if only at a subconscious level, to 'find' educational, sociological or psychological concepts staring them in the face or leaping out at them from the data. It is a common enough misconception to expect to stumble across 'authoritarianism', 'social control', or whatever, and to be disappointed – even to feel betrayed.
>
> (quoted in Silverman 1985: 50)

In moving away from the structured format, it becomes necessary to employ techniques which can make some analytic sense of the raw data. Conventional methods of achieving this involve the *coding* of open-ended replies in order to permit comparison. Coding has been defined as

> the general term for conceptualizing data; thus, coding includes raising questions and giving provisional answers (hypotheses) about categories and about their relations. A code is the term for any product of this analysis (whether a category or a relation among two or more categories).
>
> (Strauss 1988: 20–1)

Strauss's prescriptions in his detailed monograph on qualitative analysis follow the method of grounded theory (Glaser and Strauss 1967). Yet even if analysts are not a follower of this method, the ways in which they begin to categorize data will still depend upon the aims of their research and theoretical interests. These, in turn, should be open to modification and challenge by the interview data analysed. It could be, for example, that a researcher is interested in the ways in which people negotiate their roles or performances in particular contexts (Strauss 1978). The researcher would then focus upon the data in order to understand how people go about their daily lives and compare each interview in this way to see if there are similarities. If replies are similar, they can be categorized under particular headings such as 'methods of negotiation', which allows the analyst to index the data under topics and headings.

Whyte (1981) used two methods to index interview materials in his study of the social organization of 'street corner society'. First, in terms of the respondents and their relationships to each other, and second, their references to events in terms of what actually happened and how important it was to the person being interviewed (Whyte 1984: 118). By focusing upon the ways in which people spoke of one another and made sense of the events which they experienced, this enabled him to build up a picture of the meaning of relationships to people and type of language used to describe each other and the events which took place. This is a form of *ethnographic* analysis achieved through becoming familiar with the interview data in order to understand the culture that people inhabit and their relationships to each other (Spradley 1979).

The important analytic stage of becoming familiar with the data is assisted by writing up notes or transcribing tapes and simply listening to the conversations. This is further assisted if the technique of 'developmental interviewing' has been employed. By moving, chronologically, through a person's account of an event and their experiences of it, a picture is constructed. A comparison of people's accounts is enhanced by focusing on the ways in which different people relate their experiences according to the circumstances they found themselves in. If a tape recorder was used, this can be achieved by editing each tape according to various topic headings which the analyst chooses. Each tape would then comprise a part of the interview that is relevant to these categories. These, together with notes on the course of the interview and any significant non-verbal gestures employed, assist the researcher in becoming familiar with the data and the particular nuances of each interview. On the other hand, if written notes were used, once they are fully written up, they simply have to be ordered in the same way (this is assisted by writing up the interviews on a word-processor and using the cut and paste facility).

There are now computer packages for the analysis of qualitative data which search for key phrases and the frequency with which people use certain words and in what context (Fielding and Lee 1991; Kelle 1995). These packages, for example *Nudist* and *Ethnograph*, facilitate the process of comparing categories, as well as enabling exploration of the data. Here we should note that while of considerable use, the process of analysis should not come to override the need to be familiar with the data produced. Furthermore, while the use of directly inputting data on to a computer has been used in telephone surveys, it is increasingly being used in face-to-face interviews. However, once again, we encounter issues over the maintenance of rapport. As such, it may be more applicable to structured interviews, but who can say how long it will be before tape recorders are routinely linked to computers and the data downloaded without the need for manual transcription?

We should not forget that talk has to be situated. Analysts need to ascertain what Mills (1940) termed 'vocabularies of motive'. These may be given during the interview as reasons why people performed various actions within particular situations in which they found themselves. Pierre Bourdieu (1992) argues that the analysis of talk requires more than linguistic analysis, as if speech were constructed in a hermetically sealed universe. What is also required is an explanation of the position of the speaker in terms, for example, of their class, race, gender, occupational position, etc. This 'positioning' will be missed if concentrating upon the form of speech alone. Erving Goffman made a similar point:

> linguists have reason to broaden their net, reason to bring in uttering that is not talking, reason to deal with social situations, nor merely with jointly sustained talk. . . . For it seems that talk itself is intimately regulated and closely geared to its context through non-vocal gestures which are very differently distributed from the particular language and subcodes employed by any set of participants.
>
> (Goffman 1981: 122)

Other researchers have argued that accounts people give of their actions are either 'justifications' or 'excuses'. These, in turn, may be viewed as indicative of how people identify themselves and routinely negotiate their social identities (M. Scott and Lyman 1968). An account given during an interview is 'the presentation not only of reasons but of oneself' (Harré 1988: 167). Thus, in a study of domestic fires and the methods used to analyse the interview data, two researchers noted how

> the individuals normally recounted their actions in an explanatory context. In other words, they qualified the description of their actions by the reasons why they behaved as they did, generally without any prompting.
>
> (J. Brown and Sime 1981: 182)

The analysis of interviews focuses not only on motivations and reasons, but also social identities and how these are constructed within the social settings in which people live and work. In this context, Dorothy Smith and Alison Griffith, influenced by feminist standpoint epistemology, examined the relationship between mothering and schooling. They focused on

> the social relations in which the work that mothers do in relation to their children's schooling is embedded. Their ongoing practical knowledge of the concerting of their activities with those of others is expressed in how they speak about those activities.
>
> (D. Smith 1988: 189)

To express it another way, how the relationship between mothering and schooling was constructed and reflected upon within the settings in which a mother entered (the school, home, workplace, etc.).

Finally, there are also those who have moved away from the idea that interviews tell researchers the 'truth' about the actions or events which people engage in (a positivist oriented position) or that they demonstrate a relationship between position and utterances via which people routinely act and interpret events and relationships (a realist oriented position). Simply expressed, the assumption that there exists something beyond the accounts that people give is abandoned. Instead, what is examined are regularities and features of the account. Such a method was employed by Nigel Gilbert and Michael Mulkay in a study of scientists' accounts (Gilbert and Mulkay 1984). This moves towards an ethnomethodological perspective that stresses what people 'do' in performing an utterance. The emphasis is therefore upon how accounts serve as justifications, accusations, etc.

Although the above has been referred to as a form of 'discourse analysis' (Wetherell and Potter 1988; Dant 1991), it does need to be separated from poststructuralist inspired approaches to discourse analysis. Here the stress is upon how discourses can possess a life of their own. Therefore, the focus of analysis moves beyond the performance of the speech itself, to how such discourses order a domain of reality which has repercussions beyond those understood or intended by the speaker. The effect of such discourses may then be to 'silence' certain voices through their ability to construct channels of communication which authorize only certain persons to speak in particular ways (see Wetherell and Potter 1988). That noted, a focus upon these 'circuits of power' (Clegg 1989) does not necessarily mean adopting a poststructuralist methodology (see May 1994).

I have mentioned these approaches to the analysis of interview data for the interested reader and in order to show the variety of ways in which they may be interpreted (also see Gilbert and Abell 1984; Silverman 1985; 1993). Interview analysis, whatever the focus of study, can be a long process in which perseverance, theoretical acumen and an eye for detail is paramount. It is frequently said that the hard work starts only when the data are collected and analysis begins – that is often the case. The success of its execution, in turn, lies in the hands of the researcher. In this section I have simply given an overview of its main elements and the different approaches employed. Yet to be faced with many hours of tapes or pages of transcripts can be a daunting sight. However, if you choose to use interviewing yourself, don't think the hours of frustration you might experience are the result of problems peculiar to you. They are not likely to be. The process can be alleviated by experience, reading around the subject and seeking supportive individuals for their opinions on the data, the interviewing process, your coding and mode of analysis.

Issues in interviewing

I have covered a range of perspectives on interviewing. In this process it has been noted how structured interviewing does not simply reflect positivism, nor unstructured interviewing a social construction approach associated with idealism. In terms of the latter method, the section on analysis covered an ethnographic approach using cultural analysis, to a form of discourse analysis which focuses upon language use. As a result of covering such a broad spectrum I have, implicitly at least, covered many of the criticisms. However, consider the following issues.

Interviews are used as a resource for understanding how individuals make sense of their social world and act within it. However, ethno-methodological approaches are interested in interviews as topics in their own right. It is thereby assumed that the link between a person's account of an action and the action itself cannot be made: it tells the social researcher little about a reality that is 'external' to the interview. Instead, an interview is a social encounter like any other. The prescription of inter-viewing books to control the situation are just attempts to produce a false social situation which has no validity beyond the interview; they cannot be assumed to produce data which reflect a real world beyond interpre-tation. For this reason, interviews are a *topic* of social research, not a *resource* for social research:

> interview data report not on an *external* reality displayed in the respondent's utterances but on the *internal* reality constructed as both parties contrive to produce the appearances of a recognisable interview.
>
> (Silverman 1985: 165)

The focus now moves to the methods that people employ in constructing the interview, not the interview data themselves; as noted above, the use of language as performance. This leads to a form of conversation analy-sis (see Heritage 1984; Schegloff 1988; Boden and Zimmerman 1993) which has been used to study such topics as embarrassment (Heath 1988), doctor–patient interactions (Heath 1981) and opening sequences to telephone calls (Houtkoop-Steenstra 1993). Note, however, that we have taken a methodological route back into the discussion in Chapter 2, where so-called practical reasoning and the methods that people use to make sense of the social world around them were considered topics for social research and theorizing. The same criticisms of this perspective apply to this focus on interviewing as a topic for social research.

The issue of qualitative depth in focused interviews and quantitative patterns of relationships which emerge from structured interviewing also raise their heads. In Chapter 5 we saw how it was argued that questions of meaning could be understood using a structured format. Yet more instrumental and less theoretical considerations also place a schism between these methods. In-depth qualitative interviewing with a large number of people is both expensive and time consuming and these con-siderations frequently dictate the methods employed. However, this does not prevent the researcher from understanding that the aims and limi-tations of different methods still apply, nor from lobbying sponsors for the use of the method(s) which would best suit the aims of the research. Researchers therefore have a duty to themselves and to others to reflect upon and acknowledge both the strengths and weaknesses of the different methods that they employ.

There are also the feminist criticisms of interviews which have been briefly covered. The spurious distinctions between reason and experience and of objectivity as detachment, are just some of the underlying arguments which inform this critique. Yet, as noted in Chapter 5, feminists have also used structured interviewing and in the section above I concentrated on focused methods. Thus, while sharing the critiques of malestream research, there also exists a debate around interviewing methods among those who would regard themselves as feminist researchers. Further, some have argued that Ann Oakley's characterization of textbook prescriptions is inaccurate (Malseed 1987). In reply to this critique, Oakley (1987) argued that this did not detract from the substance of her arguments.

In a final criticism, I examined the contention that interviews rely on people's account of their actions as representing something beyond the interview situation. Several possibilities arise from this. First, accounts may simply be inaccurate for one reason or another. Second, while accounts may be a genuine reflection of a person's experiences, there might be circumstances or events which surrounded these of which the person was not aware. Third, a fuller understanding can be achieved only by witnessing the context of the event or circumstances to which people refer. The only way in which the researcher could examine these is to be there at the time. This, not without an element of contrivance on my part, brings us round to the subject of participant observation.

Summary

In many walks of life interviews are used on a daily basis to understand and appraise individuals in particular and gain information in general. While the aims of such interviews are different in form from those used in social research, this common usage is a point often lost on those who concentrate solely upon their validity, instead of the way they are used as instruments for gaining information and, often, employing social power for the purposes of recruitment and assessment. Interviews in social life are not just topics, but are employed as means of appraisal which may determine life chances. At the same time, interviewing utilizes particular skills. For these reasons, researchers need to maintain an interest in their interviewing practices, as well as what is said and done as a result of the interview.

Lastly, it is worth emphasizing that the data derived from interviews are not simply 'accurate' or 'distorted' pieces of information, but provide the researcher with a means of analysing the ways in which people consider events and relationships and the reasons they offer for doing so. Yet they are mediated not only by the interviewee, but also by the interviewer. It is their presuppositions in the interpretation of the data that should also be a subject of the analysis. Quite simply, if both the strengths and weaknesses of different methods of interviewing and approaches to their analysis are understood, they can provide us with an essential way of understanding and explaining social events and relations.

Questions for your reflection

1 You are asked to devise an outline for an 'interviewer handbook'. The aim of this is to explain the skills which are required for different types of interview methods. What do you consider are the essential attributes of an interviewer and why?

2 Do you believe that the choice of interview method is simply based upon the type of information you wish to collect, or do different methods of interviewing ultimately reflect incompatible ways of viewing social reality?

3 Devise a topic in which you are interested as a social researcher. Given your choice, which method would you choose and what do you think would be the issues you need to consider before, during and after the interviews themselves?

4 Is an interview a topic or resource? What perspectives inform this debate and what is your opinion on it?

Suggested further reading

Dey, I. (1993) *Qualitative Data Analysis: A User Friendly Guide for Social Scientists*. London: Routledge.

Kvale, S. (1996) *Interviews: An Introduction to Qualitative Research Interviewing*. London: Sage.

Maynard, M. and Purvis, J. (eds) (1994) *Researching Women's Lives from a Feminist Perspective*. London: Taylor and Francis.

Silverman, D. (ed.) (1997) *Qualitative Research: Theory, Method and Practice*. London: Sage.

CHAPTER 7 Participant observation: perspectives and practice

Participant observation and social research
The Chicago School and participant observation
Muddying the waters
The practice of participant observation
The researcher's role
Access
Utilizing flexibility
Field notes
Subjective adequacy
The analysis of observations
Writing ethnography
Issues in participant observation
Summary
Questions for your reflection
Suggested further reading

Jean Baudrillard, a French postmodern theorist, challenges the ability to represent reality via research instruments. For him, the ideas of the world are now so saturated by media images, that the difference between reality and its representation has collapsed: 'We tend to forget that our reality, including the tragic events of the past, has been swallowed up by the media' (Baudrillard, in Gane 1993: 160). We can no longer differentiate between appearance and reality. Adverts persuade us to consume goods by employing visual media which often have nothing whatsoever to do with the product; we have become sold on and by the images we consume.

Such ideas have not been received without scepticism (Rojek and Turner 1993; O'Neill 1995; May 1996). In examining the work of Baudrillard, Zygmunt Bauman (1992) concludes with a recommendation for him: 'It becomes a philosopher and an analyst of his time to go out and use his feet now and again. Strolling still has its uses' (Bauman 1992: 155). To 'stroll' in this sense is to listen, observe and experience and to expose theories and biographies to new and unfamiliar social settings and relations, with a view to enhancing an understanding of them. This is precisely what the historian Raphael Samuel did in his rich reflections on living history. In his footnotes one gets a sense of the origin of his ideas when he refers to 'notes on a perambulation' (Samuel 1994: 117).

This use of observation and the ideas upon which it is based are the subject of this chapter. First, it introduces the ideas and place of participant observation in social research. Second, it examines the process of conducting research using this method. Third, it considers the methods of analysing observations, and finally, moves on to discuss the problems associated with this method of social research.

Participant observation and social research

Participant observation has a quite distinct history from that of the positivist (or variable centred) approach to research. While its origins may be sought in social anthropology, it was the Chicago School of social research, particularly Robert Park, who encouraged his students to study, by observation, the constantly changing social phenomena of Chicago in the 1920s and 1930s. This led to a wide body of research on areas such as crime and deviance, race relations and urbanism (see Bulmer 1984a; Kurtz 1984). It should be noted, however, that the distinctions that are now made between quantitative and qualitative research in relation to participant observation were not intrinsic to the Chicago School at this time (see Platt 1996).

The Chicago School and participant observation

The aims of participant observation, as well as its history, are different from what is commonly termed positivism: for example, the design of questionnaires involves the researcher in developing ideas and testing or exploring these using questions. Critics argue that researchers employing this method assume that they already know what is important. In contrast, participant observation is said to make no firm assumptions about what is important. Instead, the method encourages researchers to immerse themselves in the day-to-day activities of the people whom they are attempting to understand. In contrast to testing ideas (deductive), they may be developed from observations (inductive). That said, there are those who combine methods in their quests for understanding and explanation. As William Foot Whyte puts it in reflecting upon his research practices:

> From 1948 on, working with students on surveys, I came to recognise that, while the method had limitations, it also had important strengths. Many years later, in the course of our research programme in Peru, I became convinced not only of the importance of integrating surveys with anthropological methods but also that the study of local history could enrich our knowledge.
>
> (Whyte 1984: 20)

In the Chicago tradition of research we witness a merging of two intellectual traditions. First, there is the tradition of *pragmatism* from the work of the American philosophers such as William James, Charles Peirce, John Dewey and George Mead. Within this tradition, it is emphasized that social life is not fixed, but dynamic and changing. In the words of Paul Rock (1979), social life is both 'incremental' and 'progressive'. Therefore, if people's social lives are constantly changing, we must become part of their lives in order to understand how it changes; we must participate in it and record our experiences of those transformations, their effects on people, as well as their interpretations. Knowledge of the social world does not come from the propositions of logic upon which the theorist then descends upon the world to test. Knowledge comes from experience and the undertaking of detailed and meticulous inquiries through which we generate our understandings.

Practitioners shun what is known as the *a priori* (a proposition that can be known to be true or false without reference to experience), preferring the *a posteriori* (knowing how things are by reference to how things have been or are):

> They attempt to make their research theoretically meaningful, but they assume that they do not know enough about the organization *a priori* to identify relevant problems and hypotheses and that they must discover these in the course of the research.
>
> (Becker 1979a: 312)

This is not an assumption of interviews in so far as if someone is asked for an account, the researcher does not consider it necessary to have personally experienced the event or relationship to which it refers in order to analyse or understand it. Similarly, positivists who use questionnaires are not immersing themselves in the social world in which people are busy experiencing, perceiving and acting according to their interpretations of that world. Instead, it is important to participate in social relations and seek to understand actions within the context of an observed setting. Why? Because it is argued that people act and make sense of their world by taking meanings from their environment. As such, researchers must become part of that environment for only then can they understand the actions of people who occupy and produce cultures, defined as the symbolic and learned aspects of human behaviour which include customs and language. This technique, it is argued, is least likely to lead to researchers imposing their own reality on the social world they seek to understand.

The second strand informing the Chicago School tradition is known as *formalism*. While social relationships may differ from each other, they take forms which display similarities. In this way, we do not simply talk about one setting or group being 'unique', but ask the extent to which it displays similarities or is typical of other groups or settings. The focus of social inquiry is upon the interactions of people within social settings, not individuals as such. An advocate of this idea, George Simmel, argued that in order to discover and elucidate the general features of human interaction . . . the investigator must proceed, as in all other sciences, on the basis of methodical abstraction. For Simmel this constitutes the separation of the form from the content of social interactions, the forms by which individuals and groups of individuals come to be members of society.

(Frisby 1984: 61)

As a perspective formalism is also concerned with the ways in which particular social and cultural forms of life emerge. In keeping with pragmatism, they are argued to come from the practical concerns of people's everyday lives 'but that once established they take on a life of their own' (Hammersley 1990b: 37). These forms may actually conflict with each other, but the task of the researcher is to understand how they evolve. It is not surprising that Robert Park, a student of Simmel's, encouraged his students to 'stroll'; to stroll in order to understand the flux of social life in which the individual self is also subject to change:

the empirical self is always changing, and is never self-consistent. This means that the individual cannot be viewed as a basic unit; both from the above standpoint and in terms of the systems of relationships investigated by sociology, the individual does not constitute a permanent uniformity.

(Park 1972: 29)

These strands of thought also combine with the idea of *naturalism* which 'proposes that, as far as possible, the social world should be studied in its "natural state" undisturbed by the researcher' (Hammersley and Atkinson 1995: 6). However, this does not mean that people simply react to their environments. According to this view, influenced by a number of theoretical and philosophical traditions, people are busy interpreting and acting within a social world infused with meaning. Thus, any concern with change and process must take this as its starting-point:

I wish to point out that any line of social change, since it involves change in human action, is necessarily mediated by interpretation on the part of the people caught up in the change – the change appears in the form of new situations in which people have to construct new forms of action.

(Blumer 1972: 191)

The process of learning behaviour is argued to be absent from other forms of research: for instance, a questionnaire asks questions at one particular time. It is a 'static-causal snapshot' of attitudes; how and why people change is not understood. In practice, observers record their own experiences in order to understand the cultural universes which people occupy. Participant observation may therefore be defined as:

> The process in which an investigator establishes a many-sided and relatively long-term relationship with a human association in its natural setting, for the purposes of developing a scientific understanding of that association.
>
> (Lofland and Lofland 1984: 12)

Ethnography, as it is often referred, leads to an empathic understanding of a social scene. It is said to exclude, over time, the preconceptions that researchers may have and exposes them to a new social milieu which demands their engagement. According to one view, theory is then generated from data (Glaser and Strauss 1967). Glaser and Strauss propose two criteria for this purpose. First, it should fit the data and not be forced on to it. Second, it should be meaningfully relevant to the behaviour under study. As the researcher is exposed to each new social scene, this acts as a control on hasty theoretical conclusions (Silverman 1985). The more varied the scenes of interaction that are viewed and circumstances experienced, the more one can understand actions within social contexts.

Muddying the waters

The above tradition has had a considerable impact on the aims and methods of participant observation. However, the point has been made throughout this book that perspectives do not dictate, but inform methods and different perspectives frequently use the same methods or combination of methods. Participant observation is no different in this respect and no overview of its place in social research can fail to acknowledge this state of affairs.

We have encountered a number of dichotomies in social research which, on closer examination, have tended to be less clear cut than the doctrinaire posturing of much literature on social research would suggest. Here I am thinking, in particular, of the simple distinctions made between quantitative and qualitative social research, theory and fact and modern and postmodern ideas. In the literature these differences are frequently assumed rather than subject to the rigours of analytic examination. While the methods that we use will influence the nature of the data which we collect, it is worth noting: 'Qualitative and quantitative methodology are not mutually exclusive. Differences between the two approaches are located in the overall form, focus, and emphasis of study' (Van Maanen 1979: 520).

Qualitative researchers often resort to the language of quantification in their work and while surveys are argued by researchers to tap questions of meaning, they must first understand people's frames of reference and for this reason have a qualitative dimension to their design and interpretation. In other words, there is a central ethnographic component to successful survey work.

The idea that there are facts which we can gather on the social world is also highly questionable, for it is theory which mediates our interpretations. Yet the emphasis of the above approach to participant observation has been upon induction and naturalism. Data are assumed to be collected and are somehow 'naturally occurring' – without being mediated by the theoretical concerns and biography of the researcher – while theory is derived from observations.

Again, these assumptions have been subjected to scrutiny and found wanting (Hammersley 1992). For these reasons researchers influenced by other perspectives have employed the method of participant observation and it would be an error to gloss over them and present the method as if its practice reflected a unified perspective (Stanley 1990c). However, two features certainly differentiate it from positivist oriented research. First, the subject matter of the social sciences differs from the natural sciences, and second, to assist in understanding social reality, we must also directly experience that reality (Bryman 1988a: 52).

Paul Willis (1977) used the method of participant observation within the realist tradition. Spending time with a group of 'lads', he charted their progression from school to work. From his observations on their everyday lives, he derived a theory which argued that capitalist relations structured not only their actions, but also their expectations. However, this did not assume that the 'lads' were simply cultural puppets. On the contrary, they were active in their resistance to oppressive social structures by not only understanding, but also questioning and mocking, the authority of teachers. In addition, Sam Porter (1993) has employed, following the work of Roy Bhaskar (1989a), a critical realist ethnographic method to investigate racism in doctor–nurse relations. Given an emphasis upon the generative social mechanisms which underlie these interactions, this enables the comparison of results with other social settings of this type (Porter 1993: 607).

Ethnographers influenced by Marxism have studied West Indian lifestyles in Bristol (Pryce 1986) and youth cultures more generally (Jefferson 1975). Cicourel (1976) has worked in the ethnomethodological tradition in order to show how juvenile justice was the product of negotiation between officials, parents and the juveniles. John Law (1994) has employed poststructuralist insights in order to illuminate work in a research laboratory and Catherine Casey (1995) invokes ideas on 'post-industrialism' to consider the effects of transformations in corporate cultures. Finally, feminist researchers, of differing theoretical orientations, have used observation methods to study women quantity surveyors (Greed 1990), relations within Chinese restaurants (Kay 1990), women and social class (S. Webb 1990), gendered work in the tourist industry (Adkins 1995) and the formation of friendships among 'girls' (Hey 1997).

I am now in a position to summarize the positive aspects of this method. First, it is least likely to lead researchers to impose their own reality on the social world they seek to understand. Second, the process of understanding action is omitted from other forms of research and how and why people change is not understood. Third, during interviews, there may be language or cultural differences expressed. In this case, observers may record their own experiences in order to understand the cultural universe which people occupy (subjective experiences) and convey these observations to a wider audience (from field notes) within the context of explaining their data (theoretical framework). The process by which these are achieved is the subject of the following sections.

The practice of participant observation

This method is one that those new to social research believe they can undertake with ease. On first glance it appears to be just about looking, listening, generally experiencing and writing it all down. However, it is more plausible to argue that participant observation is the most personally demanding and analytically difficult method of social research to undertake. Depending on the aims of the study and the previous relationship of researchers to those with whom they work, it requires them to spend a great deal of time in surroundings with which they may not be familiar; to secure and maintain relationships with people with whom they may have little personal affinity; to take copious notes on what would normally appear to be everyday mundane happenings; to possibly incurring some personal risk in their fieldwork and then, if that is not enough, to spend months of analysis after the fieldwork. From this point of view, it is worth bearing in mind that when the fieldwork stops, the work itself does not! Nevertheless, to those who are prepared and willing, it is also one of the most rewarding methods which yields fascinating insights into people's social lives and relationships and, more generally, assists in bridging the gap between people's understanding of alternative lifestyles and the prejudices which difference and diversity so often meet.

The researcher's role

Participant observers may work in teams, which assists in sharpening insights and generating ideas. More often, however, researchers work alone. In the process they witness the 'reflexive rationalization' of conduct, that is the continual interpretation and application of new knowledge by people (including themselves) in their social environments as an ongoing process. The ethnographer is *the* instrument of data collection (G. Brown 1984). Ethnographers gather data by their active participation in the social world; they enter a social universe in which people are already busy interpreting and understanding their environments. This can involve a number of different methods:

- It can involve gathering information by moving closely among people, sometimes quite literally 'living among people', and observing their everyday lives. . . . In other forms of study, in-depth interviews and life-histories which could never be obtained simply by 'hanging around' and 'watching the action'. Not uncommonly, different methods are mixed together.

(Pearson 1993: ix)

In adopting this first form of study it does not follow that researchers comprehend the situation as though it were 'uncontaminated' by their social presence. For this reason, among others, naturalism, in its literal sense, is regarded as 'dishonest' by denying the effect of the researcher on the social scene. Accounts of ethnography, following this course of action, are viewed as mythologies that 'present an oversimplistic account of research' (Stanley and Wise 1993: 161). On the contrary, the aim of understanding is actually enhanced by considering how they are affected by the social scene, what goes on within it and how people, including themselves, act and interpret within their social situations – hence the term *participant* observation.

In 'doing' ethnography, engagement is used to an advantage. Furthermore, being part of the social world which we study 'is not a matter of methodological commitment, it is an existential fact' (Hammersley and Atkinson 1983: 15). In this process, ethnographers have explicitly drawn upon their own biographies in the research process: for example, having been personally and politically engaged in protest as part of a group, before deciding to turn attention to its analysis (see Roseneil 1993). Our own cultural equipment is thereby used reflexively to understand social action in context. The idea of reflexivity

Implies that the orientations of researchers will be shaped by their socio-historical locations, including the values and interests that these locations confer upon them. What this represents is a rejection of the idea that social research is, or can be, carried out in some autonomous realm that is insulated from the wider society and from the particular biography of the researcher.

(Hammersley and Atkinson 1995: 16)

Depending upon the aim and history of the research, the particular roles which researchers adopt will vary and this, in turn, will affect the data produced. However, we may wish to adopt a particular role, but the circumstances do not permit it. As the experiences of Buchanan *et al.* (1988) suggest, while organizational researchers, for example, should be 'opportunistic' in their fieldwork, if the possible and desirable clash, the former will always win through! The reasons why we are not able to adopt a particular role, while frustrating, might also become the topics of our research for they may tell us a great deal about the operation of social power and relations in the setting under study.

In what is now becoming a standard reference on fieldwork roles, originally written in 1958, Gold (1969) identifies four roles of field research which assist in the process of analysing field notes. A central part of the analytic process being a reflexive consideration of the 'relations between and among investigator and research participants' (Gergen and Gergen 1991: 93) and the types of data subsequently generated.

The first role Gold identifies is the *complete participant*. The researcher employing this role attempts to engage fully in the activities of the group or organization under investigation. Their role is also covert for their intentions are not made explicit. This is the role that Humphreys (1970) adopted in his work (discussed in Chapter 3). Among its advantages, it is argued to produce more accurate information and an understanding not available by other means (for example, see Festinger *et al.* 1956; Ditton 1977; Rosenhan 1982; L. Graham 1995).

Second, there is the *participant as observer*. This person adopts an overt role and makes her or his presence and intentions known to the group (for example, see Campbell 1984; May 1991; Watson 1994). In this process they attempt 'to form a series of relationships with the subjects such that they serve as both respondents and informants' (Denzin 1978a: 188). Despite traditional concerns with 'establishing rapport' or what is called 'going native' and hence not being 'objective', for many researchers who possess the capabilities to understand, listen and learn, these are not problems and reflect a particular view of scientific inquiry which has been subjected to scrutiny and found wanting.

This role often means becoming a 'fan' (Van Maanen 1978) who desires to know and understand more from people within the setting. It does not, however, mean attempting to act as one of the group studied. This is particularly the case when it comes to research on crime and deviance. Polsky puts this forcefully: 'in doing field research on criminals you damned well better *not* pretend to be "one of them", because they will test this claim out' (Polsky 1985: 117, original emphasis). At the same time, attention to the accurate recording of events is still paramount and problems with this, or the previous role, may focus on the researcher's recall. This is particularly the case in situations where note-taking is not possible. In the case of researching motorcycle gangs, for example, two authors spoke of the physical threats they faced:

> Even seemingly insignificant remarks sometimes caused a problem. In Biloxi on one occasion, we had an appointment to visit a biker clubhouse late on a Saturday afternoon in 1986. When we were admitted into the main room of the building, two women picked up four pistols that had been lying on a coffee table and scurried into a bedroom.
>
> (Hopper and Moore 1990: 369)

Third, we move away from the idea of participation to build up, over time, an understanding of a social setting, to the role of *observer as participant*. Strictly speaking, this would not be regarded as participant observation:

The observer-as-participant role is used in studies involving one-visit interviews. It calls for relatively more formal observation than either informal observation or participation of any kind.

(Gold 1969: 36)

Due to the lack of any lasting contact with people, Gold notes the possibility in this role of misunderstanding due to unfamiliarity with the culture and the language employed. It is more of an encounter between strangers which does not utilize the strengths of time in the field and getting to understand the rules, roles and relationships within the settings observed. Similarly, the *complete observer* is a non-participant role. At this end of the spectrum, the role completely removes the researcher from observed interactions and is epitomized by laboratory experiments which simply involve the mechanical recording of behaviour through, for example, one-way mirrors.

Access

If participant observation involves becoming part of a group or organization to understand it, then it is obviously not simply a case of 'hanging around'. To become part of a social scene and participate in it requires that the researcher is accepted to some degree. This period of 'moving into' a setting is both analytically and personally important. Those aspects of action which are 'strange' to the observer may be 'familiar' to the people who are part of the study. However, how people manage and interpret their everyday lives is an important condition of understanding a social scene. In this sense, the experiences of the observer are central. As we experience a new scene it feels 'strange': Fineman and Gabriel (1996) utilized this by drawing upon the accounts of new recruits to a variety of organizations. After a time, it becomes more familiar and it is understanding 'how' people achieve this which is a legitimate focus for participant observation:

> We learn what we can in advance about this relatively unknown territory, but once we are there, the first requirement is to gain some initial familiarity with the local scene and establish a social base from which we can continue our exploration until we are able to study some parts of that territory systematically.
>
> (Whyte 1984: 35)

It becomes important to regard the normal as unfamiliar. Further, in negotiating access into an organization, for instance, the researcher should be aware of power relations within the setting. As Severyn Bruyn notes:

> The participant observer who studies a complex social organization must be aware of the fact that clearance at one level of the organization does not insure clearance at another level. It is very important

that the researcher takes into account the levels of power and decision-making extant in the group.

(Bruyn 1966: 204)

If management are your level of entry into an organization, that could mean that others in the organization may be suspicious of your intentions. After all, they may consider that you are part of a management strategy of change. In such situations, the researcher must address these issues. However, while initial suspicion may be experienced, it is important not to regard this as a personal weakness, for it may be an understandable reaction on the part of the people within the setting or organization. Of course, this could block your entry, but access is not simply a stage, as many texts suggest, through which an observer passes before 'uncontaminated' data are supposedly derived (May 1993).

Initial reactions to your presence can cause a sense of personal discomfort, but tell you a great deal about relations and concerns of people and should be recorded and not simply regarded as personal problems or weaknesses. For instance, only two days after starting research on changes in a public sector organization (May 1991), I was questioned by two people who were apparently suspicious of my intentions. The questions were forcefully put and difficult to answer at the time. Yet I learnt from this episode. I learnt that suspicion was understandable due to the politically charged atmosphere surrounding organizational change. I learnt that my credibility as an impartial researcher was to be a central issue as I moved through different levels within the organization. My level of entry was management and not to have positively acted in the light of this initial suspicion would have meant, by default, carrying this suspicion with me. I also learnt that the two people who did the questioning had a vested interest in the changes taking place within the organization and, as such, any research associated with it.

Frequently in literature on the practice of participant observation, questions of access are regarded as methodological and/or theoretical inconveniences to be overcome. Researchers' actual experiences of fieldwork are then reserved for separate volumes (see C. Bell and Newby 1977; C. Bell and Roberts 1984; Bryman 1988b; Van Maanen 1988; Roberts 1990; D. Bell et al. 1993; Hobbs and May 1993). On the contrary, experiences gained during negotiations for access to a group or organization, as well as the researcher's reflections on the research in general, are fundamental to the aims of enhancing understanding and explaining social relations.

Utilizing flexibility

One of the main advantages of participant observation is its flexibility:

If you're half-way through a survey and one of the questions isn't working, you're worried, what are you going to do? You can't change it. Whereas if I learn today something useful from my field research, my observation, I can go out tomorrow and use it.

(Becker, in Mullan 1987: 120)

Fieldwork is a continual process of reflection and alteration of the focus of observations in accordance with analytic developments. It permits researchers to witness people's actions in different settings and routinely ask themselves a myriad of questions concerning motivations, beliefs and actions. Here are just a few for your reflection which could preoccupy any fieldworker: why did that happen and to whom? What do people ordinarily do in this setting and why? What would happen if people did X? What do they think about Y? What are the usual rules of the social scene? How are the rules negotiated? What are the verbal and non-verbal gestures employed? Who said what to whom and why? What do they mean and how do they relate to particular relationships and actions? Why is X not done? What would happen if something different happened? Finally, how does physical space relate to the setting and the interactions which take place within it? (Adapted from Lofland and Lofland 1984.)

These are just a small number of possible questions that ethnographers would routinely ask themselves during the course of fieldwork. It is then possible to focus the next series of observations on answering these questions and thereby utilizing the flexibility of the method. In addition, participant observation often employs the unstructured interview technique as a routine part of its practice. The comparison of data derived from these two methods is not assumed to be incompatible. The very opposite is the case for such comparisons illuminate the researcher's understanding and provide information which is simply not available through observation:

> Observation guides us to some of the important questions we want to ask the respondent, and interviewing helps us to interpret the significance of what we are observing. Whether through interviewing or other means of data gathering, we need to place the observed scene in context, searching for the potential positive or negative sanctions, which are not immediately observable but may be important in shaping behaviour.
>
> (Whyte 1984: 96)

The questions to which we are directed are formulated according to an exposure to the social scene over time and an observation of people's everyday actions. This, together with an explicit analytic framework and aims for the study, enables us to focus research inquiries. For this purpose Whyte uses what he calls an 'orientating theory' which 'simply tells us in the most general terms what data we are likely to need at the point of analysis' (Whyte 1984: 118). Data are collected under two headings (also mentioned in Chapter 6 under analysis): first, the identification of relationships within the social setting, and second, a description of events and situations which took place. Observation and the writing up of notes under these headings, together with any relevant interview data, provide a rich insight into social relations, events and processes. Data collection and analysis and the decision as to when to withdraw from fieldwork then take place together in what Glaser and Strauss (1967) refer to as 'theoretical sampling' and 'theoretical saturation', the latter referring to the time when observations no longer serve to question or modify the theories generated from earlier observations, thus rendering the theory 'saturated' with data.

Field notes

The 'data logging process', as Lofland and Lofland (1984) call it, is often regarded as boring but 'if the researcher lacks any personal emotional attachment to the concerns of the research, project quality (even completion) may be jeopardized' (1984: 47). This relies not only upon commitment, but also on the quality of the researcher's observations, field notes and analytic abilities. In relation to field notes, there are a series of guidelines which can be given which I shall briefly overview in this section, but researchers do vary in their methods. Some prefer to use school exercise books with wide margins on the left-hand side. These margins enable you to highlight particular observations in which you are interested, make analytic notes, or notes to yourself to investigate an event or relationship in more depth and read other literature on a topic or theme which you have observed or which has arisen from your observations. (I use a particular pencil, with a rubber on top, which enables me to write fairly quickly and make corrections – we all have our quirks!)

The notes made will depend upon the focus of your inquiries. As noted, the flexibility of this method is a considerable advantage and some time will be spent in familiarizing yourself with the social setting and the people within it (and they with you). Following this initial period, to take notes on anything and everything which happens is not only impossible, but also undesirable; your observations will be guided by your theoretical interests and they, in turn, modify or alter those. You will also need to minimize the time from observations to full notes to maintain good recall and in the initial stages of your research, make a running description of events noting those questions for the ethnographer outlined above, and any others which may arise or you wish to pose.

While the nature of relationships are noted, the order and setting in which events unfolded are important to note, as are the rules employed and your reflections upon the events observed (the latter being for the left-hand margin). Over time, a picture is built up of the roles, rules and relationships between people. For instance, Bob Burgess, in his study of a school, moved from a general description to more detailed and focused records:

in the staff common room my first set of fieldnotes begin by locating the position of the individuals with whom I sat. Gradually my notes detail a wider group of individuals, their names and their positions in the school until I could subdivide the groups in the staff common room according to their major characteristics.

(Burgess 1990: 169)

A particular notation and filing system for your notes is important: for example, key words to jog your memory; different quotation marks to indicate paraphrased and verbatim quotes; files on individuals, topics and events; theoretical 'memos' (see Strauss 1988) to yourself on the research, plus any supplementary data in the form of documents or previous literature and research on the subject. Whatever method you devise, the important issues are *consistency* and *accessibility*.

Subjective adequacy

In writing notes, the feeling often arises that the observer may have missed something or is being too selective in their observations or even too general. Severyn Bruyn (1966) assists in this concern by listing six indices of what he calls 'subjective adequacy' to enhance the understanding of the researcher and thereby the validity of the research. These are time, place, social circumstances, language, intimacy and social consensus. As authors on validity and qualitative research have noted (Kirk and Miller 1986), while this concept tends to be couched in terms of a positivist framework, Bruyn's ideas do assist in the continual process of reflexivity.

Time is the first of the indices. Quite simply, the more time that the observer spends with a group, the greater the adequacy achieved. As 'process' is a focus of inquiry,

> It is time which often tells us how deeply people feel about certain subjects. It is time that tells us how long it takes an outside influence to become a meaningful part of the lives of people in a culture. Those social meanings which really count in people's lives cannot be calculated by reference to the temporally limited, stimulus–response framework of the experimentalist. Cultural influences have an incubation period which takes time and close association to study.
>
> (Bruyn 1966: 207)

Second, there is *place*. A concentration on this dimension enables the researcher to consider the influence of physical settings upon actions. The researcher should record not only the interactions observed, but also the physical environment in which it takes place. Third, and closely related to this, are *social circumstances*. The more varied the observer's opportunities to relate to the group, in both terms of status, role and activities, the greater will be his or her understanding. In work on the probation service (May 1991), I spent time with officers in prisons, day centres and different types of courts, allowing me to observe probation work in different settings and the relationship between actions and social environments.

Fourth, there is *language*. The more familiar that researchers are with the language of a social setting, the more accurate will be their interpretations of that setting. Bruyn is using the term language in its 'broadest sense' (1966: 212) to encompass not only words and the meanings that they convey, but also non-verbal communications such as facial expressions and bodily gestures in general. As researchers become more familiar with this aspect of the social setting they learn the language of the culture and record their impressions and any changes in their own behaviour: 'language threads through subject and object, creating, expressing, and representing the life and character of the people studied' (Bruyn 1966: 213).

Fifth, there is *intimacy*. The greater the personal involvement with the group and its members, the more the researcher is able to understand the meanings and actions they undertake. This not only links in with social circumstances, but also provides access to a more private or 'backstage' world, which underlies the comments of one of the greatest observers of human action, Erving Goffman. He speaks of the 'front' and 'backstage behaviour' of people which the observer can witness:

> there tends to be one informal or backstage language of behaviour, and another language of behaviour for occasions when a performance is being presented. The backstage language consists of reciprocal first-naming, co-operative decision-making, profanity. . . . The frontstage behaviour language can be taken as the absence (and in some sense the opposite) of this.
>
> (Goffman 1984: 129)

Finally, there is *social consensus*. This is the extent to which the observer is able to indicate how the meanings within the culture are employed and shared among people. This ability is clearly assisted by being exposed, over time, to the culture and noting under what conditions and in what settings the meanings are conveyed. This links into what is known at the 'principle of verifiability' which enhances the reliability of the study. As Hughes (1976) describes it, social researchers achieve 'understanding' when they know the rules of a social scene and can communicate them to another person who could then 'become a member of the actor's group' (Hughes 1976: 134). In other words, not only familiarity, but also the ability to communicate to another person the rules operating within the setting in such a way that they could enter that setting and feel part of it. This, of course, is a regulative ideal which researchers should aim at, not something which can be achieved as such.

In this section I have sought to present an overview and introduction to the main issues involved in the process of undertaking participant observation: from the researcher's role, through access to a social scene, to the flexibility of the method and finally, questions of subjective adequacy. During each of these elements of the research process, the question of reflexivity has been raised. While this is applicable to all forms of research, with participant observation in particular, researchers and their experiences and observations are the means through which the data are derived. For this reason, a process of constant questioning takes place whether in the form of considering explicit theoretical formulations, or reflecting upon personal experiences which form an important component of those. Seeing these as a central part of the process greatly assists when it comes to the final analysis and writing-up of the research. Before moving on to the next section, I just wish to note a particular issue associated with reflexivity.

While it is important to locate the ethnographer at the centre of the research in terms of their interpretations, role and interactions, the current trend for reflexive accounting sometimes reads like an excuse for introspective indulgences. This can, as John Law (1994: 190) notes, actually disempower the reader in terms of their ability to critically engage with a representation of events. What is required is an understanding of the context and nature of interactions observed, *along with* an understanding of the relationship between observation and interpretation. A preoccupation with the latter, while of clear methodological importance, can actually render little justice to the subject matter under investigation. A balance in ethnographic accounts allows connections to be made and understandings to be enhanced on the part of the reader. An active and critical engagement thereby results.

The analysis of observations

Both the concept of reflexivity and the advantages of flexibility emphasize the process of analysis as part of fieldwork itself. At the same time, it was noted that researchers will also be constrained by the setting itself which may limit their abilities to conduct in-depth analysis at that stage. Therefore, the opportunity for reflection on experiences and a detailed analysis of the data may not come until the researcher has decided to withdraw from conducting any further fieldwork.

Howard Becker (1979a) lists four distinct stages of analysis whose overall aim is the categorization of collected data in order that the events, relationships and interactions observed may be understood or explained within the context of a developed theoretical framework. The first of the stages towards this aim is the 'selection and definition of problems, concepts and indices'. At this stage, researchers seek problems and concepts within the field setting which enable them to develop their understanding of the social setting; to determine the types of data which may be available by this method and to what extent observed social phenomena are related. Once established, observed phenomena are then placed within a theoretical framework for further investigation. Thus, in his research on medical students, Becker *et al.* (1961) observed them referring to particular patients as 'crocks'. By focusing upon the interactions between students and patients, a theory of how some groups within the hospital classified other groups, and for what reasons, was developed by further observations.

The second stage is a check on the 'frequency and distribution of phenomena'. This means focusing the inquiry in order to see what events 'are typical and widespread, and by seeing how these events are distributed among categories of people and organizational sub-units' (Becker 1979a: 317). It is at this point that the distinction between quantitative and qualitative work also breaks down (but not between good and bad research), because the researcher enters the realm of probability; in other words, how likely is it that a given phenomenon is frequent in the social setting and for what reason? It is possible to check such observations through interviewing and utilizing these forms of data, together with, say, documents on events – if available. This enables a check to be made against observations but, as Becker notes, this may not always be possible in the field, so observers have to consider what other evidence they may need at the final stage of analysis and collect it accordingly. For example, collecting the minutes of organizational meetings and comparing these with your notes at those meetings if observing the policy process in an organization (May 1991; May and Landells 1994). It is not infrequent to find yourself confronted by enormous amounts of data, much of which may not be of help in your theoretical formulations. However, it is better to have it at your disposal.

Third, Becker notes the 'construction of social system models' as the final stage of analysis 'in' the field, which 'consists of incorporating individual findings into a generalized model of the social system or organization under study or some part of that organization' (Becker 1979a: 319). This is similar in form to Glaser and Strauss's (1967) movement from substantive to formal theory and the need to make broader links in observational studies (Silverman 1993). In each setting, one may derive a concept of substantive theory grounded within observations. In analysing different contexts, the researcher can then move to more formal theory composed of abstract categories. I shall give some examples.

Glaser and Strauss (1967) studied the concept of loss in the case of nurses dealing with dying patients. In each setting, nurses understandably experienced social loss which manifested itself in various ways. However, this in turn depended on the general concept of what social value was attached to individuals. So they moved from the particular (observed experiences of social loss) to the more general (how people attach social value to each other and how that affects their experiences of loss).

Becker's (1963) work on marijuana use led to an interest in the process through which people redefine experiences in order to 'neutralize' their deviant status. Yet in his eagerness to show how wrong previous literature on drug use was, he ignored a larger and more general question: that is, 'how do people learn to define their own internal experiences?' (Becker 1986: 148). This focus led to a whole series of empirical studies leading towards a general theory of self-identifying activity. As Becker notes, in using literature on the topic to help you generate theory, the moral of this story is: 'Use the literature, don't let it use you' (Becker 1986: 149).

Finally, the importance of making broader links is clearly illustrated by Laurie Graham's (1995) study of the production line at Subaru-Isuzu. Her focus is upon new management techniques which seek to enhance quality and in so doing exercise greater control over the workforce. After providing rich and detailed accounts of work on the production line itself, she then situates these changes within a broader framework of what has been termed the 'Japanization of work' (Bratton 1992). These strategies are thus examined in terms of the differential skills that workers possess and their abilities to control certain aspects of these managerial changes whose overall aim is 'to manipulate workers' social experience within production' (L. Graham 1995: 152).

Aside from the use of previous literature, this method requires the constant comparison of data on the phenomena in which the researcher is interested. Thus, triangulated inquiry allows a comparison of data from interviews, observations, documents and even surveys (see Jick 1979; Whyte 1984; Fielding and Fielding 1986). The important point to remember is the level of generality at which you are operating, for this obviously differs between substantive and formal theory:

> Both types of theory exist on distinguishable levels of generality which differ only in degree. Therefore in any one study each type of theory can shade at points into the other. The analyst, however, needs to focus clearly on one level or the other, or on a specific combination, because the strategies vary for arriving at each one. Thus, if the focus is on the higher level of generality, then the comparative analysis should be made among different kinds of substantive cases and their theories, which fall within the formal area.
>
> (Strauss 1988: 242)

The need to make comparisons between substantive cases to generate formal theory makes the task of using a consistent method of filing notes, theoretical ideas and secondary sources (other studies, books and documents on the topic) all the more important.

Assisting at this and the other stages of analysis is the use of 'units'. A 'unit is a tool to use in scrutinizing your data' (Lofland and Lofland 1984: 71). In their outline of qualitative analysis, John and Lyn Lofland note that they emerge as the scale of organization increases and each new one contains past ones. Thus, you start with *meanings* such as cultural norms and people's definitions of the situation and the variations in the scope of rules in the social scene. You may then focus on *practices* such as recurrent categories of talk and action which you consider have analytic significance. You might then consider *episodes*, for example, the remarkable and dramatic such as crowd disorder and sudden illness and then move on to *encounters* (see Goffman 1961) where two or more people in each other's presence strive to maintain a single focus of mutual involvement. While how people 'get on' with each other appears mundane, it is also part of the social fabric which is observed and is worthy of attention in its own right.

A unit of analysis called *roles* is then of use. The focus here is directed towards the labels that people and organizations use to organize their own activities and describe those of others. How are these used? What are the issues in performing a role and what difficulties are encountered in their execution? These are just some of the questions to be asked. Then there are *relationships*. Noting Whyte's suggestion above on dividing data in terms of events and relationships, we would note how people regularly interact over time. From relationships we move to *groups* defined as those who conceive of themselves as a social entity (the 'we') having hierarchies, cliques and the means to cope with circumstances by mutual support or adaption. How and why these come about would be one focus of study of this social unit.

The units increase in abstraction with a focus upon *organizations*. The questions to ask yourself at this point and how this unit is defined are summarized by John and Lyn Lofland as

Consciously formed collectivities with formal goals that are pursued in a more or less planned fashion. Some major aspects of the analysis of organizations include the circumstances of their formation, how they recruit and control members, the types and causes of goal-pursuit strategies they adopt, and the causes of their growth, change, or demise.

(Lofland and Lofland 1984: 87–8)

Continuing with the theme of more general social units which encompass previous ones, there are *settlements*. These are beyond the grasp of the participant observer given their complex history and abstract nature. They comprise complex encounters, roles, groups and organizations within a defined territory which perform a range of functions. A classic example of this type of settlement analysis would be Whyte's *Street Corner Society* (1981, originally published 1943).

A more general and abstract social unit is that of *social worlds* which manifest themselves in terms of modern transportation and communication systems providing the means for the proliferation and rise of social units. However, these are 'sprawling, shapeless entities' (Lofland and Lofland 1984: 91) which are not reducible to any one of the other units they contain. Thus, we speak of 'business worlds' or 'political worlds'. Finally, there are *lifestyles* considered as global adjustments to life by large number of similarly like-minded and situated individuals. Here we might consider the social forces that create or channel our tastes and structure our cultural lives (for example, see R. Williams 1981; Williamson 1987; Chaney 1996).

Each of these different units may have different questions asked of them by the analyst. However, as we move away from what can be observed to more abstract entities, so too we move away from substantive to more formal theories. Yet this method of analysis is very useful for orientating the researcher to data which may, on first glance, appear unmanageable. This is where the development of an analytic framework during fieldwork renders the data both manageable and intelligible.

Becker (1979a) notes a final stage: the withdrawal from the field to a final analysis and writing-up of the results. At this stage there might be a search for data which does not appear to represent your emerging theoretical considerations. If so, it requires your consideration and explanation. At the same time, evidence is systematically collected in order to illustrate a particular theme which arises from the data or to illustrate the particular way in which an episode, encounter or relationship unfolded and the practices and the meanings utilized by the people concerned. This may lend itself to a *sequential* analysis whereby the chronological unfolding of a particular topic or event is examined. This goes back to the methods described in Chapter 6 for analysing focused interviews.

Aside from the suggestions of Glaser and Strauss (1967), Becker (1979a), Lofland and Lofland (1984) and Strauss (1988), there have been a number of interesting innovations in the analysis of qualitative data, one of which, as noted, employs computer programs for the mechanical indexing of the data (Fielding and Lee 1991). Others have specifically explored the relationship between feminism and fieldwork (A. Williams 1990), the use of deconstruction in postmodern research strategies (Game 1991; Denzin 1994) and qualitative analysis and semiotics (Manning 1987). This latter method focuses upon codes and signs used in social interaction whose analysis can be used for interpretative understanding of human relations and, for the purposes of policy analysis, organizational actions. Researchers may then focus upon the relationship between the use of language and human actions or study how language is employed in the social setting. Either way, what is often a difficult area of study may be employed in interesting new directions for qualitative researchers.

No matter how well the data are analysed, the results must be presented and communicated in a way which is both persuasive, well argued and accessible to the audience, although the actual witnessing and recording of actions can cause problems when it comes to publication (see Becker 1979b). The final result of your work is a text which attempts to persuade the audience of the authenticity of your descriptions and their analyses. In this sense, writers have focused on texts not only as reporting a reality 'out there', but also in terms of their abilities to construct social reality (P. Atkinson 1990):

Once cultures are no longer prefigured visually – as objects, theaters, texts – it becomes possible to think of a cultural poetics that is an interplay of voices, of positioned utterances. In a discursive rather than a visual paradigm, the dominant metaphors for ethnography shift away from the observing eye and toward expressive speech (and gesture). The writer's 'voice' pervades and situates the analysis, and objective distancing rhetoric is renounced.

(Clifford 1986: 12)

Nevertheless, to admit of the centrality of the ethnographer in the interpretative process does not imply an automatic opening for what is termed 'postmodern ethnography'. Here there is the attempt to deny any authority for the observer through, for example, allowing the narratives of the researched to 'speak for themselves' (see Fontana 1994). In thinking about these issues, I would like to conclude this section with a brief look at the writing of ethnography, noting that many of these points are equally applicable to other methods.

Writing ethnography

Harry Wolcott (1990) suggests several points which need to be borne in mind when writing-up fieldwork. First, maintain a focus on the topic and continually ask the question: 'What is this (really) a study of?' (Wolcott 1990: 46). However, don't let yourself suffer from writer's cramp:

> you have already made many choices when you sit down to write, but probably don't know what they were. That leads, naturally, to some confusion, to a mixed-up early draft. But a mixed-up early draft is no cause for shame. Rather, it shows you what your earlier choices were, what ideas, theoretical viewpoints, and conclusions you had already committed yourself to before you began writing. Knowing that you will write many more drafts, you know that you need not worry about this one's crudeness and lack of coherence. This one is for *discovery* not *presentation*.
>
> (Becker 1986: 17, emphasis added)

Second, Wolcott suggests that data must be 'ditched' as you home in on the topic. While interesting to you, a long rambling description of an event, without analytic mileage, may not be to the audience. Third, if you do not have the evidence for some issues, do not let it grind you down. Check your materials and if it is not available, then there is little you can do. Remember, researchers cannot claim to know everything! Fourth, unless otherwise prevented, write in the first person. Do not overdo it with constant 'Is', but you were centre stage in this method of data collection and reflexivity and biography is a legitimate part of its practice. Fifth, Wolcott suggests the past tense for writing to prevent the use of present and past tenses together (Wolcott 1990: 47). Sixth, to illustrate analytic points, utilize specific instances from field notes. This is part of Clifford Geertz's (1973a) notion of 'thick description' as it aligns the analytic framework with the imagination of the reader and a description of people's relationships and the events observed. Seventh, consider the audience for whom you are writing. Wolcott's suggestion is to write for those who know little of the area of study. This is a good discipline as it enables a degree of general accessibility to areas of academic study and is particularly important when considering action or evaluation research on behalf of an organization to whom you have to report.

Finally, there is the brevity of your writing. While it is important to get it first written and not just 'right', the craft of writing remains of central importance. Corrections, additions, revising and editing of the text are all part of the writing process through which everyone has to travel (Becker 1986). Again, a supportive and knowledgeable friend or supervisor can always be asked for their opinions in cases of doubt.

Issues in participant observation

As with Chapter 6 on interviewing, I have characterized the method of participant observation as not being the preserve of one school of thought and in so doing have again pre-empted some of the criticisms which are made by one perspective on the practice and theory of another. Interactionist researchers focus upon the operation of rules in social interaction, but not upon how these rules are formulated by people in context and so are criticized for presupposing their existence. Yet I have noted that how rules are formulated, negotiated and employed within interaction is a legitimate area of inquiry for observation. This point made, the ideas which inform 'naturalism' are worthy of further consideration for they are often apparent, in various guises, in the process and production of ethnographic research. Martyn Hammersley (1990b; 1990c; 1992), in particular, has turned his attention to the problems of naturalism and those of ethnography in general.

As noted in relation to interviewing, the idea of disengagement to produce 'untainted data' is something of a myth and is based upon a particular view of 'scientific procedure' challenged by feminists, postmodernists and those who generally emphasize the importance of reflexivity in the research process. Naturalism, although different in history and aim, often becomes translated as positivism by concentrating upon the production of data about the social world whose validity is based upon it being 'untainted' by the medium of its collection. Hence a lot of material on observation is devoted to 'reactivity', 'going native' and so on. On the other hand, naturalism focuses upon social life as a process in direct contrast to the positivist viewpoint. Given this state of 'flux', the positivist criteria of being able to replicate a study in order to justify its scientific status is rendered problematic (see Marshall and Rossman 1989).

The issues surrounding data collection as mediated by the researcher is not peculiar to observation, but as it relies so heavily upon the researcher's powers of observation and selection, then it is directly reliant upon his or her abilities. It is possible that researchers will omit a whole range of data in order to confirm their own pre-established beliefs, leaving the method open to the charge of bias. Further, the observation of small-scale settings leaves it open to the charge that its findings are local, specific and not generalizable: it lacks *external validity*. This may be challenged by arguing that the observed social scene is 'typical', by adopting the perspective of realism and examining the generative mechanisms of human interaction (Porter 1993), or through using a variety of data sources. However, on the latter point, Denzin's (1978a) original prescriptions for methodological, data, investigator and theoretical triangulation often read like a positivist desire to mediate between sources of data in the search for some 'truth' about the social world *independent* of people's interpretations and creations of it:

> Underlying this suggestion is, ironically, once more, elements of a positivist frame of reference which assumes a single (undefined) reality and treats accounts as multiple mappings of this reality.
>
> (Silverman 1985: 105)

Norman Denzin would no longer subscribe to such views (Denzin 1988; 1994). Yet this does not detract from the issue that the strict separation between fact and value that is found in versions of naturalism is highly problematic. In the actual practice of this method (as noted in Chapter 1), feminist researchers have argued that women may view the social world from a greater vantage point, given their exclusion from its dominant ways of working (D. Smith 1988), while practitioners of ethnography have noted how it often 'embodies implicitly masculine perspectives' (P. Atkinson 1990: 148).

Realists, while utilizing this method, have also criticized the idea that we can observe events or relationships free from theories or concepts. Thus, any distinction between theory on the one hand, and empirical data through neutral observation on the other, must be challenged for we mediate our observations through concepts acquired in everyday life (Sayer 1992). The difference between 'natural' and 'artificial' settings as presupposed by naturalism must therefore be highly questionable. Reflexivity, biography and theory lie at the heart of research practice in general and ethnography in particular. This emphasis recognizes that we are part of the world we study; that we bring to any setting our own experiences; that there is a constant interaction between theory and data and that these issues cannot be separated from each other.

Aside from the assumptions of naturalism, the problems of external validity and a masculine bias in its practice, participant observation has, for want of a better phrase, practical limitations. It demands that researchers spend time with relatively small groups of people in order to understand fully the social milieu which they inhabit. Hammersley and Atkinson, while advocates of this method, note that 'in contrast to the social survey, it is poor at dealing with large-scale cases such as big organizations or national societies' (Hammersley and Atkinson 1983: 237).

Once again we are left with not one single method as being the answer to all the methodological problems of social research. The use of a method or combination of methods will depend upon the aim of our research, the practical difficulties which are faced in the field and the time and money available to conduct the research in the first place. Its successful execution depends upon the skills of the researchers and their understanding of the issues which inform research practice. In this there is not an either/or choice between seeing ethnography as a neutral and accurate reflection of a social milieu on the one hand and a work of fiction on the other. Instead, the reflexive ethnographer considers the methods through which their interpretations are constructed and will utilize the cultural resources at their disposal. After all:

> There is little point in the academic agonizing over epistemology and methodology, or suffering the slings and arrows of data collection, only to have no disciplined awareness of the means available to report those efforts.
>
> (Hammersley and Atkinson 1995: 243)

Summary

Participant observation is about engaging in a social scene, experiencing it and seeking to understand and explain it. The researcher is the medium through which this takes place. By listening and experiencing, impressions are formed and theories considered, reflected upon, developed and modified. Participant observation is not an easy method to perform or to analyse, but despite the arguments of its critics, it is a systematic and disciplined study which, if performed well, greatly assists in understanding human actions and brings with it new ways of viewing the social world.

Questions for your reflection

1 What are the strengths and weaknesses of participant observation compared to other methods of social research?

2 'Work of fiction, or social fact.' What do you think is the scientific status of ethnography?

3 How do different roles of participant observation affect the data which are collected?

4 What is the relationship between social theory and the data collected by observational methods?

Suggested further reading

Clifford, J. and Marcus, G. (eds) (1986) *Writing Culture: The Poetics and Politics of Ethnography.* Berkeley: University of California Press.

Coffey, A. and Atkinson, P. (1996) *Making Sense of Qualitative Data: Complementary Research Strategies.* London: Sage.

Hammersley, M. and Atkinson, P. (1995) *Ethnography: Principles in Practice,* 2nd edn. London: Routledge.

Hobbs, D. and May, T. (eds) (1993) *Interpreting the Field: Accounts of Ethnography.* Oxford: Oxford University Press.

CHAPTER 8 Documentary research: excavations and evidence

The place of documents in social research
  Sources of documentary research
The process of documentary research
  Conceptualizing documents
  Using documents
  Approaching a document
The analysis of documents
  Quantitative and qualitative approaches
  A note on presentation of findings
Issues in documentary research
Summary
Questions for your reflection
Suggested further reading

The potential use of documents in social research, alongside observational data, was noted in Chapter 7. This could allow comparisons to be made between the observer's interpretations of events and those recorded in documents relating to those events. These sources may also be utilized in their own right. They can tell us a great deal about the way in which events were constructed at the time, the reasons employed, as well as providing materials upon which to base further research investigations. As such, the method is deserving of attention and, as we shall see, covers a wide variety of sources, including official statistics. The cautionary comments made in Chapter 4 on using secondary sources for research should thus be read alongside the following accounts.

The place of documents in social research

There are a wide variety of documentary sources at our disposal for social research. Documents, as the sedimentations of social practices, have the potential to inform and structure the decisions which people make on a daily and longer-term basis; they also constitute particular readings of social events. They tell us about the aspirations and intentions of the period to which they refer and describe places and social relationships at a time when we may not have been born, or were simply not present. Nevertheless, despite their importance for research purposes and in permitting a range of research designs (Hakim 1987), relative to the other methods we have come across, this is one of the least explained research techniques in the literature. Why should this be so?

Ken Plummer (1990) offers an answer to this question. The twin influences of positivistic methodologists and abstract theories on social research lead either to documents being dismissed as 'impressionistic', or to the use of any type of data being regarded as crude empiricism. Thus, despite the richness of documents, research reports based upon these sources are often 'relegated to the dustbins of journalism and the most marginal social science journals' (Plummer 1990: 149). In contrast to these tendencies, it is clear from his book that social research has much to learn from these sources.

A further reason focuses upon the use of documents for historical research. History is often thought to sit uneasily alongside social science disciplines (Goldthorpe 1984). Another possibility focuses upon the method itself. Documentary research is, in comparison to the other methods we have covered so far,

> not a clear cut and well-recognized category, like survey research or participant observation. . . . It can hardly be regarded as constituting a method, since to say that one will use documents is to say nothing about *how* one will use them.
>
> (Platt 1981a: 31, original emphasis)

To take each of these three points in turn. Positivism has been criticized as based upon a limited concept of science which, upon examination, cannot live up to its own canons of scientific inquiry, while its methods reproduce and reflect biases already contained within society. As for the debates on the relationship between history and social research, space precludes a detailed discussion. However, history as a discipline in its own right provides us with a sense of our 'past' and with that, the ways in which our 'present' came about. The nature of past social, political and economic relations are there for us to see through acts of historical research which enable us to reflect on contemporary issues. For instance, Geoff Pearson (1983) examines the view that hooliganism is symptomatic of a contemporary moral decline following a 'permissive age'. By employing a range of documentary sources going back to Victorian times, he examines what are often thought to be these 'golden ages', only to find identical fears being expressed in each period considered. This study therefore demonstrates that this phenomenon is not peculiar to contemporary times, as is widely believed.

The ways in which documents are used is clearly a methodological and theoretical question, as well as a matter for the technicalities that surround method. Take, for example, the idea that a document is a monument to the past. We can say, from this point of view, that history, in its traditional form, undertook to 'memorize' the monuments of the past, transform them into *documents*, and lend speech to those traces which, in themselves, are often not verbal, or which say in silence something other than what they actually say; in our time, history is that which transforms *documents* into *monuments*.

(Foucault 1989: 7, original emphasis)

In order to achieve this mode of analysis, matters of relevance, scope and relations need to be established. The means for doing so is to utilize the idea of a constant that may, for example, be invoked to demonstrate the gradual unfolding of history in terms of progress. Indeed, much of the history we read about is exactly of this type. What if, however, an event is analysed without invoking its relation to other events as part of, say, the forward march of rationalization towards a supposed better world? To question necessity in this way would require us to see events and thus documents of those events, not as self-evident, but as part of the ways in which truth is produced. This investigation of the mode of ordering of the social world is precisely what Foucault used in his studies of medicine, mental illness, sexuality and criminality:

If I have studied 'practices' like those of the sequestration of the insane, or clinical medicine, or the organization of the empirical sciences, or legal punishment, it was in order to study this interplay between a 'code' which rules ways of doing things (how people are to be graded and examined, things and signs classified, individuals trained, etc.) and a production of true discourses which serve to found, justify and provide reasons and principles for these ways of doing things.

(Foucault 1991: 79)

These different approaches to documents are fundamental to how we see ourselves and our surroundings. Yet on a more instrumental level, the ambiguities and tensions surrounding documentary research are changing as more researchers utilize documents due to the increasing availability of data in modern societies. As such, researchers need to be aware of the documentary sources which may be used, as well as the ways in which they are used (Jennifer Platt's 'how'). The next section considers various documentary sources for social research and the second part of the chapter examines the perspectives and processes which inform their use and collection.

Sources of documentary research

These include historical documents, not only laws, declarations and statutes, but also secondary sources such as people's accounts of incidents or periods in which they were involved. However, while many definitions of documents are narrow in scope, John Scott offers a broad definition for research purposes which is worth quoting at length:

> a document in its most general sense is a written text. . . . Writing is the making of symbols representing words, and involves the use of a pen, pencil, printing machine or other tool for inscribing the message on paper, parchment or some other material medium. . . . Similarly, the invention of magnetic and electronic means of storing and displaying text should encourage us to regard 'files' and 'documents' contained in computers and word processors as true documents. From this point of view, therefore, documents may be regarded as physically embodied texts, where the containment of the text is the primary purpose of the physical medium.
>
> (J. Scott 1990: 12–13)

A report based on official statistics would be covered by this definition. To these we could add other government records: for example, Hansard, ministerial records, debates, political speeches, administrative and government committee records and reports, etc. In addition, the content of the mass media, novels, plays, maps, drawings, books and personal documents such as biographies, autobiographies, diaries and oral histories, the latter being used in work and life-history analyses (Samuel 1982; K. Anderson *et al.* 1990; Plummer 1990; Dex 1991). We can call biographies and diaries 'life-course documents':

> These documents are generated after the events they describe, but they are written on the basis of those events. The diary is a contemporaneous record of the psychological life-course, whereas the biography must be constructed from a past which must be revived before it can be described. In consequence, biography and autobiography are epistemologically distinct from diary.
>
> (Harré 1993: 220)

To this list we can add photographs which, although existing on the borderline between the 'aesthetic' and 'documentary' (J. Scott 1990: 13), may be records of events. For that reason, attention has also been turned to these with interesting results (Sontag 1978; Bourdieu *et al.* 1990; Farran 1990; Spence and Holland 1991; A. Young 1996). It is not surprising, given such a catalogue of sources, that Scott's book aims 'to recognise this diversity in documentary sources as a valuable feature of social research' (J. Scott 1990: 13). Let us examine both the physical and documentary sources available to researchers.

According to E. Webb *et al.* (1966) researchers may use 'physical traces' as part of what they call 'unobtrusive measures' of social research. Sherlock Holmes used 'physical' evidence in his deductions which they define as those pieces of data not specifically produced for the purpose of comparison and inference, but available to be exploited opportunistically by the alert investigator.

(E. Webb *et al.* 1966: 36)

Into this category would fall evidence left at the scene of a crime such as hair, or a piece of fabric from clothing. These are further subdivided into 'erosion' and 'accretion' measures. Erosion measures are defined as those 'where the degree of selective wear on some material yields the measure' (E. Webb *et al.* 1966: 36). One example might be the degree of wear on a carpet to determine the frequency of its use, or the wear on library books for a similar purpose. Indeed, the wear on vinyl tiles surrounding an exhibit in a museum in Chicago provided an indicator of its popularity with visitors (E. Webb *et al.* 1966: 36). In terms of the popularity of library books, this could be ascertained by using library records whether in manual or computer format. Indeed, it might even be possible to determine when people attend their places of work by whether they have collected their mail and if using a computer, how often they log in and at what times.

Accretion measures, on the other hand, are deposits of materials (E. Webb *et al.* 1966: 36). One such example, to continue with the detective analogy, is the deposit of mud on shoes. The mud can be analysed and its likely location established, telling detectives where the suspect or victim may have come from. In a similar way, archaeologists estimate the populations of ancient sites by the size of the floor area of excavated buildings.

Literature on the classification of documents (E. Webb *et al.* 1966; Denzin 1978a; Burgess 1990; J. Scott 1990; Calvert 1991; Forster 1994) tends to fall into three main groups: first, primary, secondary and tertiary documents; second, public and private documents; and third, unsolicited and solicited sources. Primary sources refer to those materials which are written or collected by those who actually witnessed the events which they describe. In Bertrand Russell's (1912) terms they represent knowledge by *acquaintance*. It is therefore assumed that they are more likely to be an accurate representation of occurrences in terms of both the memory of the author (time) and their proximity to the event (space). However, as Burgess notes (1990: 124), these sources must also be seen in social context and for this purpose, the researcher might employ secondary sources. These are written after an event which the author had not personally witnessed and the researcher has to be aware of potential problems in the production of this data. Tertiary sources enable us to locate other references. They are 'indexes, abstracts and other bibliographies. . . . There are even bibliographies to help us find bibliographies' (Calvert 1991: 120). Libraries often possess collections of abstracts and reference manuals which assist in this process.

The distinction between public and private documents is an important one. The fact that materials may exist tells us little about whether the researcher may gain access to them. For this reason, John Scott (1990) divides documents into four categories according to the degree of their accessibility. They are closed, restricted, open-archival and open-published. In his study of the life and thought of Sydney Olivier (an early Fabian thinker), Frank Lee (1988) found it necessary to seek the permission of the guardians of the private 'Olivier Family Papers', whose access is restricted.

In terms of public documents, the largest category are those produced by national and local governments and would include, for example, registrations of births, marriages and deaths and also police, taxation and housing records. Some of these documents may be protected by the Official Secrets Act and are therefore closed. Few official records, as Scott notes, fall into the restricted category; one example is the British royal papers to which access may be granted only by the monarch (J. Scott 1990: 17). Open-archived records are stored in the Public Records Office (PRO) at Kew, in Richmond, Surrey, or, in the case of the United States, the Library of Congress. Open-published documents include many of those covered in Chapter 4, plus Acts of Parliament and Hansard records of parliamentary debates.

Finally, we come to the third group: solicited and unsolicited documents. Burgess (1990) makes this distinction on the grounds that some documents would have been produced with the aim of research in mind, whereas others would have been produced for personal use. Diaries, for example, may be used in social research by asking participants to record particular events and/or express their opinions upon them. However, even if they are for personal consumption and are accessible to a researcher, they are still 'addressed to an audience' (Thompson 1982: 152), or what has been called a 'model reader' (Eco 1979). It is this sense of social context and to whom a document or text may be addressed, which brings us round to a discussion of the perspectives in and processes of documentary research.

The process of documentary research

Conceptualizing documents

There are several ways in which researchers might conceptualize a document and frame their research questions accordingly. In one guise or another, we have encountered most of them in our discussions of other methods. For some researchers a document represents a reflection of reality. It becomes a medium through which the researcher searches for a correspondence between its description and the events to which it refers. Yet if we can read off the accounts of a document, separate from the methods we employ to achieve this, are we not suggesting, once again, that there are social facts which exist independently of interpretations? We have already encountered the problems of this positivistic approach.

In contrast, other approaches consider documents as representative of the practical requirements for which they were constructed. In this focus we would examine what Cicourel (1964) has called the 'unstated meaning structures' of documents. The document itself is taken to stand for some underlying social pattern or use value. Thus, in his classic study on juvenile justice (Cicourel 1976), he examined the translation of oral conversations between juveniles and police and probation officers into written reports. These reports attempted to justify the procedures adopted for this purpose, but were also open-ended in their translation. This provided for 'various constructions of "what happened"' (Cicourel 1976: 17). They were thereby based upon a form of 'practical reasoning' which rendered the social order of juvenile justice accountable and comprehensible and yet open to negotiation and manipulation by interested parties. There are parallels here with the discussion on official statistics as 'accomplishments' and interviews as topics and not resources. Let us take one further illustrative example.

Research by Zimmerman (1974) on caseworkers' use of documents in a welfare agency firmly places the use of administrative documents within what he calls 'practical organizational purposes'. On most occasions, information contained within them is accepted without question as 'fact'. If it is questioned by, for example, a welfare claimant, the document then stands as the arbitrator of these 'facts'. Indeed, the suggestion that the document may be false was regarded by agency staff as 'incredible':

> For them, the possibilities opened up by such a doubt, including the possibility of a conspiracy between the applicant and the document-producing organization, were not matters for idle speculation. The possibility of error was admitted, but only as a departure from ordinarily accurate reportage.
>
> (Zimmerman 1974: 133)

Moving away from the idea that a document independently reports social reality, or its production is yet another method by which people accomplish social order, we now utilize our own cultural understandings in order to 'engage' with 'meanings' which are embedded in the document itself. Researchers do not then apologize for being part of the social world which they study but, on the contrary, utilize that very fact. A document cannot be read in a 'detached' manner. Instead, we must approach documents in an engaged manner. This emphasis on *hermeneutics* (discussed in Chapter 1 and elsewhere) submits the analyst to consider the differences between their own frames of meanings and those found in the text. A researcher might then begin with an analysis of the common-sense procedures which came to formulate the document in the first instance, but their analysis need not end there. The document may be located within a wider social and political context. Researchers then examine the factors surrounding the *process* of its production, as well as the social *context*. It becomes

> necessary to rise above, not only the particularity of texts, but also the particularity of the rules and recipes into which the art of understanding is dispersed. Hermeneutics was born with the attempt to raise exegesis and philology to the level of a *Kunstlehre*, that is, a 'technology' which is not restricted to a mere collection of unconnected operations.
>
> (Ricoeur 1982: 45, original emphasis)

What people decide to record is itself informed by decisions which, in turn, relate to the social, political and economic environments of which they are a part:

> fields of learning, as much as the works of even the most eccentric artist, are constrained and acted upon by society, by cultural traditions, by worldly circumstance, and by stabilizing influences like schools, libraries, and governments . . . both learned and imaginative writings are never free, but are limited in their imagery, assumptions, and intentions.
>
> (Said, in Easthope and McGowan 1992: 59)

Documents might be interesting for what they leave out, as well as what they contain. They do not simply reflect, but also construct social reality and versions of events. The search for the documents' 'meaning' continues, but with researchers also exercising 'suspicion'. It is not then assumed that documents are neutral artefacts which independently report social reality (positivism), or that analysis must be rooted in that nebulous concept, practical reasoning.

Documents are now viewed as media through which social power is expressed. They are approached in terms of the cultural context in which they were written and may be viewed 'as attempts at persuasion' (Sparks 1992). Approaching a document in this way 'tells us a great deal about the societies in which writers write and readers read' (Agger 1991: 7). It might, for example, reflect the marginalization of particular groups of people and the social characterization of others: for example, in her study of the way in which the media represented the Greenham women who protested against nuclear weapons, Alison Young did not take their reports at face value:

> This strategy of rejection and repudiation I take to be axiomatic for any critique of representational forms such as the press, which continually foster the desire for consensual world views, unifying and objective underlying orders, monolithic structures and the obscuring of differences.
>
> (A. Young 1990: 164–5)

Within this approach, the very act of reading a text may become the revision of its premises. Thus, for Adrienne Rich, a feminist reading of a text is also an act of refusal. The researcher concentrates on the way in which it constructed the contribution of women to an event, but the strategy of refusal enables women to see their contemporary social and political situation in a new light:

> the act of looking back, of seeing with fresh eyes, of entering an old text from a new critical direction – is for women more than a chapter in cultural history: it is an act of survival. Until we can understand the assumptions in which we are drenched we cannot know ourselves.
>
> (Rich, in Humm 1992: 369)

Critical approaches to documentary sources are far from being unified bodies of thought. As noted, Michel Foucault's work, for instance, is a critical project which is not so concerned with the relationship between the author and the document, but the ways in which the use of a document in linked to the present:

> For no matter how much historical writing is about dimensions or aspects of the past, and refers to events, irruptions, discourses, and social practices that can be given a particular time-space, it is in fact an activity that is irrevocably linked to its current uses.
>
> (M. Dean 1994: 14)

The poststructuralist work of both Michel Foucault and Jacques Derrida (see Game 1991; Kamuf 1991) are influenced by a 'semiotic' approach to textual analysis (mentioned in Chapter 7). This is particularly represented in the work of Roland Barthes (1967). In contrast, there are those who are critical of this approach as it appears to suggest that a text does not refer to anything beyond itself nor to the intentions of its author. We return, once again, to the issue of whether a text (which would include an interview transcript or observation field notes) corresponds to the events which it describes: is it a topic *of* social research or a resource *for* social research? It is argued that a text must be approached in terms of the intentions of its author and the social context in which it was produced.

Following from Giddens's (1979; 1984) approach, John Scott (1990) suggests that a researcher should approach a document in terms of three levels of meaning interpretation. First, the meanings that the author *intended* to produce. Second, the *received* meanings as constructed by the audience in differing social situations, and third, the *internal* meanings that semioticians exclusively concentrate upon. However, they cannot 'know' these 'independently of its reception by an audience' (J. Scott 1990: 34).

These are new directions in documentary research which move away from the positivist emphasis that Plummer (1990) identified as one impediment to their use in social research. Collectively, they represent various approaches to analysis and combine elements of realism, critical theory, feminism, postmodernism and poststructuralism. These are not easy ideas to grasp, particularly as positivism has held such a grip on social research for so long. However, to present the 'how' which Platt (1981a) referred to as being one perspective on documentary research would be an inaccurate representation of their contemporary use (as well as being counter to the philosophy underlying this book).

Using documents

The above perspectives noted, I now wish to move on to the process of collecting documents. For this purpose I shall use two examples, one drawn from the use of past documents to understand events and relationships, the other being a media research project. In the process it will become evident that the methods utilized depend not only upon the researcher's perspectives, but also on the time and resources available, the aims of the research and the problems encountered in the collection of data. As we shall see with the first example, if we are relying solely upon this technique, we cannot rectify this by producing the data ourselves. Nevertheless, with John Scott's (1990) broad definition of a document and the vast generation of information which now characterizes modern societies, this may not be a problem unless dealing with particular historical periods. A number of problems may then be encountered.

David Dunkerley's (1988) research account provides a useful summary of some of these problems in his 'case study research' (see Yin 1988; Collinson 1994; Stake 1995) which examined the relationship between a naval dockyard and the local community. This account appears in a volume which deliberately aims to show how research was actually carried out, as opposed to the ideals of methodological procedure. It demonstrates that even the most experienced researchers are subject to issues associated with time and money and the availability and accessibility of documentary evidence.

Dunkerley's study aimed to

> concentrate upon the origin of the dockyard labour force, the extent of intergenerational job transmission, internal work structure, job security and political attitudes, and the effect of mobility opportunities.
>
> (Dunkerley 1988: 85)

Three methods of documentary inquiry were chosen for this purpose. First, a sample of population censuses dated since 1851, which are kept at the Public Records Office (PRO). The aim was to gain information on levels of employment, birthplaces, and so on, across time. Second, the use of local histories, as well as Admiralty and Treasury Papers (also at the PRO). These sources would specifically relate to dockyard labour relations, employment opportunities and skills to be found within the locality. Third, the use of oral histories based on interviews with three generations of dockyard workers.

Three immediate problems arose in what the author notes was an ambitious exercise given the constraints of time and resources (Dunkerley 1988: 86). First, it was assumed that the historical records would be available. As it transpired, local information either was not available or no longer existed (due to bombing raids during the Second World War). In addition, what there was turned out to be catalogued in the PRO under obscure headings. Second, the type of material collected by the Census changed over the years, making its collection either a non-starter, or rendering the ability to compare changes, across time, untenable. Third, when it came to more recent and detailed information, it was 'subject to closure and simply not available to the bona fide researcher' (Dunkerley 1988: 86). What information there was also proved to take a considerable time to extract.

As a result of these problems and the distance that the researcher had to travel to get to the research site, the aims of the dockyard community study were altered and additional funding had to be sought. In the end, the study concentrated upon 'technological and historical development covering a period spanning the last century' (Dunkerley 1988: 87). This change of focus took account of cost and time, as well as the availability of documentary evidence.

This account demonstrates that researchers have to be aware of the possibility that the information which they seek is 'closed'. In researching people over the age of 90, for example, researchers were prevented by the Department of Social Security from obtaining sample names from records (Bury and Holme 1990). Furthermore, even if documents are available, if they are hand-written the researcher may have problems in reading them, or they may have been damaged over time. Diaries and other personal documents, in particular, use abbreviations and coded references to individuals or events which may be difficult to interpret. One of the most famous diarists, Samuel Pepys (1633–1703), often used codes in his diary entries (J. Scott 1990: 179). Finally, in terms of the use of documents generally, as well as specifically in relation to organizational research, it is worth remembering:

> They should never be taken at face-value. In other words, they *must* be regarded as information which is context-specific and as data which must be contextualized with other forms of research. They should, therefore, only be used with caution.
>
> (Forster 1994: 149, original emphasis)

The second example is based upon a field of study which examined the relationship between the media and their depictions of criminal or deviant activity (also see Cameron and Frazer 1987; Caputi 1987; Sparks 1992; A. Young 1996). While they differ in their methodological and theoretical approaches, they all employ documentary sources in one form or another. In order to consider this process, I shall concentrate on the works of Richard Ericson and his colleagues.

A study by Ericson *et al.* (1991) examined the content of news sources on crime, law and justice. Following their previous work (1987; 1989) their perspective viewed news as not only reflecting but also actively constructing our sense of the social reality to which it refers. Journalists themselves are implicated within societal apparatuses of social control by constructing news which visualizes and symbolizes crime and attempts to convince the audience of the authority of its descriptions. After all, most people learn of crime, law and order via the media:

> Through dramatized descriptions, metaphoric language, and pictures, news depicts events that are called up in the mind (visualized) even while they remain invisible to the eye. News representations are symbolic in the sense they embody, stand for, or correspond to persons, events, processes, or states of affairs being reported. News representation involves authorization of who can be a representative or spokesperson of a source organization, of what sources are 'authorized knowers'.
>
> (Ericson *et al.* 1991: 5)

The aim of this study was to examine the ways in which different media sources operated according to the markets they were located within. For this purpose the authors took a sample of radio, television and newspaper outlets, covering issues of crime, legal control, deviance and justice in the Toronto region of Canada. This provided a comparison of the different ways in which news was depicted. These sources were also grouped into 'quality' and 'popular' so the variations between markets could be examined. However, this was a study of news 'content'. Yet it has been emphasized that social 'context' is fundamental to understanding the meanings contained within documents. The authors were only too aware of this point:

> News, like law and science, is a socially constructed product that is highly self-referential in nature. That is, news content is used by journalists and sources to construct meanings and expectations about their organizations. This means that the analyst of news *content* must examine the meaning used by news producers in the *construction* of their product.
>
> (Ericson *et al.* 1991: 49, emphasis added)

In order to locate the study of patterns of meanings in media texts by the use of *content analysis*, they drew upon their previous ethnographic work on journalists and the construction of news sources (Ericson *et al.* 1987; 1989). The texts themselves were sampled over a period of 33 days to study them across time. The aim was to compare quality and popular newspapers, with an evening broadcast on quality and popular television and an evening quality and popular radio broadcast. The newspapers were sampled by pages; the television broadcasts were videotaped and the radio broadcasts audiotaped. The radio and television reports were transcribed – verbatim – along with notes on the use of 'visuals' and the use of sounds other than words. The result was a vast number of data which were analysed in considerable detail and located within their previous studies on news construction.

Approaching a document

Having discussed these examples, it remains to consider in this section with what questions a researcher should approach a document? This is not an exhaustive list, but points to the main themes raised in the process of documentary research. John Scott (1990) proposes four criteria for assessing the quality of the evidence available from documentary sources. This section considers each of these: authenticity, credibility, representativeness and meaning.

The issue of a document's *authenticity* is essential to the conduct of this form of research: 'Judgement of authenticity from the internal evidence of the text comes only when one is satisfied that it is technically possible that the document is genuine' (Calvert 1991: 121).

Even an unauthentic document, however, could be of interest because 'it cannot be fully and correctly understood unless one knows that it is not authentic' (Platt 1981a: 33). Platt therefore provides several guidelines for assessing their authenticity. First, it contains obvious errors or is not consistent in its representation. Second, different versions of the same document exist. Third, there are internal inconsistencies in terms of style, content, handwriting, etc. Fourth, the document has passed through the hands of several copyists. Fifth, the document has been in the hands of a person or persons with a vested interest in a particular reading of its contents. Sixth, the version derives from a suspect secondary source. Seventh, it is inconsistent in relation to other similar documents. Finally, it is 'too neat' in terms of being representative of a certain group of documents (Platt 1981a: 34). Forster, in his suggestions for analysing company documentation, sums up these checks on authenticity by suggesting that the researcher ask the following questions:

> Are the data genuine? Are they from a primary or secondary source? Are they actually what they appear to be? Are they authentic copies of originals? Have they been tampered with or corrupted? Can authorship be validated? Are the documents dated and placed? Are they accurate records of the events or processes described? Are the authors of documents believable?
>
> (Forster 1994: 155)

In her own study of the history of research methods in the United States, for example, Jennifer Platt (1996) examines writings on method using articles in leading journals and textbooks of the period in question (1920–60). While not assuming that they were representative of commitments to particular methods, this allowed her to consider to what extent reports of practice conformed to particular theoretical commitments at the time. By using various sources, including interviews, she was able to build up a picture of the relationship between theory and method and argued that the former could not explain the adoption or genesis of the latter (see May 1997).

Following the questioning of a document's authenticity, there is its *credibility*. This 'refers to the extent to which the evidence is undistorted and sincere, free from error and evasion' (J. Scott 1990: 7). Questions to ask at this point include the following: are the people who record the information reliable in their translations of the information that they receive? How accurate were their observations and records? To achieve this, we may employ other sources on the life and political sympathies of the author. This will enable the researcher to establish the social and political context in which the document was produced.

Representativeness has been referred to as a question of 'typicality' in Chapter 7. The issue of whether a document is typical depends on the aim of the research. 'Untypical' documents may be of interest, so we should not become too obsessed with this issue as it is driven as much by the aims of the study. Nevertheless, if we are concerned with drawing conclusions which are intended to argue that there is a 'typical document' or a 'typical method' of representing a topic in which we are interested, then this is an important consideration in order to demonstrate how one interpretation of an event predominates to the exclusion of others. For instance, Calvert (1991) notes how some documents are deliberately destroyed and protests in the United States over the 'systematic bias' of a series entitled *Foreign Relations of the United States*.

Finally, there is the question of a document's *meaning*. This refers to the clarity and comprehensibility of a document to the analyst. Two questions are of concern: 'what is it, and what does it tell us?' (J. Scott 1990: 8). However, these are far from easy questions to answer. Going back to the example of the media research of Ericson and his colleagues, meanings were set within a social context derived from previous studies. Thus, while meanings change and the use of words varies, an idea of social context enables understanding.

The method of documentary research, like all of those we covered so far, requires not only some practice, but also a reflexivity on the part of the researcher. So far I have endeavoured to provide you with an introduction to a method which has, in the past, been subsumed under the dominance of the others we have discussed. This, I believe, is a shortfall. As I hope to have shown, it is a valuable method for understanding and explaining social relations. It now remains for me to consider the analysis of documents and issues in their use.

The analysis of documents

We have considered a document in terms of its authenticity, representativeness, credibility and meaning; Scott (1990) divides 'meaning' into intended, received and content meaning. Building on these themes, this section will follow the same pattern as in Chapters 5–7 in presenting an overview of approaches in order that readers may pursue particular areas of interest. This is particularly pertinent given that a number of theoretical issues have been raised, from mainstream positivism, through the interpretation of documents in terms of practical reasoning, to semiotic, hermeneutic, feminist and critical approaches. Differences of emphasis clearly exist in terms of how a document is approached. In terms of life histories, Plummer's (1990) approach considers the intentions and purposes of the author. Yet to those influenced by Barthes (1967), the text takes on a life of its own, separate from the author. Given these differing perspectives, it is not surprising to find documents analysed in both quantitative and qualitative ways.

Quantitative and qualitative approaches

Documents do not stand on their own, but need to be situated within a theoretical frame of reference in order that its content is understood. For this purpose we can use *content* analysis which comprises three stages: stating the research problem, retrieving the text and employing sampling methods and interpretation and analysis. This focus considers the frequency with which certain words or particular phrases occur in the text as a means of identifying its characteristics. The resultant analytic framework makes sense of the data through generated theoretical categories. This method takes both quantitative and qualitative forms. Quantitative content analysis

> seeks to show patterns of regularities in content through repetition, and qualitative content analysis . . . emphasizes the fluidity of the text and content in the interpretive understanding of culture.
>
> (Ericson *et al.* 1991: 50)

As with interviewing and observation, the use of computer packages in the analysis of texts is helpful towards these ends. These assist in searching for individual words and phrases and their frequency or context in the text; they can also help in analysing connections between codes or categories of behaviour that the production of the document might represent (see Fielding and Lee 1991). Content analysis is employed on a commercial basis by those interested in the computing, communications and media sectors and it is possible to retrieve newspaper text on either CD-ROM or commercial on-line databases, bearing in mind the cost differential:

> Having the text on CD-ROM offers advantages in terms of unlimited use (once the disc has been purchased), unlike the use of on-line

data-bases where usage is restricted by the cost of on-line time and the cost of lines of text read.

(Hansen 1995: 150–1)

As with discussions on standardization in Chapter 5, the quantitative analyst would seek to derive categories from the data in order that it can be compared. Words or phrases in the document are transformed into numbers. The number of times in which a word occurs in the text is taken as an indicator of its significance; a strategy assumed to enhance both the reliability and validity of the classified data. Therefore, it is taken for granted 'that there exists a defensible correspondence between the trans-formed account and the way the information was meant in its original form' (Garfinkel 1967: 190–1).

In considering the problems of a quantitative count, the issues covered in previous chapters are again raised. First, this method considers product and says little of process. In the context of this discussion, it deals only with what has been produced, not the decisions which informed its pro-duction which tell us so much about its received and intended meanings. Second, an empiricist problem is raised for it deals only with information which can be measured and standardized and for this reason considers only data which can be simplified into categories. Third, in this preoccu-pation, it reproduces the meanings used by authors in the first instance, as opposed to subjecting them to critical analysis in terms of the political, social and economic context of their production. Fourth, from an ethno-methodological perspective, it fails to understand the practical organiza-tional context of their production and interpretation as part of the methods by which people make sense of their social world (Benson and Hughes 1991). Fifth, it assumes that the audience who receive the message must translate it as the analyst does. By default, it thereby negates the idea that a text is open to a number of possible readings by its audience. (Would all people read the same meanings into a diary account or news-paper report? If not, why?) To return to the discussion in Chapter 1, this can so easily become a crude stimulus–response model of human behav-iour: that is, what people read is what they think. Analysts have only to read the text to know what the audience is automatically thinking.

The frequency with which words or phrases occur in a text (a quanti-tative emphasis) may therefore say nothing about its 'significance within the document' (a qualitative emphasis):

It may be that a single striking word or phrase conveys a meaning out of all proportion to its frequency; and a non-quantitative approach may be better able to grasp the significance of such isolated references. The content analyst must engage in an act of qualitative synthesis when attempting to summarise the overall meaning of the text and its impact on the reader.

(J. Scott 1990: 32)

Thus, to return to the points made earlier, the text (be it a document, diary, etc.), the audience of the text and its author become three essential components in a process of Scott's meaning construction (intended, received and content meaning). According to Scott, for researchers to grasp its significance, they should concentrate upon what the author intended when he or she produced the document; the meaning given to it by the potential audience (including the analyst who, by an act of reading, is part of that audience and thus needs to act reflexively) and finally, between these two, the text itself which the content analysts and semioticians concentrate upon. These components add up to a simple observation: 'A document's meaning cannot be understood unless one knows what genre it belongs to, and what this implies for its interpretation' (Platt 1981b: 53).

Qualitative content analysis, on the other hand, starts with the idea of process, or social context, and views the author as a self-conscious actor addressing an audience under particular circumstances. The task of the analyst becomes a 'reading' of the text in terms of its symbols. With this in mind, the text is approached through understanding the context of its production by the analyst themselves. This may be derived either through the use of secondary sources or, as in the above example, other methods such as observational studies:

> In the process, the analyst picks out what is relevant for analysis and pieces it together to create tendencies, sequences, patterns and orders. The process of deconstruction, interpretation, and reconstruction breaks down many of the assumptions dear to quantitative analysts.
>
> (Ericson *et al.* 1991: 55)

The flexibility of this method, as with participant observation, is regarded as a prime advantage. It enables the researcher to consider not only the ways in which meaning is constructed, but also the ways in which new meanings are developed and employed. Thus, Alison Anderson's (1997) study provides us with a detailed insight into the relationship between the media and the cultural construction of environmental issues. In particular, she undertakes an in-depth examination of pressure politics and the environmental lobby and casts a critical eye over the production, transmission and negotiation of news discourses. In the process, theory is generated, modified and tested from the particulars of the document to a general understanding of its context and ways of representing the social world.

From the above we can say that although it is important, as Scott argues, to link the text to its author (the writer's intended meanings, as a diarist, journalist or the writer of an autobiography), texts are also used in ways which depend on the social situation of the audience (the reader's received meaning). This allows, contrary to the emphasis of quantitative analysis, for a variety of readings. As with interviews and observational data, analysis using computing programs may assist in this process (see Fielding and Lee 1991; R.M. Lee 1995).

Aside from this emphasis on intended and received meaning, there is also content meaning upon which content analysts and semioticians focus their attention. Semiotics is a complicated area of study, but one definition we can use comes from what Umberto Eco calls a 'specific semiotics':

> A specific semiotics is, or aims at being, the 'grammar' of a particular sign system, and proves to be successful insofar as it describes a given field of communicative phenomena as ruled by a system of signification. Thus there are 'grammars' of the American Sign Language, of traffic signals, of a playing-card 'matrix' for different games or a particular game (for instance, poker).
>
> (Eco 1984: 5)

From a methodological point of view we can say that semiotics is concerned with examining the relationship between a signifier and a signified (the idea or concept to which the signifier refers). The latter may not refer to a material object, but the way in which a system of language, through its signs, organizes the world. A semiotician thus approaches a document in order to explain its principles of signification; the overall aim being, as Peter Manning puts it,

> to explain how the meanings of objects, behaviours, or talk is produced, transformed and reproduced. . . . The interpretant connects an *expression* or signifier (a word, a picture, a sound) with a *content* or signified (another word, image or depiction).
>
> (Manning 1988: 82, original emphasis)

For this focus to be meaningful, in Scott's sense, the text must be located and analysed alongside intended and received meanings. In other words, the writer will assume a competence on the part of her or his audience and it is these assumptions which the analyst needs to engage with by employing, reflexively, their own cultural understandings alongside an understanding of the context in which the document was produced.

In practical terms, the questions asked of a document at the level of content meaning focus upon relationships *within* the text and its relationships to *other* texts:

> What is the relationship of a text's parts to each other? What is the relationship of the text to other texts? What is the relationship of the text to those who participated in constructing it? What is the relationship of the text to realities conceived of as lying outside of it? What empirical patterns are evident in these intra- and intertextual relations and what do these indicate about the meaning?
>
> (Ericson *et al.* 1991: 48)

A critical-analytic stance would consider how the document represents the events which it describes and closes off potential contrary interpretations by the reader. This considers the ways in which a text attempts to stamp its authority upon the social world it describes. In so doing, the social world might be characterized by the exclusion of valuable information and the characterization of events and people in particular ways according to certain interests.

The above characterization has tended to assume a simple dichotomy between quantitative and qualitative approaches. While there are clear differences of emphasis, throughout this book questions have continually been raised regarding this dualism. It is not surprising, therefore, to find researchers from different theoretical vantage points utilizing both methods with interesting results. However, they do not necessarily share the underlying assumptions of much content analysis as outlined above. Indeed, Marsh, whose comments on meaning and quantitative analysis were noted in Chapter 5, has employed computer packages to examine work history data (C. Marsh and Gershuny 1991) in a volume which attempts to challenge the quantitative–qualitative divide (Dex 1991). In addition, Silverman (1985) and Billig (1988), from different theoretical vantage points, have employed simple counting methods to analyse the speeches of a trade union leader and politician, respectively and Platt (1996) employs a similar method in her study of the history of American research methods. According to John Scott (1990), computer programs for the analysis of documents can still be usefully employed if using his threefold criteria of meaning interpretation. Nevertheless, the use of quantitative analysis does not sidestep the need for researchers to account for the interpretations they have employed in analysing the document(s).

A note on presentation of findings

In the second of two articles on documentary research, Jennifer Platt (1981b) notes the connection between the justification of the interpretative procedure used in the analysis of documents and how the research results are presented in an authoritative manner. As with research in general, the art of communication is fundamental to the research process. As she notes (Platt 1981b: 60), this differs when it comes to the presentation of a small number of cases or instances of a social phenomenon. The author then attempts to appeal to the authority of their interpretations in particular ways. One method is to resort to presenting all the data which substantiate a point that you wish to make. Another is to make liberal use of footnotes in order to elaborate upon the text. This is not an easy problem to solve. However, she suggests three ways in which to steer a middle course between total data display and an appeal to authority. Before moving on to issues in documentary research, I shall summarize these below.

The first strategy is to provide an account of the method utilized at the outset. This removes the obligation to elaborate on the procedure when you wish to make a particular point in the interpretation of the document(s). However, the problem with this strategy is that the method is not demonstrated at each point in the analysis, but asserted at the beginning. As a result, it requires a high level of trust in the author (Platt 1981b). The researcher could then use a second strategy and give an account of the method as each conclusion unfolds; a method similar to the historian's use of footnotes. Each positive and negative instance in relation to the results would be reported in order to substantiate the inferences. However, 'the danger here is that it could become as cumbrous as giving all the data' (Platt 1981b: 61).

Finally, the researcher might employ an 'illustrative style' as a strategy. Data are then selected in relation to the ability to illustrate general themes which emerge and which can be supported by the use of specific examples. Again, however, the reader must trust the authority of the interpretations. Not surprisingly, therefore, given the advantages and dis-advantages of each strategy, Platt (1981b) advocates the use of all three depending upon the nature of the data used and the types of conclusions reached. For large amounts of data, a sampling and coding procedure would need to be explained. In terms of small-scale data, the sources and methods of inferences would need to be described. If examples are used to illustrate points and if others are available, how were they chosen? Finally, there is the possible use of a general account of the process of analysis and checks on the interpretative procedures employed:

> This amounts to saying that where a systematic procedure has been used it should be described, and the results reported will then carry the conviction which the procedure deserves. The issue thus comes back to that of devising satisfactory systematic procedures of analy-sis and interpretation.
>
> (Platt 1981b: 62)

Issues in documentary research

Criticisms of documentary research tend to stem from how they are used, as opposed to their use in the first place. Both implicitly and explicitly, many of these have been covered. Here, I shall consider the bias of docu-ments and selectivity in their analysis.

The importance of seeing a document in terms of its potential bias has been emphasized. History itself and our understanding of it can be informed by a selective reading of documents or those documents them-selves may also be selective. Thus, what people decide to record, to leave in or take out, is itself informed by decisions which relate to the social, political and economic environment of which they are a part. History, like all social and natural sciences, is amenable to manipulation and selec-tive influence. In undertaking documentary research, we should be aware of these influences and not assume that documents are simply neutral artefacts from the past. Due to an often uncritical approach to this form of research, it has been criticized for marginalizing people along, for example, race, class, ethnic, gender and cultural lines.

Another issue relates to using documents without due regard to the process and social context of their construction. Semioticians, for example, examine the text itself in terms of meaning 'content', without a consideration of Scott's 'intended' and 'received' components of meanings. The tradition of social thought which underlies these comments stands in contrast to approaches, such as those of Plummer, which regard the intention and purposes of the author as an important part of their analysis. Authors of this perspective would, in contrast, not regard a document as simply reflecting the social 'reality' to which it refers, as some positivist approaches advocate.

Summary

The title 'documentary research' reflects a very broad spectrum of both perspectives and research sources. Documents may well be part of the practical contingencies of organizational life, but as we have also seen, they are viewed as part of a wider social context. They have been considered in terms of the centrality of their authorship, while others, particularly influenced by recent strands of French poststructuralist social theory, do not consider the author as being of immediate consequence. These latter influences have seen a move towards more literary styles of analysis which sit uneasily alongside the positivist legacy which may be detected in social research. In considering this issue we might bear in mind the philosophy that underpinned Raphael Samuel's approach to historical writing as one applicable to the social sciences as a whole:

> history is not the prerogative of the historian, nor even, as postmodernism contends, a historian's 'invention'. It is, rather, a social form of knowledge; the work, in any given instance, of a thousand different hands. If this is true, the point of address in any discussion of historiography should not be the work of the individual scholar, nor yet rival schools of interpretation, but rather the ensemble of activities and practices in which ideas of history are embedded or a dialectic of past–present relations is rehearsed.
>
> (Samuel 1994: 10)

With an increase in information available through the means discussed here, documentary research will become more popular and relevant. It will, therefore, alongside other methods, yield valuable insights into societies and the dynamics of social life.

Questions for your reflection

1 List ten different data sources for undertaking documentary research.

2 When it comes to understanding a document, what are the issues to be considered in examining intended and received meanings?

3 What questions would you ask of a document before using it?

4 You are asked to devise a study which employs 'unobtrusive measures' of police performance. Clearly, you would first have to define the idea of 'performance'. However, holding that aside, what sources would you use? To get you started, is the level of graffiti in public places an indicator? Or the number of pairs of boots an officer goes through in a year of beat patrols?

Suggested further reading

Plummer, K. (1990) *Documents of Life: An Introduction to the Problems and Literature of a Humanistic Method*. London: George Allen and Unwin.

Samuel, R. (1994) *Theatres of Memory Volume 1: Past and Present in Contemporary Culture*. London: Verso.

Scott, J. (1990) *A Matter of Record: Documentary Sources in Social Research*. Cambridge: Polity.

Stake, R. E. (1995) *The Art of Case Study Research*. London: Sage.

CHAPTER 9 Comparative research: potential and problems

Globalization and comparative social research
    The place of comparison in social research
The process of cross-national research
    The potential of comparative research
    Problems in comparative research
    Potential and problems: an overview
Summary
Questions for your reflection
Suggested further reading

In the first edition I wrote of comparative research being an 'evolving' topic, yet one with a long and rich history. As a methodological statement this largely remains the case. However, it is a growing area fostered, for example, by international organizations and institutions such as the European Union. In terms of its collective methods and theories, we may characterize it as a pluralist approach centred mainly, but not exclusively, around the theme of comparing countries under the umbrella term 'cross-national' studies. While all research involves comparison, using the term cross-national will restrict most of our discussion to comparison between countries.

The results of research using cross-national studies can be found in books and journals in comparative politics, human geography, history, economics, sociology, social policy and business studies. In the process, attention is increasingly being turned to the methodological sphere. With this variable field in mind, the following account of cross-national research is written in a less systematic and structured fashion than Chapters 5–8. To assist in a general understanding of this topic, it begins with a discussion of the place and growth of comparison in social research. The second section then considers the issues involved in cross-national research. Increasing sums of money are attached to comparative work and the pressures in social research institutions to attract funds and engage in the dissemination of findings via publications, make it more fashionable. The intention of this section, therefore, is to offer an overview of its potential and problems, as opposed to wholesale and uncritical adoption. It is thus worth bearing in mind the following observations that remain of relevance:

> The contemporary situation ... is one distinguished by methodological pluralism, with many open-minded initiatives and a corresponding diversity of priorities concerning research goals and techniques of analysis. But this state of affairs is not an end in itself. Pluralism is good but it does leave us with some peculiar questions. To what extent is open-endedness a snare for the unsuspecting?
>
> (Apter 1973: 3)

Globalization and comparative social research

As nation-states developed, so too did the opportunities for cross-national research. In contemporary times, with increases in communications and technological advances, the world is 'getting smaller'. The invention of the wireless, for example, created what Barbara Adam has termed a 'global present' in collective grief when news of the sinking of the *Titanic* was announced (1995: 111). Nowadays, news programmes keep us up-to-date on events on the other side of the globe and telephones and e-mails enable those who can afford it to converse with friends, relatives or business people in other countries – almost in an instant. Documents are sent via telephone lines and video conferencing can link us across national boundaries and oceans. This has a clear impact on the organization of societies and cultures.

Due to these changes it becomes less possible to speak of a 'society', given that modern industrial societies are open to these influences and not hermetically sealed off from the world. The social bonds of old are often seen to be giving way to a process of 'detraditionalization' whereby the certainties of old are replaced by chaos and uncertainty (see Heelas *et al.* 1996). Further, to simply employ the idea of a 'society' can also ignore or stifle the differences that exist within it. A recognition of these differences is, in part, generated by the development in mass communications which provide for the mediation of different cultural representations across national boundaries. As Poster observes: 'Electronically mediated communication to some degree supplements existing forms of sociability but to another extent substitutes for them' (Poster 1990: 154). Given this diversity, accompanied by increases in mass communications and the workings of multinational companies and international markets 'globalization' may be defined as

> the intensification of worldwide social relations which link distant localities in such a way that local happenings are shaped by events occurring many miles away and vice versa.
>
> (Giddens 1990: 64)

Research has followed this process as an increased generation of information has accompanied these transformations. Insights into our own lives are thought to be enhanced by studying the ways in which different cultures and societies organize their social and political affairs and everyday lives. This underlies Butler and Stokes's comment that comparisons of political systems 'can extend our understanding of British politics and lead to still more general formulations of the process of change' (1969: 533). This optimistic-based impression is characterized by O'Reilly (1996) as a universal approach centred upon ideas of convergence in which, it is argued, 'there are shared, universally identifiable, pressures and trends working across all industrialized societies' (1996: 4.1).

This desire to seek universal explanations across different contexts via an examination of the process of convergence is seen to be counterbalanced by the increased complications of social and political life that have accompanied globalization: differences and diversities exist not only within, but also between nations. Therefore, from a postmodernist perspective, it is increasing divergence which questions the goals of cross-national empirical generalizations and the possibility of what have been termed 'metanarratives' of theoretical explanation (Lyotard 1984). Contingency becomes celebrated over generalization. Add to this Baudrillard's (1983a, 1983b) arguments that signs no longer indicate a reality beyond them and any attempt at seeking a basis for cross-national research appears futile and without foundation. As Frank Webster notes in summarizing Baudrillard's arguments in relation to the study of the information age:

> viewers of television news may watch with the presumption that the signs indicate a reality beyond them – 'what is going on in the world'. But on a moment's reflection we can appreciate that the news we receive is a version of events, one shaped by journalists' contacts and availability, moral values, political dispositions and access to news-makers. Yet, if we can readily demonstrate that television news is not 'reality' but a construction of it, then how is it possible that people can suggest that beyond the signs is a 'true' situation?
>
> (Webster 1995: 178)

In the face of this situation, uncertainties as to the future, particularly given a resurgence of nationalism and the 'breaking-up' of previous nation-states, opens up the possibilities of fatalism and pessimism. At the same time, however, this ambivalence renders comparative research of importance. As past assumptions of similarity between and homogeneity within societies breaks down, an opportunity presents itself:

> Understanding the reason why the complex conditions within which we live are bound to remain, in significant respects, beyond our

control, paradoxically provides us with the opportunity of con-
tributing more effectively to the shaping of social futures.

(Smart 1992: 221)

We can now say that one aim of comparative research is to understand
and explain the ways in which different societies and cultures experience
and act upon social, economic and political changes.

Institutions and governments, for different reasons and motivations,
release funds to undertake research. This might take the form of applied
research where the desire is to collect information for governmental purposes or, on a more commercial basis, examine an economy in terms of
the organization of its manufacturing, financial and service sectors; this
being the case in employing Japanese work-based practices that were
believed to enhance the efficiency, effectiveness and economy of the business enterprise (Bratton 1992; Beale 1994). The collection of information, and the subsequent decision-making based upon it, can then have
an effect on different cultures and nation-states – for better or worse,
depending upon the vantage point from which such developments are
viewed.

The place of comparison in social research

While cross-national comparative research is a growing phenomenon,
we all use the idea of comparison when making judgements in everyday
life and the practice of social and natural sciences is inconceivable without it (as with the discussion on value judgements and comparative
assessment in Chapter 3). Methodologically speaking, nowhere is this
more evident than in the experimental method of research. Here, the
epitome of 'high science' is thought to find its representation among
research practitioners. In pursuing a belief in the parallels between the
natural and human sciences, there are those who seek to emulate its techniques.

Broadly speaking, the experimental method randomly allocates people
to particular groups and then subjects them to controlled stimuli. Behavioural or physiological changes can then be measured as the scientist
monitors the effect of these controls. A sequence of *cause* and *effect* is
then established in the observed pattern of events. Thus, in medical trials,
one group may be given a test drug and another group is given either no
drug or a placebo (a drug without effect in order to act as a control on
the group). Differences between the two groups are measured and any
'real' physiological or biological effects of the new drug established.
However, the experimental method has a number of methodological and
theoretical flaws when applied to the social world. For instance, in order
to observe the relation between cause and effect a number of standing
conditions must be specified in order to allow for genuine comparison.
Given that social life is more complicated than experiments can allow for

and subject to numerous forces at any one moment, social researchers frequently resort to what are known as quasi-experiments. In these instances, the researcher has less control over 'outside' or *exogenous* variables which could influence the group's 'internal' behaviour (see Kidder 1981; Moser and Kalton 1983; Shipman 1988).

These methods are still practised and appear to be enjoying a resurgence of interest with the growth of research which seeks to evaluate whether a particular programme of activity is achieving its stated ends. As one of a series of texts on *evaluation research* puts it:

> Without any *comparison* group, it is hard to know how good the results are, whether the results would have been as good with some other program, and even whether the program has any effect on the results at all.
> (Fitz-Gibbon and Lyons Morris 1987: 26, original emphasis)

Moving away from the narrow idea of comparison in experiment and design and evaluation research, there is a more general idea of comparison which social researchers constantly engage in. When they choose to study a part of human relations the choice inevitably represents selectivity through comparison:

> Normal behaviour and norms cannot be studied without acknowledging deviations from the normal. Actually, no social phenomenon can be isolated and studied without comparing it to other social phenomena. . . .Trying to understand and explain variation is a process which cannot be accomplished without previous reflections on similarities and dissimilarities underlying the variation.
> (Øyen 1990b: 4)

At an analytic level we make comparisons between the influences of variables from questionnaire results, or accounts in interview transcripts, or documentary sources and field notes on observational settings. On a more general level, we compare within societies (*intra-societal* comparison) and between societies (*inter-societal* comparison). The former method might examine differences between the ways in which white and black people are processed through the criminal justice system (as per the example in Chapter 4), or the industrial geography of the UK (Massey 1995). The latter method might compare societies which display both similarities and differences, for example, in relation to their provision of welfare (Esping-Andersen 1990). This idea is certainly not new. As one contribution to a reader on comparative policy research begins: 'States, kingdoms and principalities have been compared for approximately 2,500 years' (Deutsch 1987: 5).

In the field of politics, a strong legacy of comparative work exists which can be traced back to the work of the Greek philosopher Aristotle (384–322 BC; see Blondel 1990; R. Rose 1991). Among more recent examples are the works of Emile Durkheim on suicide (1952), Max

Weber on religion (1930; 1965) and Richard Titmuss on blood donation (1970). Indeed, the discipline of social anthropology studies the lives of people in non-industrial or pre-modern societies and therefore requires a comparative understanding from both its students and its practitioners (La Fontaine 1985). Attention has focused on its importance for research purposes, teaching and disciplinary development in many other areas of study: for example, sociology (Armer and Grimshaw 1973; Lash and Urry 1994); criminology and the study of deviant actions (Newman 1976; Mawby 1990); the social effects of free-market policies (I. Taylor 1990); social policy (Higgins 1981; Jones 1985; Esping-Andersen 1990; Dominelli 1991; Hill 1996) and policy analysis and social research in general (Warwick and Osherson 1973; Dierkes et al. 1987; Øyen 1990a; Hantrais and Mangen 1996).

The above samples of comparative work add to an increasingly expanding area of interest with a long established history. As I write, no doubt, new volumes, research reports and articles are being produced and research grants applied for. In the next section, I wish to concentrate on the questions which arise in comparing societies.

The process of cross-national research

Examining comparative research in terms of being cross-national appears to enable us to focus upon a simple definition and compare along the dimension of demarcated national boundaries. However, within these societies there are ethnic and cultural differences which governments and the general public cannot afford to ignore, nor researchers gloss over if their aim is systematic understanding and explanation.

The central methodological question which faces comparative research is: does it require a different practice from other forms of research? Within the literature, there appear to be several responses to this question. First, there are those who consider that comparative work is no different from any other. The units of analysis, whether it be political parties or welfare systems, needs no special theoretical accounts or methodological discussions. This group Øyen (1990a) calls the 'purists', adding the caveat that this is a tendency to which many researchers succumb. Second, there are those, like many researchers if they were honest, who are ethnocentric in their approach. They are not sensitive to social context and historical and cultural differences and simply 'add on' their findings to existing ways of understanding and explaining, the consequence being that cross-national data are not assumed to add to the complexity of social science research (Øyen calls this group the 'ignorants').

Third, there are those whom Øyen refers to as the 'totalists'. This group appears to be aware of the issues involved in cross-national research and its methodological and theoretical pitfalls. At the same time:

They consciously ignore the many stumbling blocks of the non-equivalence of concepts, a multitude of unknown variables interacting in an unknown context and influencing the research question in unknown ways.

(Øyen 1990a: 5)

Finally, there are the 'comparativists'. This group recognizes the arguments of the purists and totalists, but believes that cross-national research is a distinctive topic. As a result, they undertake their work in a different manner and frame their research questions accordingly.

Clearly, these four groups are ideal types. However, many researchers now compete for the position of 'comparative expert'. This has desirable consequences, but the nature of what is meant by 'comparative study' is, as these different responses suggest, another matter. Simply tacking on preconceived ideas and even prejudices on the operation of societies does little to advance our understanding and counters the idea of a reflexive basis to research practice. Thus, to be able to consider issues of practice and how these five approaches may be evaluated, the following sections provide an overview of the potential and problems associated with comparative research.

The potential of comparative research

There are several benefits in undertaking comparative research. I shall characterize these as the *import-mirror* view, the *difference* view, the *theory-development* view and finally, the *prediction* view. It will be clear from the following discussions that these are not distinct, but interrelated themes. That noted, their adoption assists in extracting arguments from the literature written by those who see comparative research as having the potential to enhance our understanding and explanation of human relations. Let us consider each of these in turn.

The import-mirror view suggests that the project of comparative analysis is worthwhile because in producing findings on the practices of other countries, we are better able to see the basis of our own practices. On an instrumental level, this means the borrowing of ideas from other countries: 'the goal is lessons rather than creating or testing theory. Countries that are similar are more likely to borrow from one another' (Teune 1990: 58). According to this view, the results generated by comparative study may permit the importation of different methods of organizing a society's affairs to improve their efficiency. On a less instrumental dimension, this also allows us to reflect upon our own social systems and cultural ways of behaving. It thereby possesses the potential to challenge our 'background assumptions' (Gouldner 1971) by producing findings on different social contexts and cultural practices.

At the same time, this can allow those who are studying other countries to have a particular insight into their practices. While it is advantageous to be an 'insider', 'outsiders' (as researchers) can raise questions which may not have been thought of by those who take their own practices for granted. Of course, we do not necessarily require cross-national research for this purpose as there may be sufficient diversity within our own societies. However, societies and the systems they devise reveal variable historical conditions leading to current practices and policies. Thus, and this brings us round to the second advantage, comparative analysis is undertaken to explain and understand difference.

By examining different societies, we can ask why some have developed in similar ways and others in diverse ways. This adds to an understanding and explanation of the complicated relationship between economic, social and political systems without, by theoretical fiat, opting for the convergence or contingent perspective (beyond which generalization is not possible). For instance, Esping-Andersen's (1990) study is centred on the belief 'that only comparative empirical research will adequately disclose the fundamental properties that unite or divide modern welfare states' (Esping-Andersen 1990: 3). Further, the contributors to the volume by Ian Taylor (1990) examine the 'cultural specificities' which any adoption of free-market policies has to take account of, thereby blending the contingent with the convergent models. Through comparative accounts of five western-style societies, the limits to market-based policies are illuminated. Differences within and between these societies expose the problem of adopting a philosophy of 'free markets' given the profound social costs which this ideology entails.

Comparisons which reveal difference and diversity and, in the above example, cultural impediments to the implementation of policy enable us to consider the macro factors which influence social and political change and the micro factors peculiar to each social setting. This relates to a third advantage, which sees an improvement in theoretical development resulting from the growth of comparative research. For those who consider that the goal of social research is the discovery of general theories which explain the way societies are organized: 'comparative studies are absolutely essential' (Holt, quoted in Grimshaw 1973: 19). This has both positive and negative aspects, depending upon how the research is conducted.

From a positive viewpoint, cross-national studies can have the effect of altering the focus of research efforts with considerable implications for policy initiatives. Consider, for example, the drift from measurements of poverty, to those associated with 'social exclusion'. In an insightful discussion of this issue in relation to Europe, Jos Berghman (1995) notes how the European Observatory on Policies to Combat Social Exclusion, along with the European Community Programme to Foster Economic and Social Integration of the Least Privileged Groups, acted as catalysts for an analytic shift with practical consequences. Poverty can be measured both directly (in relation to consumption patterns and living conditions) and indirectly (income). Poverty tends to be measured in terms of income, providing a baseline below which active membership of a society is highly problematic, if not impossible. Yet income may be at a minimum level, or just above, but it does not follow that one has access to the resources of a society. Here we would need to take account of citizenship expressed in terms of social, civil and political rights (see Barbalet 1988). The focus now moves away from the household as such, to encompass the societal institutions that enable a person to participate as a full member of society:

> So, the conceptual differences become somewhat clearer: there is the traditional concept of poverty, which by now is restricted to denote a lack of disposable income, and there is the comprehensive concept of social exclusion, that refers to a breakdown or malfunctioning of the major societal systems that should guarantee full citizenship.
>
> (Berghman 1995: 20)

While this change of analytic focus has profound practical outcomes, the issue remains (as noted in the discussion in Chapter 2) that any generated theories may be stated at such a level of abstraction they are not useful for the interpretation of data. Furthermore, such abstraction may ignore important differences between countries through, for example, a preoccupation with structure over culture; a point noted by O'Reilly (1996) in relation to the attempts made by what organizational theorists call contingency theory. This form of contingency theory attempts to generalize across social contexts by explaining the success of an organization in terms of the 'fit' between its structure and environment. Therefore, it is not to be confused with postmodern ideas on contingency, as I have been employing the term here (see Cole 1994).

Given these issues, there are those who would steer a middle course between universalistic theories which are assumed to be generally relevant to societies across time and space and particularistic theories which are only applicable to particular social settings and thus not generalizable. This is said to take account of differences within societies, as well as similarities between them. Richard Rose expresses this succinctly. Indeed, at the end of this quote, he links the 'theoretical' and 'difference' potentials of comparative research:

> Anyone who engages in comparative research immediately notices differences between countries. Yet anyone who persists in wide-ranging comparative analysis also recognizes boundaries to these differences: for example, among two dozen countries, the variations in methods of electing a Parliament are limited. Since the time of Aristotle, the first task of comparison is to observe the extent to which countries differ or are similar. The second task is to ask why. Under what circumstances do differences occur?
>
> (R. Rose 1991: 447)

To allow for the possibility of diversity and similarity, comparative analysis considers both *endogenous* and *exogenous* factors. The former are those which are peculiar to the country which is being studied, while the latter are those elements, such as international capital, gender and race relations, which while influencing that country's social and political relations, are not simply peculiar to it. However, as the discussion on Ian Taylor's (1990) work indicated, comparative researchers need to be sensitive to the 'cultural specificities' which affect *how* exogenous factors influence each country.

Esping-Andersen's comparative study could be summarized as an example of this middle-course genre. The need for theoretical generation was the second belief, aside from that of empirical comparison mentioned above, which informed his work:

> existing theoretical models of the welfare state are inadequate. The ambition is to offer a reconceptualization and re-theorization on the basis of what we consider important about the welfare state. The existence of a social program and the amount of money spent on it may be less important than what it does. We shall devote many pages to arguing that issues of decommodification, social stratification, and employment are keys to a welfare state's identity.
>
> (Esping-Andersen 1990: 2)

I have deliberately included the latter part of this quote which refers to the concepts which he employed to understand and compare the identity of welfare states. This is a central point in theory development. The use of such concepts, it is argued, enables the researcher to have a common point of reference in order to group empirical data which is differentiated along both linguistic and geographical dimensions (Ferrari 1990; R. Rose 1991). By approaching the comparison of welfare states in this way, Esping-Andersen (1990) was able to show, using a considerable amount of data and 'ideal-type' welfare regimes (liberal, conservative and social democratic), how countries' welfare states evolved as a result of different historical forces. Thus, he compares, but in so doing does not ignore, differences between countries. The result is a novel theoretical analysis of contemporary changes in welfare states (although it has been criticized for the absence of gender as a significant social category in comparative welfare-state analysis: Langan and Ostner 1991).

Finally, we come to the fourth view: that is, the prediction of programme outcomes is enhanced through comparative work. According to this view, not only can the potential for the success of particular policies, systems or practices in a given society be understood, but also their outcomes can be predicted, once experiences of their effects in other societies and social and cultural contexts is examined. Therefore, organizations or governments may embark upon particular courses of action knowing their likely consequences. Yet, one must exercise caution here in terms of the positivist connotations of this view. While there may be a degree of predictability that may be attributed to aggregated social phenomena, it does not follow that the intentions of policy are aligned with outcome.

Quite simply, there are unintended consequences to social actions, at whatever level they may arise. Thus, in her comparison of women's employment in Britain and France, Veronica Beechey notes the similarity of developments in these countries in terms of economic restructuring, but a clear variation in their form (1989: 377).

Problems in comparative research

Comparative research is considered to have potential around one or more of the above four themes. However, the picture is, as you can imagine, more complicated than this simple characterization allows for. In both the process of undertaking comparative research and in the potential for theoretical development, a number of problems have been raised in the literature.

One of the primary problems with comparative analysis is not only the ability of researchers to understand adequately cultures and societies which are different from their own, but more specifically, to generalize and explain social relations across societies and social contexts. Following the work of Winch (1990), it has been argued that in order to understand a culture, we have to know the rules which are employed in that culture; only then can we understand the ways in which the culture views the social world. So far, so good. However, and this is the important point, there is nothing 'beyond' this understanding: for example, establishing whether a culture or society beliefs are valid through a comparison with other societies. As three sympathizers of this view express it, Winch sees the creation of a comparative social research programme as requiring

> the comparison of like with like. . . . In order to decide which institutions of one society – our own in many cases – to compare with those of another we shall need to be able to match those institutions, to say what kind of part they play in their respective societies. . . . However, if we are in a position to say what part each institution plays in the life of its society then we have already achieved a very good understanding of it.
>
> (R. Anderson *et al.* 1986: 184)

In other words, this understanding is the aim of comparison and its finishing point. We cannot explain its history and development in terms of social forces which are external to a culture. This renders the ability to generate particular forms of cross-cultural and societal explanations untenable.

The potential of comparative research in allowing the outsider to 'look in' and see things in a different way which is theoretically useful is also untenable; at least, according to this view. Researchers can understand only from the inside – from the social context which is peculiar and *relative* to that time and place. We have actually returned to the discussion in

Chapter 1. Social research should look for and seek to understand the *meanings* within a social context where people act according to the rules of the social setting. This excludes, by definition, the search for *causal* explanations which may provide for generalizations across societies. Instead, the 'stranger' must be prepared to grasp what Winch (1990) calls 'forms of life' which are fundamentally different from their own, but which can be evaluated only in terms of the indigenous culture. Beyond this, there is no way of establishing a general explanation of beliefs beyond their social context. To this extent, Winch's arguments may seem to parallel those of postmodernism in terms of the absence of universal criteria upon which different societies may be meaningfully compared to each other. As Ernest Gellner, a critic of Winch's views, succinctly summarizes this position in terms of people speaking:

> their own lives and pursue their manifold interests in the context of 'forms of life', cultural/linguistic traditions, and the concepts they employ derive their validity from, and *only* from, possessing a place in these forms of life.
>
> (Gellner 1974: 143, emphasis added)

Winch's arguments can be further located and based in relation to those arguments in Chapter 2 on common sense as a basis of theorizing. The researcher cannot legitimately consider, in theoretical or empirical terms, anything other than the practical use of language in everyday life or the methods which people use in interpreting the social world in *context*. This position has actually been raised in all the four previous chapters in one form or another, for it occurs throughout discussions on social research (on the meaning-equivalence of attitude scales in questionnaires, interviews as topics not resources and documents analysed in terms of practical reasoning). However, conflict around the exercise of power, within the same societies, questions the idea that there are beliefs which are beyond question in its own terms, let alone those of the outsider. The question to be formulated here is 'why' does this occur? These are questions to which those such as Esping-Andersen (1990), R. Rose (1991) and Hirst and Thompson (1996) address themselves. The influence of global capital on a culture, or the development of whole societies, affects that culture as an *exogenous* factor, particularly in terms of the relationships between western societies and the Third World. For this reason, among others, critical social researchers would not regard Winch's arguments as tenable, while they are argued to be contradictory (Lukes 1994).

The implications of Winch's arguments are reflected in the literature on comparative work. Both Esping-Andersen (1990) and R. Rose (1991) are not only aware of the importance of being sensitive to social context, but also note the similarities which are found between societies. Comparative researchers are also aware of the issue of comparing like with like (see R. Marsh 1967; Armer 1973; Teune 1990). This finds its outlet in discussions on *appropriateness* and *equivalence* in comparative research.

Appropriateness refers to the methods employed and the conceptualization of issues when undertaking comparative research. Researchers cannot assume that what is appropriate for their culture will necessarily be appropriate for another. A sensitivity and understanding of cultural context is thereby required:

> Appropriateness requires feasibility, significance, and acceptability in each foreign culture as a necessary (but not sufficient) condition for insuring validity and successful completion of comparative studies.
>
> (Armer 1973: 50–1)

Equivalence is a related issue. As Winch (1990) rightly suggests, meanings vary between cultures. This raises a particular problem in the use of surveys in cross-national research where meaning-equivalence is an important component of a questionnaire's validity (see Verba 1971; Scheuch 1990). In terms of the process of study, unless researchers have an understanding of the social context with which they are dealing, two samples, although random, may actually sample different age ranges or population characteristics which are not comparable. This often results from indigenous factors which the researcher either has overlooked, or is simply not sensitive to. A survey might then measure different aspects of the phenomena under investigation and treat them as similar. For this reason:

> a second major methodological task in comparative research is to devise and select theoretical problems, conceptual schemes, samples, and measurement and analysis strategies that are comparable or equivalent across the societies involved in a particular study.
>
> (Armer 1973: 51)

A more general problem relates to appropriateness and equivalence. As Robert Marsh comments: 'the task of linguistic translation falls heavily upon the shoulders of the comparativist' (R. Marsh 1967: 272). Language differences, even if researchers have a proficient understanding of a language, require a cultural understanding of words to allow for the equivalence of meaning. This becomes particularly important when dealing with dialects where the meanings of words varies, or entirely different words may be employed in referring to the same phenomena. From a methodological vantage point, it has therefore been argued that a sensitivity to the context in which beliefs are generated needs to be accompanied by the employment of

> complementary methodologies to investigate the language, vocabulary and structure of people's attitudes and beliefs. . . .This means a far greater use of qualitative techniques, ethnographic research, and discourse and rhetorical analysis.
>
> (Golding 1995: 231)

When it comes to examining available data on countries, it is worth bearing in mind that if not conversant with the language, the use of English translations can lead to issues of selectivity and thus bias. Problems of language, together with a drive to increase comparative work and the high costs of comparative survey and observational research, leads many researchers to rely on official publications (Manis 1976). Any analysis based upon such documents may then produce partial and incomplete theories. In other words, the stereotype of English visitors abroad continuing to speak English and simply raising their voice if not understood by 'those foreigners', has its methodological equivalent.

As researchers have pointed out (Lawrence 1988), the language issue *may* be becoming less problematic as English comes to dominate as a world language. However, issues of meaning equivalence still remain, to say nothing of the desirability for non-English speakers of this state of affairs. For instance, dialogues between the researcher and interviewees, as well as the translation of documents and a reliance on official publications, are still matters of interpretation. Lawrence refers to this in his account of studying comparative management. Here he considers not only a delicate balancing act between inferring actions from observations in social settings by utilizing nationalist stereotypes, but also the possible misapprehensions which occur in interview situations:

> One is never quite sure that they have understood the question, or at least its nuances or comparative thrust; one worries that interviewees are responding to the question they think you asked (but you think you asked something different). The problem is compounded by the admirable vagueness of English: there is no other language more suited to the framing of open-ended questions or projective try-ons.
> (Lawrence 1988: 102)

Due to these ambiguities, he recommends that even if a researcher's command of the language is not 'perfect', misapprehension can still be reduced by its use (Lawrence 1988: 102). In addition, if English is employed for the interview, the use of key words in the interviewee's own language helps to maintain meaning equivalence. Further, even if interviewees' command of English is good, there may be terms in their own language for which they do not know the English equivalent and this can also lead to ambiguity. One example that Lawrence notes is Dutch managers who say 'agenda' rather than 'diary'. As he suggests, the interviewer must accept this: the purpose of their research 'is to end up with an enlarged understanding, not to teach other people English' (Lawrence 1988: 102).

Potential and problems: an overview

The potential for theoretical development is a strong component of comparative research. Yet there are those who regard this potential as a problem – if by this we mean the ability to generalize across societies and produce explanations of social and political phenomena. While Jones is speaking of comparative social policy, her comments characterize this debate as one between

> those who see cross-national analysis as furnishing a welcome additional dimension to assist in the task of policy analysis and those who regard any attempts at cross national 'theory building' (as opposed to constructive description) as hopelessly premature, given the present far-from-perfect grasp of home-country let alone other people's social policy.
>
> (Jones 1985: 7–8)

Much literature on the practice of comparative research is aware of these disputes and therefore focuses upon the issues of equivalence, appropriateness and language. These are central for we can all, despite our most determined attempts, often find ourselves succumbing to the belief that our ways of acting and thinking are in some ways better than others. This is personified by the neo-colonialism that characterizes particular attitudes.

Comparative researchers cannot assume that their own countries, or those of others, are characterized on the basis of a single culture or shared value-consensus. This allows for a continuum between difference and similarity which is open to comparative empirical examination. A note of caution should be added here lest people think that the process of globalization will automatically combat such thinking. This may simply result in more global forms of ethnocentrism. The world may move beyond the researcher's shores, only to finish at the frontiers of 'the west'. Disputes over the exploitation of Third World countries by western societies are being constantly raised and these changes will not necessarily alleviate this situation (Rattansi and Westwood 1994). At the same time, comparative research has the potential to check against narrow thinking by its production of studies on alternative cultures and societies. This raises the possibility for a greater understanding and explanation of social, political and economic forces and their relationship to specific policies and human relations and cultures in general.

Summary

Comparative research is clearly a two-edged sword having both potential and problems. Nevertheless, this does not constitute a reason for its abandonment. If that were the case, all forms of research, both in the social and natural sciences, would cease overnight. On the contrary, as the earlier quote from Smart (1992) indicated, increasing complexity still requires understanding and explanation. The implications of this ambivalence for individual researchers is that it requires an awareness of both its strengths and limitations for good practice. This means an understanding of different social contexts and cultures and the various issues which form part of the actual process of comparative research: for example, those of the relationship between theory and data and the power relations which exist within and between societies which affect the design, production, interpretation and dissemination of research results. Clearly, there are important differences between the practice of cross-national research and the other methods of social inquiry that this book has covered. Yet, as has been argued throughout this book, issues and methods are not mutually exclusive topics. To that extent, it is no different and the researcher thus needs to act reflexively in their practice.

Questions for your reflection

1 When it comes to the topic of comparative research and its practice, are you a comparativist, purist, totalist, ignorant or something else? What are the reasons for your answer?

2 In considering Winch's (1990) arguments on 'forms of life', does this negate a researcher from one culture explaining the beliefs and practices of another in causal terms?

3 What is your opinion on the promise of comparative social research? Is it a good or bad idea?

4 Given the types of information which tend to be generated (increased media focus, etc.) how does the phenomenon of 'globalization' relate to the development of social research?

Suggested further reading

Hantrais, L. and Mangen, S. (eds) (1996) *Cross-National Research Methods in the Social Sciences*. London: Pinter.

Hill, M. (1996) *Social Policy: A Comparative Analysis*. London: Harvester Wheatsheaf.

Øyen, E. (ed.) (1990a) *Comparative Methodology*. London: Sage.

Room, R. (ed.) (1995) *Beyond the Threshold: The Measurement and Analysis of Social Exclusion*. University of Bristol: Policy Press.

Bibliography

Abrams, P., Deem, R., Finch, J. and Rock, P. (eds) (1981) *Practice and Progress: British Sociology 1950–1980*. London: George Allen and Unwin.

Acker, J., Barry, K. and Esseveld, J. (1991) Objectivity and truth: problems in doing feminist research, in M. M. Fonow and J. A. Cook (eds) *Beyond Methodology: Feminist Scholarship as hired Research*. Bloomington and Indianapolis: Indiana University Press.

Ackers, L. (1993) Race and sexuality in the ethnographic process, in D. Hobbs and T. May (eds) *Interpreting the Field: Accounts of Ethnography*. Oxford: Oxford University Press.

Ackroyd, S. and Hughes, J. (1983) *Data Collection in Context*. Harlow: Longman.

Adam, B. (1995) *Timewatch: The Social Analysis of Time*. Cambridge: Polity.

Adkins, L. (1995) *Gendered Work: Sexuality, Family and the Labour Market*. Buckingham: Open University Press.

Adler, M. and Asquith, S. (eds) (1981) *Discretion and Welfare*. London: Heinemann.

Adorno, T., Frankel-Brunswik, E., Levinson, D. and Sanford, R. (1950) *The Authoritarian Personality*. New York: Harper Row.

Agger, B. (1991) *A Critical Theory of Public Life: Knowledge, Discourse and Politics in an Age of Decline*. London: Falmer.

Allan, G. and Skinner, C. (eds) (1991) *Handbook for Research Students in the Social Sciences*. London: Falmer.

Anderson, A. (1997) *Media, Culture and the Environment*. London: UCL Press.

Anderson, R., Hughes, J. and Sharrock, W. (1986) *Philosophy and the Human Sciences*. London: Routledge.

Anderson, K., Armitage, S., Jack, D. and Wittner, J. (1990) Beginning where we are: feminist methodology in oral history, in J. McCarl Nielsen (ed.) *Feminist Research Methods: Exemplary Readings in the Social Sciences*. London: Westview.

Antaki, C. (ed.) (1988) *Analysing Everyday Explanation: A Casebook of Methods*. London: Sage.

Apter, D. (1973) Comparative studies: a review with some projections, in I. Vallier (ed.) (1971) *Comparative Methods in Sociology: Essays on Trends and Applications*. Los Angeles: University of California Press.

Aramov, D. (ed.) (1997) *Emergency and Transitory Housing for Homeless People: Needs and Best Practices.* Brussels: FEANTSA.

Archer, M. S. (1995) *Realist Social Theory: The Morphogenetic Approach.* Cambridge: Cambridge University Press.

Armer, M. (1973) Methodological problems and possibilities in comparative research, in M. Armer and A. Grimshaw (eds) *Comparative Social Research: Methodological Problems and Strategies.* London: John Wiley.

Armer, M. and Grimshaw, A. (eds) (1973) *Comparative Social Research: Methodological Problems and Strategies.* London: John Wiley.

Atkinson, J. M. (1978) *Discovering Suicide: Studies in the Social Organisation of Sudden Death.* London: Macmillan.

Atkinson, P. (1990) *The Ethnographic Imagination: Textual Constructions of Reality.* London: Routledge.

Atkinson, P. and Heath, C. (eds) (1981) *Medical Work: Realities and Routines.* Aldershot: Gower.

Baldamus, W. (1984) The category of pragmatic knowledge in sociological analysis, in M. Bulmer (ed.) *Sociological Research Methods*, 2nd edn. London: Macmillan.

Banks, J. A. (1957) The group discussion as an interview technique. *Sociological Review*, 5 (1).

Barbalet, J. (1988) *Citizenship.* Milton Keynes: Open University Press.

Barnes, B. (ed.) (1972) *Sociology of Science: Selected Readings.* Harmondsworth: Penguin.

Barnes, B. (1991) Thomas Kuhn, in Q. Skinner (ed.) *The Return of Grand Theory in the Human Sciences.* Cambridge: Cambridge University Press.

Barnes, J. A. (1979) *Who Should Know What?* Harmondsworth: Penguin.

Barrett, M. (1991) *The Politics of Truth: From Marx to Foucault.* Cambridge: Polity.

Barthes, R. (1967) *Elements of Semiology.* London: Jonathan Cape.

Baudrillard, J. (1983a) *Simulations.* New York: Semiotext(e).

Baudrillard, J. (1983b) *In the Shadow of the Silent Majorities.* New York: Semiotext(e).

Bauman, Z. (1988) Is there a postmodern sociology? *Theory, Culture and Society*, 5 (2–3): 217–37.

Bauman, Z. (1992) *Intimations of Postmodernity.* London: Routledge.

Beale, D. (1994) *Driven by Nissan: A Critical Guide to New Management Techniques.* London: Lawrence and Wishart.

Beck, U. (1992) *Risk Society: Towards a New Modernity.* London: Sage.

Becker, H. (1963) *Outsiders: Studies in the Sociology of Deviance.* New York: The Free Press.

Becker, H. (1967) Whose side are we on? *Social Problems*, 14: 239–47.

Becker, H. (1979a) Problems of inference and proof in participant observation, in J. Bynner and K. Stribley (eds) *Social Research: Principles and Procedures.* Harlow: Longman.

Becker, H. (1979b) Problems in the publication of field studies, in J. Bynner and K. Stribley (eds) *Social Research: Principles and Procedures.* Harlow: Longman.

Becker, H. (1986) *Writing for Social Scientists: How to Start and Finish Your Thesis, Book, or Article.* Chicago: University of Chicago Press.

Becker, H., Geer, B., Hughes, E. and Strauss, A. (1961) *Boys in White: Student Culture in a Medical School.* Chicago: University of Chicago Press.

Beechey, V. (1986) Women and employment in contemporary Britain, in V. Beechey and E. Whitelegg (eds) *Women in Britain Today*. Milton Keynes: Open University Press.

Beechey, V. (1989) Women's employment in France and Britain: some problems of comparison. *Work, Employment and Society,* 3 (3): 369–78.

Beechey, V. and Whitelegg, E. (eds) (1986) *Women in Britain Today*. Milton Keynes: Open University Press.

Bell, C. and Newby, H. (eds) (1977) *Doing Sociological Research*. London: George Allen and Unwin.

Bell, C. and Roberts, H. (eds) (1984) *Social Researching: Politics, Problems and Practice*. London: Routledge and Kegan Paul.

Bell, D., Caplan, P. and Karim, W. J. (eds) (1993) *Gendered Fields: Women, Men and Ethnography*. London: Routledge.

Benney, M. and Hughes, E. (1984) Of sociology and the interview, in M. Bulmer (ed.) *Sociological Research Methods*, 2nd edn. London: Macmillan.

Benson, D. and Hughes, J. (1991) Method: evidence and inference – evidence and inference for ethnomethodology, in G. Button (ed.) *Ethnomethodology and the Human Sciences*. Cambridge: Cambridge University Press.

Berghman, J. (1995) Social exclusion in Europe: policy context and analytical framework, in R. Room (ed.) *Beyond the Threshold: The Measurement and Analysis of Social Exclusion*. University of Bristol: Policy Press.

Bernstein, R. (1976) *The Restructuring of Social and Political Theory*. Oxford: Basil Blackwell.

Bernstein, R. (1983) *Beyond Objectivism and Relativism: Science, Hermeneutics and Praxis*. Oxford: Basil Blackwell.

Berridge, V. and Thom, B. (1996) Research and policy: what determines the relationship? *Policy Studies,* 17 (1): 23–34.

Bhaskar, R. (1975) *A Realist Theory of Science*. Leeds: Leeds Books.

Bhaskar, R. (1989a) *Reclaiming Reality: A Critical Introduction to Contemporary Philosophy*. London: Verso.

Bhaskar, R. (1989b) *The Possibility of Naturalism*, 2nd edn. Hemel Hempstead: Harvester.

Bhaskar, R. (1993) *Dialectic: The Pulse of Freedom*. London: Verso.

Bhat, A., Carr-Hill, R. and Ohri, S. (eds) (1988) *Britain's Black Population: A New Perspective*. Aldershot: Gower.

Billig, M. (1988) Methodology and scholarship in understanding ideological explanation, in C. Antaki (ed.) *Analysing Everyday Explanation: A Casebook of Methods*. London: Sage.

Bishop, Y., Fienburg, S. and Holland, P. (1975) *Discrete Multivariate Analysis*. Cambridge, MA: MIT Press.

Blaikie, N. (1993) *Approaches to Social Enquiry*. Cambridge: Polity.

Blalock, H. (1984) *Social Statistics*, 2nd edn. London: McGraw-Hill.

Blondel, J. (1990) *Comparative Government*. London: Philip Allan.

Blumer, H. (1972) Society as symbolic interaction, in A. Rose (ed.) *Human Behaviour and Social Processes: An Interactionist Approach*. London: Routledge and Kegan Paul.

Boden, D. and Zimmerman, D. H. (eds) (1993) *Talk and Social Structure: Studies in Ethnomethodology and Conversation Analysis*. Cambridge: Polity.

Bourdieu, P. (1992) *Language and Symbolic Power*. Edited and introduced by J. Thompson. Translated by G. Raymond and M. Adamson. Cambridge: Polity.

Bourdieu, P. (1993) *Sociology in Question*. Translated by R. Nice. London: Sage.

Bourdieu, P. and Wacquant, L. J. (1992) *An Invitation to Reflexive Sociology*. Cambridge: Polity.

Bourdieu, P., Boltanski, L., Castel, R. and Chamboredon, J. C. (1990) *Photography: A Middle-brow Art*. Cambridge: Polity.

Bratton, J. (1992) *Japanization at Work: Managerial Studies for the 1990s*. London: Macmillan.

British Sociological Association (1993) Statement of Ethical Practice. Durham: British Sociological Association.

Brown, G. (1984) Accounts, meaning and causality, in G. Gilbert and P. Abell (eds) *Accounts and Action*. Aldershot: Gower.

Brown, G. and Harris, T. (1978) *The Social Origins of Depression: A Study of Psychiatric Depression in Women*. London: Tavistock.

Brown, J. and Sime, J. (1981) A methodology for accounts, in M. Brenner (ed.) *Social Method and Social Life*. New York: Academic Press.

Bruyn, S. T. (1966) *The Human Perspective in Sociology: The Methodology of Participant Observation*. Englewood Cliffs, NJ: Prentice-Hall.

Bryant, C. G. (1995) *Practical Sociology: Post-empiricism and the Reconstruction of Theory and Application*. Cambridge: Polity.

Bryman, A. (1988a) *Quantity and Quality in Social Research*. London: Unwin Hyman.

Bryman, A. (ed.) (1988b) *Doing Research in Organizations*. London: Routledge.

Bryman, A. and Cramer, D. (1990) *Quantitative Data Analysis for Social Scientists*. London: Routledge.

Buchanan, D., Boddy, D. and McCalman, J. (1988) Getting in, getting on, getting out and getting back, in A. Bryman (ed.) *Doing Research in Organizations*. London: Routledge.

Bulmer, M. (ed.) (1978) *Social Policy Research*. London: Macmillan.

Bulmer, M. (ed.) (1979a) *Censuses, Surveys and Privacy*. London: Macmillan.

Bulmer, M. (1979b) Maintaining public confidence in quantitative social research, in M. Bulmer (ed.) *Censuses, Surveys and Privacy*. London: Macmillan.

Bulmer, M. (ed.) (1982a) *Social Research Ethics: An Examination of the Merits of Covert Participant Observation*. London: Macmillan.

Bulmer, M. (1982b) *The Use of Social Research: Social Investigation in Public Policy-Making*. London: George Allen and Unwin.

Bulmer, M. (1984a) *The Chicago School of Sociology*. Chicago: University of Chicago Press.

Bulmer, M. (ed.) (1984b) *Sociological Research Methods*, 2nd edn. London: Macmillan.

Bulmer, M. (1984c) Why don't sociologists make more use of official statistics?, in M. Bulmer (ed.) *Sociological Research Methods*, 2nd edn. London: Macmillan.

Bulmer, M. (1986a) The role of theory in applied social science research, in M. Bulmer with K. Banting, S. Blume, M. Carley and C. Weiss, *Social Science and Social Policy*. London: George Allen and Unwin.

Bulmer, M. (1986b) The use and abuse of social science, in M. Bulmer with K. Banting, S. Blume, M. Carley and C. Weiss, *Social Science and Social Policy*. London: George Allen and Unwin.

Bulmer, M., Banting, K., Blume, S., Carley, M. and Weiss, C. (1986) *Social Science and Social Policy*. London: George Allen and Unwin.

Bulmer, M., Lewis, J. and Piachaud, D. (eds) (1989) *The Goals of Social Policy*. London: Unwin Hyman.

Burchell, G., Gordon, C. and Miller, P. (eds) (1991) *The Foucault Effect: Studies in Governmentality*. London: Harvester Wheatsheaf.

Burgess, R. (ed.) (1982) *Field Research: A Sourcebook and Field Manual*. London: George Allen and Unwin.

Burgess, R. (1990) *In the Field: An Introduction to Field Research*, 4th impression. London: George Allen and Unwin.

Bury, M. and Holme, A. (1990) Researching very old people, in S. Peace (ed.) *Researching Social Gerontology: Concepts, Methods and Issues*. London: Sage.

Butler, A. (1994) 'Taking ourselves seriously: a feminist exploration into mental health and autobiography', unpublished MA thesis. Department of Social Policy and Social Work, University of Plymouth.

Butler, D. and Stokes, D. (1969) *Political Change in Britain: Forces Shaping Electoral Choice*. London: Macmillan.

Button, G. (1987) Answers as interactional products: two sequential practices used in interviews. *Social Psychology Quarterly*, 50 (2): 160–71.

Button, G. (ed.) (1991) *Ethnomethodology and the Human Sciences*. Cambridge: Cambridge University Press.

Bynner, J. and Stribley, K. (eds) (1979) *Social Research: Principles and Procedures*. Harlow: Longman.

Cain, M. (1990) Realist philosophy and standpoint epistemologies or feminist criminology as a successor science, in L. Gelsthorpe and A. Morris (eds) *Feminist Perspectives in Criminology*. Milton Keynes: Open University Press.

Calhoun, C. (1995) *Critical Social Theory: Culture, History and the Challenge of Difference*. Oxford: Blackwell.

Callahan, D. and Jennings, B. (eds) (1983) *Ethics, the Social Sciences, and Policy Analysis*. London: Plenum.

Calvert, P. (1991) Using documentary sources, in G. Allan and C. Skinner (eds) *Handbook for Research Students in the Social Sciences*. London: Falmer.

Cambridge Women's Studies Group (eds) (1981) *Women in Society: Interdisciplinary Essays*. London: Virago.

Cameron, D. and Frazer, E. (1987) *The Lust to Kill: A Feminist Investigation of Sexual Murder*. Oxford: Polity.

Campbell, A. (1984) *The Girls in the Gang*. Oxford: Basil Blackwell.

Caputi, J. (1987) *The Age of Sex Crime*. London: The Women's Press.

Carr-Hill, R. and Drew, D. (1988) Blacks, police and crime, in A. Bhat, R. Carr-Hill and S. Ohri (eds) *Britain's Black Population: A New Perspective*. Aldershot: Gower.

Casey, C. (1995) *Work, Self and Society: After Industrialism*. London: Routledge.

Cassell, C. and Symon, G. (eds) (1994) *Qualitative Methods in Organizational Research: A Practical Guide*. London: Sage.

Central Office of Information (1994) *Britain 1994: An Official Handbook*. London: HMSO.

Central Statistical Office (CSO) (1990) Social Trends, 20. London: HMSO.

Chalmers, A. F. (1982) *What is This Thing Called Science?*, 2nd edn. Milton Keynes: Open University Press.

Chaney, D. (1996) *Lifestyles*. London: Routledge.

Cicourel, A. (1964) *Method and Measurement in Sociology*. London: Macmillan.

Cicourel, A. (1976) *The Social Organisation of Juvenile Justice*, 2nd edn. London: Heinemann.

Clegg, S. R. (1989) *Frameworks of Power.* London: Sage.

Clifford, J. (1986) Introduction: partial truths, in J. Clifford and G. Marcus (eds) *Writing Culture: The Poetics and Politics of Ethnography.* Berkeley: University of California Press.

Clifford, J. and Marcus, G. (eds) (1986) *Writing Culture: The Poetics and Politics of Ethnography.* Berkeley: University of California Press.

Coffey, A. and Atkinson, P. (1996) *Making Sense of Qualitative Data: Complementary Research Strategies.* London: Sage.

Cohen, S. and Taylor, L. (1972) *Psychological Survival: The Experience of Long-Term Imprisonment.* Harmondsworth: Penguin.

Cole, S. E. (1994) Evading the subject: the poverty of contingency theory, in H. W. Simons and M. Billig (eds) *After Postmodernism: Reconstructing Ideology Critique.* London: Sage.

Coleman, C. and Moynihan, J. (1996) *Understanding Crime Data: Haunted by the Dark Figure.* Buckingham: Open University Press.

Collinson, D. (1994) Strategies of resistance: power, knowledge and subjectivity in the workplace, in J. Jermier, D. Knights and W. Nord (eds) *Resistance and Power in Organizations.* London: Routledge.

Cook, D. and Hudson, B. (eds) (1993) *Racism and Criminology.* London: Sage.

Cook, J. and Fonow, M. (1990) Knowledge and women's interests: issues of epistemology and methodology in sociological research, in J. McCarl Nielsen (ed.) *Feminist Research Methods: Exemplary Readings in the Social Sciences.* London: Westview.

Croall, H. (1992) *White Collar Crime.* Buckingham: Open University Press.

Crow, I. (1987) Black people and criminal justice in the U.K. *Howard Journal of Criminal Justice,* 26 (4): 303–14.

Curtis, J. and Petras, J. (eds) (1970) *The Sociology of Knowledge: A Reader.* London: Duckworth.

Dale, A., Arber, S. and Procter, M. (1988) *Doing Secondary Analysis.* London: Unwin Hyman.

Dale, J. and Foster, P. (1986) *Feminists and State Welfare.* London: Routledge and Kegan Paul.

Dant, T. (1991) *Knowledge, Ideology and Discourse.* London: Routledge.

Davies, A. (1981) *Women, Race and Class.* London: The Women's Press.

Dean, J. and William Foot Whyte, W. F. (1979) How do you know if the informant is telling the truth?, in J. Bynner and K. Stribley (eds) *Social Research: Principles and Procedures.* Harlow: Longman.

Dean, M. (1994) *Critical and Effective Histories: Foucault's Methods and Historical Sociology.* London: Routledge.

Denzin, N. K. (1978a) *The Research Act in Sociology.* London: Butterworths.

Denzin, N. K. (ed.) (1978b) *Sociological Methods: A Sourcebook,* 2nd edn. London: McGraw-Hill.

Denzin, N. K. (1988) Blue velvet: postmodern contradictions. *Theory, Culture and Society.* 5: 461–73.

Denzin, N. K. (1994) Postmodernism and deconstructionism, in D. R. Dickens and A. Fontana (eds) *Postmodernism and Social Inquiry.* London: UCL Press.

Denzin, N. K. and Lincoln, Y. S. (eds) (1994) *Handbook of Qualitative Research.* London: Sage.

Deutsch, K. (1987) Prologue: achievements and challenges in 2000 years of comparative research, in M. Dierkes, H. Weiler and A. Berthoin Antal (eds) *Comparative Policy Research: Learning from Experience.* Aldershot: Gower.

de Vaus, D. (1991) *Surveys in Social Research*. London: UCL Press.

Dex, S. (ed.) (1991) *Life and Work History Analyses: Qualitative and Quantitative Developments*. London: Routledge.

Dey, I. (1993) *Qualitative Data Analysis: A User Friendly Guide for Social Scientists*. London: Routledge.

Dickens, D. R. and Fontana, A. (eds) (1994) *Postmodernism and Social Inquiry*. London: UCL Press.

Dierkes, M., Weiler, H. and Berthoin Antal, A. (eds) (1987) *Comparative Policy Research: Learning from Experience*. Aldershot: Gower.

Ditton, J. (1977) *Part-Time Crime: An Ethnography of Petty Crime*. London: Macmillan.

Dobson, A. (1990) *An Introduction to Generalized Linear Models*. London: Chapman and Hall.

Dominelli, L. (1991) *Women Across Continents: Feminist Comparative Social Policy*. Brighton: Wheatsheaf.

Douglas, J. (1979) Living morality versus bureaucratic fiat, in C. Klockars and F. O'Connor (eds) *Deviance and Decency: The Ethics of Research with Human Subjects*. London: Sage.

Douglas, J. (1985) *Creative Interviewing*. London: Sage.

Drew, P. and Wootton, A. (eds) (1988) *Erving Goffman: Exploring the Interaction Order*. Cambridge: Polity.

Dreyfus, H. and Rabinow, P. (1982) *Michel Foucault: Beyond Structuralism and Hermeneutics*. Chicago: University of Chicago Press.

Driver, E. (1989) Introduction, in E. Driver and A. Droisen (eds) *Child Sexual Abuse: Feminist Perspectives*. London: Macmillan.

Driver, E. and Droisen, A. (eds) (1989) *Child Sexual Abuse: Feminist Perspectives*. London: Macmillan.

Dunkerley, D. (1988) Historical methods and organizational analysis: the case of a naval dockyard, in A. Bryman (ed.) *Day Research in Organization*. London: Routledge.

Dunleavy, P. and Husbands, C. (1985) *British Democracy at the Crossroads: Voting and Party Competition in the 1980s*. London: George Allen and Unwin.

Durkheim, E. (1952) *Suicide*. London: Routledge and Kegan Paul.

Durkheim, E. (1964) *The Rules of Sociological Method*. Glencoe, IL: The Free Press.

Easthope, A. and McGowan, K. (eds) (1992) *A Critical and Cultural Theory Reader*. Buckingham: Open University Press.

Eaton, M. (1986) *Justice for Women: Family, Court and Social Control*. Milton Keynes: Open University Press.

Eco, U. (1979) *The Role of the Reader*. London: Hutchinson.

Eco, U. (1984) *Semiotics and the Philosophy of Language*. London: Macmillan.

Edwards, S. (1990) Provoking her own demise: from common assault to homicide, in J. Hanmer and M. Maynard (eds) *Women, Violence and Social Control*. London: Macmillan.

Eichler, M. (1988) *Nonsexist Research Methods: A Practical Guide*. London: Unwin Hyman.

Eldridge, J. (1986) Facets of 'Relevance' in sociological research, in F. Heller (ed.) *The Use and Abuse of Social Science*. London: Sage.

Elias, N. (1987) *Involvement and Detachment*. Edited by M. Schrotter. Translated by E. Jephcott. Oxford: Blackwell.

Emmet, E. R. (1981) *Learning to Philosophize*. Harmondsworth: Penguin.

Erickson, B. and Nosanchuk, T. (1992) *Understanding Data*, 2nd edn. Buckingham: Open University Press.

Ericson, R., Baranek, P. and Chan, J. (1987) *Visualizing Deviance: A Study of News Organization*. Milton Keynes: Open University Press.

Ericson, R., Baranek, P. and Chan, J. (1989) *Negotiating Control: A Study of News Sources*. Milton Keynes: Open University Press.

Ericson, R., Baranek, P. and Chan, J. (1991) *Representing Order: Crime, Law, and Justice in the News Media*. Milton Keynes: Open University Press.

Esping-Andersen, G. (1990) *The Three Worlds of Welfare Capitalism*. Cambridge: Polity.

Eurostat (1992) *Europe in Figures*, 3rd edn. Luxembourg: Statistical Office of the European Communities.

Evans, J. (1995) *Feminist Theory Today: An Introduction to Second-Wave Feminism*. London: Sage.

Farran, D. (1990) Analysing a photograph of Marilyn Monroe, in L. Stanley (ed.) *Feminist Praxis: Research, Theory and Epistemology in Feminist Sociology*. London: Routledge.

Fennell, G., Phillipson, C. and Evers, H. (1988) *The Sociology of Old Age*. Milton Keynes: Open University Press.

Ferber, R., Sheatsley, P., Turner, A. and Waksberg, J. (1980) *What is a Survey?* Washington, DC: American Statistical Association.

Ferrari, V. (1990) Socio-legal concepts and their comparison, in E. Øyen (ed.) *Comparative Methodology*. London: Sage.

Festinger, L., Riecken, H. W. and Schachter, S. (1956) *When Prophecy Fails*. New York: Harper and Row.

Feyerabend, P. (1978) *Against Method*. London: Verso.

Fielding, A. (1992) Migration and social mobility: south east England as an escalator region. *Regional Studies*, 26.

Fielding, N. (1981) *The National Front*. London: Routledge and Kegan Paul.

Fielding, N. (1982) Observational research on the National Front, in M. Bulmer (ed.) *Social Research Ethics: An Examination of the Merits of a Covert Participation*. London: Macmillan.

Fielding, N. (1988a) *Joining Forces: Police Training, Socialization and Occupational Competence*. London: Routledge.

Fielding, N. (ed.) (1988b) *Actions and Structure: Research Methods and Social Theory*. London: Sage.

Fielding, N. and Fielding, J. (1986) *Linking Data: The Articulation of Quantitative and Qualitative Methods in Social Research*. London: Sage.

Fielding, N. and Lee, R. (eds) (1991) *Using Computers in Qualitative Research*. London: Sage.

Filstead, W. (ed.) (1971) *Qualitative Methodology*. Chicago: Markham.

Finch, J. (1984) It's great to have someone to talk to: the ethics and politics of interviewing women, in C. Bell and H. Roberts (eds) *Social Researching: Politics, Problems and Practice*. London: Routledge and Kegan Paul.

Finch, J. (1987) The vignette technique in survey research. *Sociology*, 21 (1): 105–14.

Fineman, S. and Gabriel, Y. (1996) *Experiencing Organizations*. London: Sage.

Fink, A. and Kosecoff, J. (1985) *How to Conduct Surveys: A Step-By-Step Guide*. London: Sage.

Fishman, P. (1990) Interaction: the work women do, in J. McCarl Nielsen (ed.) *Feminist Research Methods: Exemplary Readings in the Social Sciences*. London: Westview.

Fitz-Gibbon, C. and Lyons Morris, L. (1987) *How to Design a Program Evaluation*. London: Sage.

Flew, A. (ed.) (1984) *A Dictionary of Philosophy*. London: Pan.

Fonow, M. M. and Cook, J. A. (eds) (1991) *Beyond Methodology: Feminist Scholarship as Lived Research*. Bloomington and Indianapolis: Indiana University Press.

Fontana, A. (1994) Ethnographic trends in the postmodern era, in D. R. Dickens and A. Fontana (eds) *Postmodernism and Social Inquiry*. London: UCL Press.

Fontana, A. and Frey, J. H. (1994) Interviewing: the art of science, in N. K. Denzin and Y. S. Lincoln (eds) *Handbook of Qualitative Research*. London: Sage.

Forster, N. (1994) The analysis of company documentation, in C. Cassell and G. Symon (eds) *Qualitative Methods in Organizational Research: A Practical Guide*. London: Sage.

Foucault, M. (1971) *Madness and Civilization*. London: Tavistock.

Foucault, M. (1977) *Discipline and Punish: The Birth of the Prison*. London: Allen Lane.

Foucault, M. (1980) *Power/Knowledge, Selected Interviews and Other Writings 1972–1977*, edited by C. Gordon. Brighton: Harvester.

Foucault, M. (1984) What is an author?, in P. Rabinow (ed.) *The Foucault Reader*. Harmondsworth: Penguin.

Foucault, M. (1989) *The Archaeology of Knowledge*, originally published 1969. Translated by A. M. Sheridan Smith. London: Routledge.

Foucault, M. (1991) Questions of method, in G. Burchell, C. Gordon and P. Miller (eds) *The Foucault Effect: Studies in Governmentality*. London: Harvester Wheatsheaf.

Fowler, F. J. (1988) *Survey Research Methods*. London: Sage.

Fowler, F. (1995) *Improving Survey Questions: Design and Evaluation*. London: Sage.

Fowler, F. and Mangione, T. (1990) *Standardised Survey Interviewing. Minimizing Interviewer-Related Error*. London: Sage

Fraser, N. (1989) *Unruly Practices: Power, Discourse and Gender in Contemporary Social Theory*. Cambridge: Polity.

Freedman, D., Pisani, R., Purves, R. and Adhikari, A. (1991) *Statistics*. London: W. W. Norton.

Frisby, D. (1984) *George Simmel*. London: Tavistock.

Game, A. (1991) *Undoing the Social: Towards a Deconstructive Sociology*. Buckingham: Open University Press.

Gane, M. (ed.) (1993) *Baudrillard Live: Selected Interviews*. London: Routledge.

Garfinkel, H. (1967) *Studies in Ethnomethodology*. Englewood Cliffs, NJ: Prentice Hall.

Gearing, B. and Dant, T. (1990) Doing biographical research, in S. Peace (ed.) *Researching Social Gerontology: Concepts, Methods and Issues*. London: Sage.

Geertz, C. (1973a) Thick description, in C. Geertz (ed.) *The Interpretation of Cultures*. New York: Basic Books.

Geertz, C. (ed.) (1973b) *The Interpretation of Cultures*. New York: Basic Books.

Gellner, E. (1974) The new idealism: cause and meaning in the social sciences, in A. Giddens (ed.) *Positivism and Sociology*. London: Heinemann.

Gelsthorpe, L. (1990) Feminist methodologies in criminology: a new approach or old wine in new bottles?, in L. Gelsthorpe and A. Morris (eds) *Feminist Perspectives in Criminology*. Milton Keynes: Open University Press.

Gelsthorpe, L. and Morris, A. (eds) (1990) *Feminist Perspectives in Criminology*. Milton Keynes: Open University Press.

Gergen, K. and Gergen, M. (1991) Toward reflexive methodologies, in F. Steier (ed.) *Research and Reflexivity*. London: Sage.

Gerth, H. and Mills, C. W. (eds) (1948) *From Max Weber: Essays in Sociology*. London: Routledge and Kegan Paul.

Giddens, A. (ed.) (1974) *Positivism and Sociology*. London: Heinemann.

Giddens, A. (1976) *New Rules of Sociological Method*. London: Hutchinson.

Giddens, A. (1979) *Central Problems in Social Theory*. London: Macmillan.

Giddens, A. (1984) *The Constitution of Society: Outline of the Theory of Structuration*. Cambridge: Polity.

Giddens, A. (1990) *The Consequences of Modernity*. Cambridge: Polity.

Giddens, A. (1993) *Sociology*, 2nd edn. Cambridge: Polity.

Giddens, A. (1996) *In Defence of Sociology: Essays, Interpretations and Rejoinders*. Cambridge: Polity.

Gilbert, N. (1981) *Modelling Society: An Introduction to Loglinear Analysis for Social Researchers*. London: George Allen and Unwin.

Gilbert, N. (1993) *Analyzing Tabular Data: Loglinear and Logistic Models for Social Researchers*. London: UCL Press.

Gilbert, N. and Abell, P. (eds) (1984) *Accounts and Action*. Aldershot: Gower.

Gilbert, N. and Mulkay, M. (1984) *Opening Pandora's Box: A Sociological Analysis of Scientists' Discourse*. Cambridge: Cambridge University Press.

Ginn, J. and Duggard, P. (1994) Statistics: a gendered agenda. *Radical Statistics*, 58: 2–15.

Glaser, B. and Strauss, A. (1965) *Awareness of Dying*. Chicago: Aldine.

Glaser, B. and Strauss, A. (1967) *The Discovery of Grounded Theory*. Chicago: Aldine.

Glastonbury, B. and MacKean, J. (1991) Survey methods, in G. Allan and C. Skinner (eds) *Handbook for Research Students in the Social Sciences*. London: Falmer.

Goffman, E. (1961) *Encounters: Two Studies in the Sociology of Interaction*. Harmondsworth: Penguin.

Goffman, E. (1968) *Asylums: Essays on the Social Situation of Mental Patients and Other Inmates*, originally published 1961. Harmondsworth: Penguin.

Goffman, E. (1981) *Forms of Talk*. Philadelphia: University of Pennsylvania Press.

Goffman, E. (1984) *The Presentation of Self in Everyday Life*, originally published 1959. Harmondsworth: Penguin.

Gold, R. (1969) Roles in sociological field observation, in G. McCall and J. Simmons (eds) *Issues in Participant Observation: A Text and Reader*. London: Addison Wesley.

Golding, P. (1995) Public attitudes to social exclusion: some problems of measurement and analysis, in R. Room (ed.) *Beyond the Threshold: The Measurement and Analysis of Social Exclusion*. University of Bristol: Policy Press.

Goldthorpe, J. (1984) The relevance of history to sociology, in M. Bulmer (ed.) *Sociological Research Methods*, 2nd edn. London: Macmillan.

Gouldner, A. (1962) Anti-Minotaur: the myth of a value-free sociology. *Social Problems*, 9 (3): 199–213.

Gouldner, A. (1971) *The Coming Crisis in Western Sociology*. London: Heinemann.

Government Statisticians' Collective (1993) How official statistics are produced: views from the inside, originally published 1979, in M. Hammersley (ed.) *Social Research: Philosophy, Politics and Practice*. London: Sage.

Graham, H. (1984) Surveying through stories, in C. Bell and H. Roberts (eds) *Social Researching: Politics, Problems and Practice*. London: Routledge and Kegan Paul.

Graham, L. (1995) *On the Line at Subaru-Isuzu: The Japanese Model and the American Worker*. Ithaca, NY: Cornell University Press.

Gramsci, A. (1971) *Selections from the Prison Notebooks*. London: Lawrence and Wishart.

Greed, C. (1990) The professional and the personal: a study of women quantity surveyors, in L. Stanley (ed.) *Feminist Praxis: Research, Theory and Epistemology in Feminist Sociology*. London: Routledge.

Griffiths, M. and Whitford, M. (eds) (1990) *Feminist Perspectives in Philosophy*. London: Macmillan.

Grimshaw, A. (1973) Comparative sociology: in what ways different from other sociologies?, in M. Armer and A. Grimshaw (eds) *Comparative Social Research: Methodological Problems and Strategies*. London: John Wiley.

Grosz, E. (1994) Sexual difference and the problem of essentialism, in N. Schor and E. Weed (eds) *The Essential Difference*. Bloomington and Indianapolis: Indiana University Press.

Gwilliam, P. (1988) *Basic Statistics*. Harmondsworth: Penguin.

Habermas, J. (1973) *Theory and Practice*. Boston, MA: Beacon.

Habermas, J. (1984) *Theory of Communicative Action. Vol. 1: Reason and the Rationalization of Society*. Translated by T. McCarthy. Cambridge: Polity.

Habermas, J. (1987) *Theory of Communicative Action. Vol. 2: Lifeworld and System: A Critique of Functionalist Reason*. Translated by T. McCarthy. Cambridge: Polity.

Habermas, J. (1989) *Knowledge and Human Interests*, originally published 1968. Translated by J. J. Shapiro. Cambridge: Polity.

Habermas, J. (1990) *On the Logic of the Social Sciences*, originally published in 1970. Translated by S. W. Nicholsen. and J. A. Stark. Cambridge: Polity.

Habermas, J. (1992) *Moral Consciousness and Communicative Action*. Translated by C. Lenhardt and S. Nicholsen. Introduction by T. McCarthy. Cambridge: Polity.

Habermas, J. (1994) *The Past as Future*. Interviews by M. Haller. Translated and edited by M. Pensky. Cambridge: Polity.

Hacking, I. (1986) Making up people, in T. Heller, M. Sosna and D. Wellbery with A. Davidson, A. Swidler and I. Watt (eds) *Reconstructing Individualism: Autonomy, Individuality, and the Self in Western Thought*. Stanford, CA: Stanford University Press.

Hage, J. (ed.) (1994) *Formal Theory in Sociology: Opportunity or Pitfall?* New York: State University of New York Press.

Hage, J. and Meeker, B. (1988) *Social Causality*. London: Unwin Hyman.

Hakim, C. (1982) *Secondary Analysis in Social Research: A Guide to Data Sources and Methods with Examples*. London: Macmillan.

Hakim, C. (1987) *Research Design*. London: George Allen and Unwin.

Hall, S. (1988) The toad in the garden: Thatcherism among the theorists, in C. Nelson and L. Grossberg (eds) *Marxism and the Interpretation of Culture*. London: Macmillan.

Hall, S. and Jacques, M. (eds) (1983) *The Politics of Thatcherism*. London: Lawrence and Wishart.

Hall, S., Cutcher, C., Jefferson, T. and Roberts, B. (1978) *Policing the Crisis: Mugging, The State and Law and Order*. London: Macmillan.

Hammersley, M. (1990a) *Classroom Ethnography*. Milton Keynes: Open University Press.

Hammersley, M. (1990b) *The Dilemma of Qualitative Method: Herbert Blumer and the Chicago Tradition*. London: Routledge.

Hammersley, M. (1990c) What's wrong with ethnography? The myth of theoretical description. *Sociology*, 24 (4): 597–615.

Hammersley, M. (1992) *What's Wrong with Ethnography? Methodological Explorations*. London: Routledge.

Hammersley, M. (ed.) (1993) *Social Research: Philosophy, Politics and Practice*. London: Sage.

Hammersley, M. (1995) *The Politics of Social Research*. London: Sage.

Hammersley, M. and Atkinson, P. (1983) *Ethnography: Principles in Practice*. London: Routledge.

Hammersley, M. and Atkinson, P. (1995) *Ethnography: Principles in Practice*, 2nd edn. London: Routledge.

Hanmer, J. and Maynard, M. (eds) (1990) *Women, Violence and Social Control*. London: Macmillan.

Hansen, A. (1995) Using information technology to analyze newspaper content, in R. M. Lee (ed.) *Information Technology for the Social Scientist*. London: UCL Press.

Hantrais, L. and Mangen, S. (eds) (1996) *Cross-National Research Methods in the Social Sciences*. London: Pinter.

Harding, S. (1986) *The Science Question in Feminism*. Milton Keynes: Open University Press.

Harding, S. (ed.) (1987a) *Feminism and Methodology*. Bloomington, Indianapolis/Milton Keynes: Indiana Press/Open University Press.

Harding, S. (1987b) Is there a feminist method?, in S. Harding (ed.) *Feminism and Methodology*. Bloomington, Indiana/Milton Keynes: Indiana Press/Open University Press.

Harding, S. (1991) *Whose Science? Whose Knowledge? Thinking from Women's Lives*. Milton Keynes: Open University Press.

Harré, R. (1988) Accountability within a social order: the role of pronouns, in C. Antaki (ed.) *Analysing Everyday Explanation: A Casebook of Methods*. London: Sage.

Harré, R. (1993) *Social Being*, 2nd edn. Oxford: Basil Blackwell.

Hartsock, N. (1987) The feminist standpoint: developing the ground for a specifically historical materialism, in S. Harding (ed.) *Feminism and Methodology*. Bloomington, Indiana/Milton Keynes: Indiana Press/Open University Press.

Harvey, L. (1990) *Critical Social Research*. London: Unwin Hyman.

Heath, C. (1981) The opening sequence in doctor–patient interaction, in P. Atkinson and C. Heath (eds) *Medical Work: Realities and Routines*. Aldershot: Gower.

Heath, C. (1988) Embarrassment and interactional organization, in P. Drew and A. Wootton (eds) *Erving Goffman: Exploring the Interaction Order*. Cambridge: Polity.

Heelas, P., Lash, S. and Morris, P. (eds) (1996) *Detraditionalization: Critical Reflections on Authority and Identity*. Oxford: Blackwell.

Heller, A. and Fehér, F. (1988) *The Postmodern Political Condition*. Cambridge: Polity.

Heller, F. (ed.) (1986) *The Use and Abuse of Social Science*. London: Sage.

Heller, T., Sosna, M. and Wellbery, D. with Davidson, A., Swidler, A. and Watt, I. (eds) (1986) *Reconstructing Individualism: Autonomy, Individuality, and the Self in Western Thought*. Stanford, CA: Stanford University Press.

Henerson, M., Lyons Morris, L. and Fitz-Gibbon, C. (1987) *How to Measure Attitudes*. London: Sage.

Heritage, J. (1984) *Garfinkel and Ethnomethodology*. Cambridge: Polity.

Hester, M., Kelly, L. and Radford, J. (eds) (1996) *Women, Violence and Male Power*. Buckingham: Open University Press.

Hey, V. (1997) *The Company She Keeps: An Ethnography of Girls' Friendship*. Buckingham: Open University Press.

Higgins, J. (1981) *States of Welfare: Comparative Analysis in Social Policy*. Oxford: Basil Blackwell.

Hill, M. (1996) *Social Policy: A Comparative Analysis*. London: Harvester Wheatsheaf.

Hirst, P. and Thompson, G. (1996) *Globalization in Question: The International Economy and the Possibilities of Governance*. Cambridge: Polity.

Hobbs, D. and May, T. (eds) (1993) *Interpreting the Field: Accounts of Ethnography*. Oxford: Oxford University Press.

Hoinville, G. and Jowell, R. in association with Airey, C., Brook, L., Courtenay, C. *et al.* (1987) *Survey Research Practice*. London: Heinemann.

Homan, R. (1991) *The Ethics of Social Research*. London: Longman.

Home Office (1991) *Digest of Information on the Criminal Justice System*. London: Home Office.

Hood, R. (1992) *Race and Sentencing: A Study in the Crown Court*. Oxford: Clarendon.

Hopper, C. B. and Moore, J. (1990) Women in outlaw motorcycle gangs. *Journal of Contemporary Ethnography*, 18 (4): 363–87.

Hörning, K., Gerhard, A. and Michailow, M. (1995) *Time Pioneers: Flexible Working Time and New Lifestyles*. Translated by A. Williams. Cambridge: Polity.

Hough, M. and Mayhew, P. (1983) *The British Crime Survey: First Report*. Home Office Research Study no. 76. London: HMSO.

Hough, M. and Mayhew, P. (1985) *Taking Account of Crime: Key Findings from the Second British Crime Survey*. Home Office Research Study no. 85. London: HMSO.

Houtkoop-Steenstra, H. (1993) Opening sequences in Dutch telephone conversations, in D. Boden and D. H. Zimmerman (eds) *Talk and Social Structure: Studies in Ethnomethodology and Conversation Analysis*. Cambridge: Polity.

Huff, D. (1981) *How to Lie with Statistics*. Harmondsworth: Penguin.

Hughes, J. (1976) *Sociological Analysis*. London: Nelson.

Humm, M. (ed.) (1992) *Feminisms: A Reader*. London: Harvester Wheatsheaf.

Humm, M. (1995) *A Dictionary of Feminist Theory*, 2nd edn. London: Harvester Wheatsheaf.

Humphreys, L. (1970) *Tea Room Trade*. London: Duckworth.

Husbands, C. (1981) The anti-quantitative bias in postwar British sociology, in P. Abrams, R. Deem, J. Finch and P. Rock (eds) *Practice and Progress: British Sociology 1950–1980*. London: George Allen and Unwin.

Irvine J., Miles, I. and Evans, I. (eds) (1979) *Demystifying Social Statistics.* London: Pluto.

Jefferson, T. (ed.) (1975) *Resistance through Rituals.* Birmingham: Centre for Contemporary Cultural Studies, University of Birmingham.

Jermier, J., Knights, D. and Nord, W. (eds) (1994) *Resistance and Power in Organizations.* London: Routledge.

Jick, T. (1979) Mixing qualitative and quantitative methods: triangulation in action. *Administrative Science Quarterly*, 24: 602–11.

Johnson, T., Dandeker, C. and Ashworth, C. (1990) *The Structure of Social Theory.* London: Macmillan.

Jolliffe, F. R. (1974) *Commonsense Statistics for Economists and Others.* London: Routledge and Kegan Paul.

Jones, C. (1985) *Patterns of Social Policy: An Introduction to Comparative Analysis.* London: Tavistock.

Kamuf, P. (ed.) (1991) *A Derrida Reader: Between the Blinds.* London: Harvester Wheatsheaf.

Kay, C. Y. (1990) At the Palace: researching gender and ethnicity in a Chinese restaurant, in L. Stanley (ed.) *Feminist Praxis: Research, Theory and Epistemology in Feminist Sociology.* London: Routledge.

Keat, R. and Urry, J. (1975) *Social Theory as Science.* London: Routledge and Kegan Paul.

Kelle, U. (ed.) (1995) *Computer-Aided Qualitative Data Analysis.* London: Sage.

Kelly, L. and Radford, J. (1987) The problem of men: feminist perspectives on sexual violence, in P. Scraton (ed.) *Law, Order and the Authoritarian State.* Milton Keynes: Open University Press.

Kent, R. (1981) *A History of British Empirical Sociology.* Aldershot: Gower.

Kidder, L. (1981) *Research Methods in Social Relations*, 4th edn. New York: Holt-Saunders.

Kimmel, A. (1988) *Ethics and Values in Applied Social Research.* London: Sage.

Kinnear, P. and Gray, C. (1994) *SPSS For Windows Made Simple.* Hove: Lawrence Erlbaum.

Kirk, J. and Miller, M. (1986) *Reliability and Validity in Qualitative Research.* London: Sage.

Klockars, C. and O'Connor, F. (eds) (1979) *Deviance and Decency: The Ethics of Research with Human Subjects.* London: Sage.

Knorr-Cetina, K. and Cicourel, A. (eds) (1981) *Advances in Social Theory and Methodology: Towards an Integration of Micro and Macro Theories.* London: Routledge and Kegan Paul.

Kuhn, T. (1970) *The Structure of Scientific Revolutions.* Chicago: University of Chicago Press.

Kuhn, T. (1972) Scientific paradigms, in B. Barnes (ed.) *Sociology of Science: Selected Readings.* Harmondsworth: Penguin.

Kurtz, L. (1984) *Evaluating Chicago Sociology: A Guide to the Literature with an Annotated Bibliography.* Chicago: Chicago University Press.

Kvale, S. (1996) *Interviews: An Introduction to Qualitative Research Interviewing.* London: Sage.

Laclau, E. and Mouffe, C. (1985) *Hegemony and Socialist Strategy: Towards a Radical Democratic Politics.* London: Verso.

La Fontaine, J. (1985) *What is Social Anthropology?* London: Edward Arnold.

Lakatos, I. and Musgrave, A. (eds) (1970) *Criticism and the Growth of Knowledge.* Cambridge: Cambridge University Press.

Langan, M. and Ostner, I. (1991) Gender and welfare: towards a comparative framework, in G. Room (ed.) *Towards a European Welfare State?* School for Advanced Urban Studies. Bristol: SAUS Publications.

Lapiere, R. (1934) Attitudes versus actions. *Social Forces*, 13: 230–7.

Lash, S. and Urry, J. (1994) *Economics of Signs and Space*. London: Sage.

Lash, S., Szerszynski, B. and Wynne, B. (eds) (1996) *Risk, Environment and Modernity: Towards a New Ecology*. London: Sage.

Latour, B. (1988) The politics of explanation: an alternative, in S. Woolgar (ed.) *Knowledge and Reflexivity: New Frontiers in the Sociology of Knowledge*. London: Sage.

Lavrakas, P. (1987) *Telephone Survey Methods: Sampling, Selection, and Supervision*. London: Sage.

Law, J. (1994) *Organizing Modernity*. Oxford: Basil Blackwell.

Lawrence, P. (1988) In another country, in A. Bryman (ed.) *Doing Research in Organisations*. London: Routledge.

Lee, F. (1988) *Fabianism and Colonialism: The Life and Political Thought of Lord Sydney Olivier*. London: Defiant Books.

Lee, R. M. (ed.) (1995) *Information Technology for the Social Scientist*. London: UCL Press.

Levitas, R. (1996) Fiddling while Britain burns? The 'measurement' of unemployment, in R. Levitas and W. Guy (eds) (1996) *Interpreting Official Statistics*. London: Routledge.

Levitas, R. and Guy, W. (eds) (1996) *Interpreting Official Statistics*. London: Routledge.

Lieven, E. (1981) If it's natural, we can't change it, in Cambridge Women's Studies Group (eds) *Women in Society: Interdisciplinary Essays*. London: Virago.

Lipsky, R. (1982) *An Introduction to Positive Economics*, 5th edn. London: Weidenfeld and Nicolson.

Lloyd, G. (1984) *The Man of Reason: 'Male' and 'Female' in Western Philosophy*. London: Methuen.

Lofland, J. and Lofland, L. (1984) *Analysing Social Settings: A Guide to Qualitative Observation and Analysis*, 2nd edn. Belmont, CA: Wadsworth.

Lorde, A. (1992) An open letter to Mary Daly, in M. Humm (ed.) *Feminism: A Reader*. London: Harvester Wheatsheaf.

Luhmann, N. (1993) *Risk: A Sociological Theory*. Translated by R. Barrett. New York: Walter de Gruyter.

Lukes, S. (1981) *Emile Durkheim: His Life and Work – A Historical and Critical Study*. Harmondsworth: Penguin.

Lukes, S. (1994) Some problems about rationality, in M. Martin and L. C. McIntyre (eds) *Readings in the Philosophy of Social Science*. Cambridge, MA: MIT Press.

Lyon, D. (1994) *Postmodernity*. Buckingham: Open University Press.

Lyotard, J. (1984) *The Postmodern Condition: A Report on Knowledge*. Manchester: Manchester University Press.

McCall, G. and Simmons, J. (eds) (1969) *Issues in Participant Observation: A Text and Reader*. London: Addison Wesley.

McCarl Nielsen, J. (ed.) (1990) *Feminist Research Methods: Exemplary Readings in the Social Sciences*. London: Westview.

McGregor, P. and Borooah, V. (1992) Is low spending or low income a better indicator of whether or not a household is poor?: some results from the 1985 family expenditure survey. *Journal of Social Policy*, 21 (1): 53–69.

McLaughlin, E. (1991) Oppositional poverty: the quantitative/qualitative divide and other dichotomies. *Sociological Review*, 39 (2): 292–308.

McMiller, P. and Wilson, M. (1984) *A Dictionary of Social Science Methods*. London: John Wiley.

McPherson, T. (1974) *Philosophy and Religious Belief*. London: Hutchinson.

Majchrzak, A. (1984) *Methods for Policy Research*. Beverly Hills, CA: Sage.

Malseed, J. (1987) Straw men: a note on Ann Oakley's treatment of textbook prescriptions for interviewing. *Sociology*, 21 (4): 629–31.

Manis, J. (1976) *Analyzing Social Problems*. New York: Praeger.

Mann, P. (1985) *Methods of Social Investigation*. Oxford: Basil Blackwell.

Manning, P. (1987) *Semiotics and Fieldwork*. London: Sage.

Manning, P. (1988) Semiotics and social theory: the analysis of organizational beliefs, in N. Fielding (ed.) *Actions and Structure: Research Methods and Social Theory*. London: Sage.

Manning, P. and Van Maanen, J. (eds) (1978) *Policing: A View from the Streets*. Santa Monica, CA: Goodyear.

Marsh, C. (1979) Opinion polls – social science or political manoeuvre?, in J. Irvine, I. Miles and J. Evans (eds) *Demystifying Social Statistics*. London: Pluto.

Marsh, C. (1982) *The Survey Method*. London: George Allen and Unwin.

Marsh, C. (1984) Problems with surveys: method or epistemology?, in M. Bulmer (ed) *Sociological Research Methods*, 2nd edn. London: Macmillan.

Marsh, C. (1988) *Exploring Data: An Introduction to Data Analysis for Social Scientists*. Cambridge: Polity.

Marsh, C. and Gershuny, J. (1991) Handling work history data in standard statistical packages, in S. Dex (ed.) *Life and Work History Analyses: Qualitative and Quantitative Developments*. London: Routledge.

Marsh, R. (1967) *Comparative Sociology: A Codification of Cross-Societal Analysis*. New York: Harcourt and Brace.

Marshall, C. and Rossman, G. (1989) *Designing Qualitative Research*. London: Sage.

Martin, J. and Manners, T. (1995) Computer assisted personal interviewing in survey research, in R. Lee (ed.) *Information Technology for the Social Scientist*. London: UCL Press.

Martin, M. and McIntyre, L. C. (eds) (1994) *Readings in the Philosophy of Social Science*. Cambridge, MA: MIT Press.

Massey, D. (1995) *Spatial Divisions of Labour: Social Structures and the Geography of Production*, 2nd edn. London: Macmillan.

Mawby, R. I. (1990) *Comparative Policing Issues: The British and American Experience in International Perspective*. London: Unwin Hyman.

Mawby, R. I. (1991) *Look After Your Heart: First Report from the Plymouth Health Survey*. Plymouth: Department of Applied Social Science, University of Plymouth.

May, T. (1986) 'Neglected territory: victims of car theft', unpublished MSc thesis. Department of Sociology, University of Surrey.

May, T. (1991) *Probation: Politics, Policy and Practice*. Milton Keynes: Open University Press.

May, T. (1993) Feelings matter: inverting the hidden equation, in D. Hobbs and T. May (eds) *Interpreting the Field: Accounts of Ethnography*. Oxford: Oxford University Press.

May, T. (1994) Transformative power: a study in a human service organisation. *Sociological Review*, 42 (4): 618–38.

May, T. (1995) *Study Skills in Higher Education*. Durham: Department of Sociology and Social Policy, University of Durham.

May, T. (1996) *Situating Social Theory*. Buckingham: Open University Press.

May, T. (1997) When theory fails? The history of American sociological research methods. *History of Human Sciences*, 10 (1): 163–71.

May, T. and Landells, M. (1994) Administrative rationality and the delivery of social services: an organisation in flux. Paper delivered to the International Conference on Children, Family Life and Society, University of Plymouth, July.

Maynard, M. and Purvis, J. (eds) (1994) *Researching Women's Lives from a Feminist Perspective*. London: Taylor and Francis.

Merton, R. (1957) *Social Theory and Social Structure*. New York: The Free Press.

Merton, R. and Kendal, P. (1946) The focused interview. *American Journal of Sociology*, 51: 541–57.

Mills, C. W. (1940) Situated accounts and vocabularies of motive. *American Sociological Review*, 6: 904–13.

Mills, C. W. (1959) *The Sociological Imagination*. New York: Oxford University Press.

Mirrlees-Black, C., Mayhew, P. and Percy, A. (1996) *The 1996 British Crime Survey: England and Wales*. London: HMSO.

Mishra, R. (1989) The academic tradition in social policy, in M. Bulmer, J. Lewis and D. Piachaud (eds) *The Goals of Social Policy*. London: Unwin Hyman.

Morrow, R. A. with Brown, D. D. (1994) *Critical Theory and Methodology*. London: Sage.

Moser, C. and Kalton, G. (1983) *Survey Methods in Social Investigation*. London: Heinemann.

Mullan, B. (1987) *Sociologists on Sociology*. London: Croom Helm.

Nagel, E. (1961) *The Structure of Science*. London: Routledge and Kegan Paul.

Nelson, C. and Grossberg, L. (eds) (1988) *Marxism and the Interpretation of Culture*. London: Macmillan.

Newman, G. (1976) *Comparative Deviance: Perception and Law in Six Cultures*. New York: Elsevier.

Newton, T. (1996) Agency and discourse: recruiting consultants in a life insurance company. *Sociology*, 30 (4): 717–39.

Oakley, A. (1979) *From Here to Maternity: Becoming a Mother*. Harmondsworth: Penguin.

Oakley, A. (1984) *Taking it Like a Woman*. London: Fontana.

Oakley, A. (1987) Comment on Malseed. *Sociology*, 21 (4): 632.

Oakley, A. (1990) Interviewing women: a contradiction in terms, in H. Roberts (ed.) *Doing Feminist Research*. London: Routledge and Kegan Paul.

Oakley, A. and Oakley, R. (1979) Sexism in official statistics, in J. Irvine, I. Miles and J. Evans (eds) *Demystifying Social Statistics*. London: Pluto.

Okin, S. M. (1980) *Women in Western Political Thought*. London: Virago.

O'Neill, J. (1995) *The Poverty of Postmodernism*. London: Routledge.

O'Reilly, J. (1996) Theoretical considerations in cross-national employment research. *Sociological Research Online*, 1 (1).

Oppenheim, A. N. (1973) *Questionnaire Design and Attitude Measurement*. London: Heinemann.

Outhwaite, W. (1991) Hans-George Gadamer, in Q. Skinner (ed.) *The Return of Grand Theory in the Human Sciences*. Cambridge: Cambridge University Press.

Øyen, E. (ed.) (1990a) *Comparative Methodology*. London: Sage.

Øyen, E. (1990b) The imperfection of comparisons, in E. Øyen (ed.) *Comparative Methodology*. London: Sage.

Padfield, M. and Procter, I. (1996) Effects of interviewer's gender on interviewing: a comparative inquiry. *Sociology*, 30 (2): 355–66.

Pahl, R. (1995) *After Success: Fin de Siècle Anxiety and Identity*. Cambridge: Polity.

Papineau, D. (1978) *For Science in the Social Sciences*. London: Macmillan.

Park, R. E. (1972) *The Crowd and the Public and Other Essays*, edited by H. Elsner. Translated by C. Elsner. Chicago: University of Chicago Press.

Parker, H. (1974) *View from the Boys*. Newton Abott: David and Charles.

Pascall, G. (1986) *Social Policy: A Feminist Analysis*. London: Tavistock.

Patton, M. (1987) *How to Use Qualitative Methods in Evaluation*. London: Sage.

Peace, S. (ed.) (1990) *Researching Social Gerontology: Concepts, Methods and Issues*. London: Sage.

Pearson, G. (1983) *Hooligan: A History of Respectable Fears*. London: Macmillan.

Pearson, G. (1993) Talking a good fight: authenticity and distance in the ethnographer's craft, in D. Hobbs and T. May (eds) *Interpreting the Field: Accounts of Ethnography*. Oxford: Oxford University Press.

Penal Affairs Consortium (1996) *Race and Criminal Justice*. London: National Association for the Care and Resettlement of Offenders.

Phoenix, A. (1993) Practising feminist research: the intersection of gender and 'Race' in the research process, in M. Maynard and J. Purvis (eds) *Researching Women's Lives from a Feminist Perspective*. London: Taylor and Francis.

Pinker, R. (1971) *Social Theory and Social Policy*. London: Heinemann.

Platt, J. (1981a) Evidence and proof in documentary research: 1 Some specific problems of documentary research. *Sociological Review*, 29 (1): 31–52.

Platt, J. (1981b) Evidence and proof in documentary research: 2 Some shared problems of documentary research. *Sociological Review*, 29 (1): 53–66.

Platt, J. (1996) *A History of Sociological Research Methods in America 1920–1960*. Cambridge: Cambridge University Press.

Plummer, K. (1990) *Documents of Life: An Introduction to the Problems and Literature of a Humanistic Method*. London: George Allen and Unwin.

Polsky, N. (1985) *Hustlers, Beats and Others*. Chicago: Chicago University Press.

Popper, K. R. (1959) *The Logic of Scientific Discovery*. London: Hutchinson.

Popper, K. R. (1970) The sociology of knowledge, in J. Curtis and J. Petras (eds) *The Sociology of Knowledge: A Reader*. London: Duckworth.

Porter, S. (1993) Critical realist ethnography: the case of racism and professionalism in a medical setting. *Sociology*, 27 (4): 591–609.

Poster, M. (1990) *The Mode of Information: Poststructuralism and Social Context*. Cambridge: Polity.

Pryce, K. (1986) *Endless Pressure: A Study of West Indian Life Styles in Bristol*, 2nd edn. University of Bristol: Bristol Classical Press.

Pugh, A. (1990) My statistics and feminism – a true story, in L. Stanley (ed.) *Feminist Praxis: Research, Theory and Epistemology in Feminist Sociology*. London: Routledge.

Rabinow, P. (ed.) (1984) *The Foucault Reader*. Harmondsworth: Penguin.

Radford, J. (1990) Policing male violence – policing women, in J. Hanmer and M. Maynard (eds) *Women, Violence and Social Control*. London: Macmillan.

Radford, J. and Stanko, E. (1996) Violence against women and children: the contradictions of crime control under patriarchy, in M. Hester, L. Kelly and J. Radford (eds) *Women, Violence and Male Power*. Buckingham: Open University Press.

Ramazanoglu, C. (1990) *Feminism and the Contradictions of Oppression*. London: Routledge.

Ramazanoglu, C. (1992) On feminist methodology: male reason versus female empowerment. *Sociology*, 26 (2): 207–12.

Rattansi, A. and Westwood, S. (eds) (1994) *Racism, Modernity and Identity on the Western Front*. Cambridge: Polity.

Ravn, I. (1991) What should guide reality construction?, in F. Steier (ed.) *Research and Reflexivity*. London: Sage.

Rice, M. (1990) Challenging orthodoxies in feminist theory: a Black feminist critique, in L. Gelsthorpe and A. Morris (eds) *Feminist Perspectives in Criminology*. Milton Keynes: Open University Press.

Ricoeur, P. (1982) *Hermeneutics and the Human Sciences*, edited and translated by J. B. Thompson. Cambridge: Cambridge University Press.

Roberts, H. (ed.) (1990) *Doing Feminist Research*. London: Routledge and Kegan Paul.

Rock, P. (1979) *The Making of Symbolic Interactionism*. London: Macmillan.

Rojek, C. and Turner, B. (eds) (1993) *Forget Baudrillard?* London: Routledge.

Room, G. (ed.) (1991) *Towards a European Welfare State?* School for Advanced Urban Studies, Bristol: SAUS Publications.

Room, R. (ed.) (1995) *Beyond the Threshold: The Measurement and Analysis of Social Exclusion*. University of Bristol: Policy Press.

Rorty, R. (1989) *Contingency, Irony and Solidarity*. Cambridge: Cambridge University Press.

Rorty, R. (1992) We anti-representationalists. *Radical Philosophy*, 60: 40–2.

Rose, A. (ed.) (1972) *Human Behaviour and Social Processes: An Interactionist Approach*. London: Routledge and Kegan Paul.

Rose, D. and Sullivan, O. (1996) *Introducing Data Analysis for Social Scientists*, 2nd edn. Buckingham: Open University Press.

Rose, G. (1982) *Deciphering Sociological Research*. London: Macmillan.

Rose, N. (1991) *Governing the Soul: The Shaping of the Private Self*. London: Routledge.

Rose, R. (1991) Comparing forms of comparative analysis. *Political Studies*, 39 (3): 446–62.

Rosenberg, M. (1968) *The Logic of Survey Analysis*. New York: Basic Books.

Rosenberg, M. (1984) The meaning of relationships in social surveys, in M. Bulmer (ed.) *Sociological Research Methods*, 2nd edn. London: Macmillan.

Roseneil, S. (1993) Greenham revisited: researching myself and my sisters, in D. Hobbs and T. May (eds) *Interpreting the Field: Accounts of Ethnography*. Oxford: Oxford University Press.

Rosenhan, D. (1982) On being sane in insane places, in M. Bulmer (ed.) *Social Research Ethics: An Examination of the Merits of Covert Participant Observation*. London: Macmillan.

Rowntree, D. (1981) *Statistics Without Tears: A Primer for Non-Mathematicians*. Harmondsworth: Penguin.

Russell, B. (1912) *Problems of Philosophy*. Oxford: Oxford University Press.

Ryan, A. (1984) *The Philosophy of the Social Sciences*. London: Macmillan.

Sainsbury, R., Ditch, J. and Hutton, S. (1993) Computer assisted personal interviewing. *Social Research Update* 3. Guildford: Department of Sociology, University of Surrey.

Samuel, R. (1982) Local and oral history, in R. Burgess (ed.) *Field Research: A Sourcebook and Field Manual*. London: George Allen and Unwin.

Samuel, R. (1994) *Theatres of Memory Volume 1: Past and Present in Contemporary Culture*. London: Verso.

Sayer, A. (1992) *Method in Social Science: A Realist Approach*, 2nd edn. London: Routledge.

Schegloff, E. (1988) Goffman and the analysis of conversation, in P. Drew and A. Wootton (eds) *Erving Goffman: Exploring the Interaction Order*. Cambridge: Polity.

Scheuch, E. (1990) The development of comparative research: towards causal explanations, in E. Øyen (ed.) *Comparative Methodology*. London: Sage.

Schor, N. and Weed, E. (eds) (1994) *The Essential Difference*. Bloomington and Indianapolis: Indiana University Press.

Schuman, H. and Presser, S. (1996) *Questions and Answers in Attitude Surveys: Experiments on Question Form, Wording and Context*. London: Sage.

Schutz, A. (1979) Concept and theory formation in the social sciences, in J. Bynner and K. Stribley (eds) *Social Research: Principles and Procedures*. Harlow: Longman.

Scott, J. (1990) *A Matter of Record: Documentary Sources in Social Research*. Cambridge: Polity.

Scott, M. and Lyman, S. (1968) Accounts. *American Sociological Review*, 33 (1): 46–62.

Scraton, P. (ed.) (1987) *Law, Order and the Authoritarian State*. Milton Keynes: Open University Press.

Seidman, S. (1994) *Contested Knowledge: Social Theory in the Postmodern Era*. Oxford: Blackwell.

Shallice, A. and Gordon, P. (1990) *Black People, White Justice? Race and the Criminal Justice System*. London: Runnymede Trust.

Sharrock, W. and Watson, R. (1988) Autonomy among social theories, in N. Fielding (ed.) *Actions and Structure: Research Methods and Social Theory*. London: Sage.

Shaw, C. (1930) *The Jack Roller: A Delinquent Boy's Own Story*. Chicago: Chicago University Press.

Shibley Hyde, J. (1990) How large are cognitive differences? A meta analysis using W^2 and d, in J. McCarl Nielsen (ed.) *Feminist Research Methods: Exemplary Readings in the Social Sciences*. London: Westview.

Shils, E. and Finch, H. (eds) (1949) *Max Weber on the Methodology of the Social Sciences*. Glencoe, IL: The Free Press.

Shipman, M. (1988) *The Limitations of Social Research*, 3rd edn. London: Longman.

Sieber, S. (1978) The integration of fieldwork and survey methods, in N. K. Denzin (ed.) *Sociological Methods: A Sourcebook*, 2nd edn. London: McGraw-Hill.

Silverman, D. (1985) *Qualitative Methodology and Sociology*. Aldershot: Gower.

Silverman, D. (1993) *Interpreting Qualitative Data: Methods for Analysing Talk, Text and Interaction*. London: Sage.

Silverman, D. (ed.) (1997) *Qualitative Research: Theory, Method and Practice*. London: Sage.

Simeoni, D. and Diani, M. (1995) The sociostylistics of life histories: taking Jenny at her word(s). *Current Sociology*, 43 (2/3): 27–39.

Simons, H. W. and Billig, M. (eds) (1994) *After Postmodernism: Reconstructing Ideology Critique*. London: Sage.

Skinner, Q. (ed.) (1991) *The Return of Grand Theory in the Human Sciences*. Cambridge: Cambridge University Press.

Smart, B. (1992) *Modern Conditions, Postmodern Controversies*. London: Routledge.

Smith, D. (1988) *The Everyday World as Problematic: A Feminist Sociology*. Milton Keynes: Open University Press.

Smith, G. (1977) The place of professional ideology in the analysis of social policy: some theoretical conclusions from a pilot study of the children's panels. *Sociological Review*, 25 (4): 843–65.

Social and Community Planning Research (SCPR) (1981) Survey methods newsletter on open-ended questions. Autumn.

Solomos, J. (1993) Construction of Black criminality: racialisation and criminalisation in perspective, in D. Cook and B. Hudson (eds) *Racism and Criminology*. London: Sage.

Sontag, S. (1978) *On Photography*. London: Allen Lane.

Sparks, R. (1992) *Television and the Drama of Crime: Moral Tales and the Place of Crime in Public Life*. Buckingham: Open University Press.

Spence, J. and Holland, P. (eds) (1991) *Family Snaps: The Meanings of Domestic Photography*. London: Virago.

Spender, D. (1982) *Women of Ideas (and What Men Have Done to Them)*. London: Ark.

Spradley, J. (1979) *The Ethnographic Interview*. New York: Holt, Rinehart and Winston.

Spradley, J. (1980) *Participant Observation*. New York: Holt, Rinehart and Winston.

Sprent, P. (1988) *Understanding Data*. Harmondsworth: Penguin.

Squires, P. (1990) *Anti-Social Policy: Welfare, Ideology and the Disciplinary State*. London: Harvester Wheatsheaf.

Stake, R. E. (1995) *The Art of Case Study Research*. London: Sage.

Stanko, B. (1990) When precaution is normal: a feminist critique of crime prevention, in L. Gelsthorpe and A. Morris (eds) *Feminist Perspectives in Criminology*. Milton Keynes: Open University Press.

Stanko, B. (1994) Dancing with denial: researching women and questioning men, in M. Maynard and J. Purvis (eds) *Researching Women's Lives from a Feminist Perspective*. London: Taylor and Francis.

Stanley, L. (ed.) (1990a) *Feminist Praxis: Research, Theory and Epistemology in Feminist Sociology*. London: Routledge.

Stanley, L. (1990b) Feminist praxis and the academic mode of production, in L. Stanley (ed.) *Feminist Praxis: Research, Theory and Epistemology in Feminist Sociology*. London: Routledge.

Stanley, L. (1990c) Doing ethnography, writing ethnography: a comment on Hammersley. *Sociology*, 24 (4): 617–27.

Stanley, L. and Wise, S. (1990) Method, methodology and epistemology in feminist research processes, in L. Stanley (ed.) *Feminist Praxis Research, Theory and Epistemology in Feminist Sociology*. London: Routledge.

Stanley, L. and Wise, S. (1993) *Breaking Out Again: Feminist Ontology and Epistemology*, 2nd edn. London: Routledge and Kegan Paul.

Steier, F. (ed.) (1991) *Research and Reflexivity*. London: Sage.

Stewart, D. and Shamdasani, P. (1990) *Focus Groups: Theory and Practice*. London: Sage.

Steyaert, C. and Bouwen, R. (1994) Group methods of organizational analysis, in C. Cassell and G. Symon (eds) *Qualitative Methods in Organizational Research: A Practical Guide*. London: Sage.

Strauss, A. (1978) *Negotiations, Varieties, Contexts, Processes and Social Order.* San Francisco: Jossey-Bass.

Strauss, A. (1988) *Qualitative Analysis for Social Scientists.* Cambridge: Cambridge University Press.

Sudman, S. and Bradburn, N. (1982) *Asking Questions: A Practical Guide to Questionnaire Design.* San Francisco: Jossey-Bass.

Sudman, S., Sirken, M. and Cowan, C. (1988) Sampling rare and elusive populations. *Science,* 240: 991–6.

Sydie, R. (1987) *Natural Women, Cultured Men: A Feminist Critique of Sociological Theory.* Milton Keynes: Open University Press.

Taylor, C. (1994) Neutrality in political science, in M. Martin and L. C. McIntyre (eds) *Readings in the Philosophy of Social Science,* Cambridge: MA: MIT Press.

Taylor, I. (ed.) (1990) *The Social Effects of Free Market Policies: An International Text.* London: Harvester Wheatsheaf.

Taylor, I., Walton, P. and Young, J. (1973) *The New Criminology: For a Social Theory of Deviance.* London: Routledge and Kegan Paul.

Taylor Fitz-Gibbon, C. and Lyons Morris, L. (1987) *How to Analyze Data.* London: Sage.

Teune, H. (1990) Comparing countries: lessons learned, in E. Øyen (ed.) *Comparative Methodology.* London: Sage.

Thomas, R. (1996) Statistics as organizational products. *Sociological Research Online,* 1 (3).

Thompson, E. (1982) Anthropology and the discipline of historical context, in R. Burgess (ed.) *Field Research: A Sourcebook and Field Manual.* London: George Allen and Unwin.

Titmuss, R. (1970) *The Gift Relationship.* London: George Allen and Unwin.

Titmuss, R. (1974) *Social Policy: An Introduction.* London: George Allen and Unwin.

Tong, R. (1989) *Feminist Thought: A Comprehensive Introduction.* London: Unwin Hyman.

Townsend, P. (1996) The struggle for independent statistics on poverty, in R. Levitas and W. Guy (eds) *Interpreting Official Statistics.* London: Routledge.

Turner, R. (ed.) (1974) *Ethnomethodology.* Harmondsworth: Penguin.

Vallier, I. (ed.) (1971) *Comparative Methods in Sociology: Essays on Trends and Applications.* Los Angeles: University of California Press.

Van Maanen, J. (1978) On watching the watchers, in P. Manning and J. Van Maanen (eds) *Policing: A View for the Streets.* Santa Monica, CA: Goodyear.

Van Maanen, J. (1979) Reclaiming qualitative methods for organizational research: a preface. *Administrative Science Quarterly,* 24: 520–6.

Van Maanen, J. (1988) *Tales of the Field: On Writing Ethnography.* Chicago: University of Chicago Press.

van Zijl, V. (1993) *A Guide to Local Housing Needs Assessment.* Coventry: Institute of Housing.

Verba, S. (1971) Cross-national survey research: the problem of credibility, in I. Vallier (ed.) *Comparative Methods in Sociology: Essays on Trends and Applications.* Los Angeles: University of California Press.

Viinikka, S. (1989) Child sexual abuse and the law, in E. Driver and A. Droisen (eds) *Child Sexual Abuse: Feminist Perspectives.* London: Macmillan.

Voakes, V. and Fowler, Q. (1989) *Sentencing, Race and Social Enquiry Reports.* Wakefield: West Yorkshire Probation Service.

Vogt, W. (1993) *Dictionary of Statistics and Methodology.* London: Sage.

Warwick, D. (1982) Tearoom trade: means and ends in social research, in M. Bulmer (ed.) *Social Research Ethics: An Examination of the Merits of Covert Participation Observation*. London: Macmillan.

Warwick, D. and Osherson, S. (eds) (1973) *Comparative Research Methods*. Englewood Cliffs, NJ: Prentice-Hall.

Warwick, D. and Pettigrew, T. (1983) Towards ethical guidelines for social science research in public policy, in D. Callahan and B. Jennings (eds) *Ethics, the Social Sciences, and Policy Analysis*. London: Plenum.

Watson, T. J. (1994) *In Search of Management: Culture, Chaos and Control in Managerial Work*. London: Routledge.

Webb, E., Campbell, D., Schwartz, R. and Sechrest, L. (1966) *Unobtrusive Measures: Nonreactive Research in the Social Sciences*. Chicago: Rand McNally.

Webb, S. (1990) Counter-arguments: an ethnographic look at women and class, in L. Stanley (ed.) *Feminist Praxis: Research, Theory and Epistemology in Feminist Sociology*. London: Routledge.

Weber, M. (1930) *The Protestant Ethic and the Spirit of Capitalism*. London: George Allen and Unwin.

Weber, M. (1949) *The Methodology of the Social Sciences*. Glencoe, IL: The Free Press.

Weber, M. (1965) *The Sociology of Religion*. London: Methuen.

Webster, F. (1995) *Theories of the Information Society*. London: Routledge.

Wetherell, M. and Potter, J. (1988) Discourse analysis and the identification of interpretative repertoires, in C. Antaki (ed.) *Analysing Everyday Explanation: A Casebook of Methods*. London: Sage.

Whitford, M. (1988) Luce Irigaray's critique of rationality, in M. Griffiths and M. Whitford (eds) *Feminist Perspectives in Philosophy*. London: Macmillan.

Whyte, W. F. (1981) *Street Corner Society*, originally published 1943. Chicago: Chicago University Press.

Whyte, W. F. (1984) *Learning from the Field: A Guide from Experience*, with the collaboration of Kathleen King Whyte. London: Sage.

Williams, A. (1990) Reading feminism in fieldnotes, in L. Stanley (ed.) *Feminist Praxis: Research, Theory and Epistemology in Feminist Sociology*. London: Routledge.

Williams, F. (1989) *Social Policy: A Critical Introduction*. Cambridge: Polity.

Williams, M. (1997) The homeless count in Plymouth: using 'capture–recapture' to estimate the size of the homeless population. Evidence from Plymouth, England, in D. Aramov (ed.) *Emergency and Transitory Housing for Homeless People: Needs and Best Practices*. Brussels: FEANTSA.

Williams, M. and May, T. (1996) *Introduction to the Philosophy of Social Research*. London: UCL Press.

Williams, R. (1981) *Culture*. London: Fontana.

Williams, R. (1983) *Keywords: A Vocabulary of Culture and Society*. London: Fontana.

Williamson, J. (1987) *Consuming Passions: The Dynamics of Popular Culture*. London: Marion Boyers.

Willis, C. (1983) *The Use, Effectiveness and Impact of Police Stop and Search Powers*. Home Office Research Unit, London: Home Office.

Willis, P. (1977) *Learning to Labour: How Working Class Kids Get Working Class Jobs*. Farnborough: Saxon House.

Winch, P. (1990) *The Idea of a Social Science and its Relation to Philosophy*, 2nd edn, originally published 1958. London: Routledge.

Wolcott, H. (1990) *Writing Up Qualitative Research*. London: Sage.

Wollheim, R. (1977) *Freud*. London: Fontana.

Woolgar, S. (ed.) (1988) *Knowledge and Reflexivity: New Frontiers in the Sociology of Knowledge*. London: Sage.

Wright, D. (1997) *Understanding Statistics – An Introduction for the Social Sciences*. London: Sage.

Yin, R. (1988) *Case Study Research: Design and Methods*. London: Sage.

Young, A. (1990) *Femininity in Dissent*. London: Routledge.

Young, A. (1996) *Imagining Crime: Textual Outlaws and Criminal Conversations*. London: Sage.

Young, K. (1977) 'Values' in the policy process. *Policy and Politics*, 5 (3): 1–22.

Young, K. (1981) Discretion as an implementation problem, in M. Adler and S. Asquith (eds) *Discretion and Welfare*. London: Heinemann.

Zimmerman, D. (1974) Facts as practical accomplishment, in R. Turner (ed.) *Ethnomethodology*. Harmondsworth: Penguin.

Author index

Acker, 52
Adorno, 107
Agger, 34, 164
Anderson, 14, 113, 189
Apter, 180
Armer, 191
Atkinson, 125, 135, 139, 155

Baldamus, 40
Barnes, 33, 49, 54, 56, 60
Baudrillard, 132, 181
Bauman, 132
Becker, 51, 121, 134, 143, 148, 149, 152
Beechey, 19
Benney, 111, 124
Berghman, 186, 187
Bernstein, 9, 35
Bhaskar, 11, 30
Blalock, 102
Blumer, 135
Bourdieu, 45, 47
Bratton, 149
Bronfenbreener, 56
Brown, 127
Bruyn, 141, 142, 145, 146
Bryman, 112, 137
Bulmer, 11, 30, 79
Burgess, 119, 145, 162

Calvert, 169
Chalmers, 8
Cicourel, 115, 163
Clegg, 128
Clifford, 152

Coleman, 70

Dale, 66, 67
Dant, 115
de Vaus, 85, 86, 104, 105
Dean, 165
Denzin, 140
Deutsch, 183
Douglas, 56
Dreyfus, 40
Dunkerley, 166, 167

Easthope, 164
Eco, 162, 174
Eichler, 20, 98, 99
Emmett, 44
Ericson, 168, 171, 173, 174
Esping-Andersen, 186, 188

Ferber, 85
Fielding, 70, 108, 111
Finch, 123
Fishman, 123
Fitz-Gibbon, 183
Flew, 54
Forster, 169
Foucault, 15, 40, 159
Fowler, 92
Fraser, 37
Frisby, 135

Gane, 132
Garfinkel, 39, 117, 172

Gearing, 115
Geertz, 153
Gellner, 190
Gelsthorpe, 52
Gergen, 140
Gerth, 50, 57
Giddens, 8, 29, 35, 36, 181
Gilbert, 128
Glaser, 125, 136, 144
Goffman, 120, 127, 146
Gold, 141
Golding, 191
Gouldner, 185
Griffith, 127
Grimshaw, 186
Grosz, 23

Habermas, 28
Hakim, 66, 91
Hall, 37
Hammersley, 53, 135, 139, 155
Hansen, 172
Harding, 21, 22, 23
Harré, 127, 160
Harvey, 37
Heritage, 78
Hoinville, 90, 117
Holt, 186
Hopper, 119, 140
Huff, 79
Hughes, 111, 124
Humm, 51
Humphreys, 58, 59

Johnson, 13, 37
Jones, 193
Jowell, 90, 117

Kalton, 116
Keat, 11
Kidder, 68, 93
Kimmel, 59
Kuhn, 33

Lapiere, 105, 106
Law, 147
Lawrence, 192
Lee, 162
Lipsky, 43
Lofland, 136, 144, 149, 150

Lorde, 24
Lyons Morris, 183
Lyotard, 181

McGowan, 164
McLaughlin, 106
McMiller, 84
Majchrzak, 46
Malseed, 130
Manning, 174
Marsh, 106, 191
May, 75, 83, 89, 105, 142, 146, 170
Mills, 29, 50, 57, 127
Mirrlees-Black, 77
Moore, 119, 140
Moser, 116
Moynihan, 70
Mulkay, 128
Mullan, 123, 143

Nagel, 49

Oakley, 121, 122, 123
Oppenheim, 94, 96, 98
Øyen, 183, 185

Padfield, 124
Pahl, 113, 120
Papineau, 33
Park, 135
Pascall, 19
Pearson, 139
Pettigrew, 54, 55
Pinker, 50, 51
Platt, 26, 158, 169, 173, 176
Plummer, 30
Popper, 32
Porter, 137
Procter, 124
Pugh, 107

Rabinow, 40
Radford, 69, 70
Ramazanoglu, 24, 52
Ravn, 51
Rex, 29
Rice, 25
Rich, 165
Ricoeur, 164
Rock, 134

Rose, 75, 95, 103, 187
Rosenhan, 60
Russell, 161

Said, 164
Samuel, 133, 177
Schutz, 38
Scott, 160, 162, 165, 167, 170, 172
Shamdasani, 113
Shaw, 121
Shipman, 61
Silverman, 125, 129, 154
Sime, 127
Simeoni, 112
Smart, 182
Smith, 127
Social and Community Planning
    Research, 95
Solomos, 73
Sparks, 164, 167
Spradley, 117, 119
Stanko, 68, 69, 122
Stanley, 22, 23, 122
Stewart, 113
Strauss, 125, 136, 149
Sullivan, 95, 103

Taylor, 40, 41, 78, 186

Teune, 185
Thomas, 75
Thompson, 162
Titmuss, 53

Urry, 11

Van Maanen, 136
Viinikka, 76
Vogt, 93

Warwick, 54, 55, 59
Webb, 160, 161
Weber, 50, 57
Webster, 181
Whitford, 20
Whyte, 118, 126, 133, 141, 143
Williams, 83, 105
Willis, 137
Wilson, 84
Winch, 14, 190
Wise, 22, 23, 122, 139
Wolcott, 152
Wollheim, 12

Young, 107, 164

Zimmerman, 163

Subject index

access, 141
  gatekeepers, 54
accretion measures, 161
Admiralty papers, 166
analysis
  methods of, 101
  qualitative content, 173
  quantitative content, 171
anti-foundationalist, 16
argumentation, 35
assumptive worlds, 107
attitude scales, 96

behaviourism, 10
belief systems, 43
bias, 90, 95
bivariate analysis, 102
bivariate relationship, 102
British Crime Survey, 69, 77
British Social Attitudes Survey, 66

causal factors, 106
census, 87
  of population, 66, 166
Central Office of Information, 66
chi-square, 102
Chicago School, 120, 133
  formalism, 134
  pragmatism, 134
classification, pre-coded, 95
coding, defined, 125
cognition, 116
common-sense methods, 38
comparative
  assessment, 44

  expert, 185
comparative research, 185
  difference view, 185
  import mirror view, 185
  potential of, 189
  prediction view, 185
  problems in, 189
  research, 185
    appropriateness of, 190
    equivalence in, 190
  theory developent view, 185
comparison
  inter-societal, 183
  intra-societal, 183
comparitivists, 185
consequentialism, 55
content analysis, 168
  qualitative, 173
  quantitative, 171
correlation, 104
covering laws, 10
Cramers V, 103
crime statistics
  construction of, 67
  and discretionary procedures, 70
  reliability of, 68
  validity of, 68
critical theory, 37
cross-national
  pitfalls of, 184
  research, 184
  studies, 179
  theory building, 193
cultural specificities, 186

data
    logging, 144
    untainted, 153
decisions
    ethical, 54
deduction, 30
dependent variable, 102
deontology, 55
detraditionalization, 180
diachronic concept, 69
difference view, 185
discourse analysis, 128
documentary, 39
documentary research, 157
    accretion measures, 161
    erosion measures, 161
    physical traces, 160
    sources, 159–60
        primary, 161
        secondary, 159
        tertiary, 161
    unobtrusive measures, 160

documents
    authenticity, 169
    closed, 162, 167
    credibility, 170
    historical, 159
    life-course, 160
    meaning , 170
    open archival, 162
    open published, 162
    representativeness, 170
    restricted, 162
    solicited, 162
    unsolicited, 162
double hermeneutic, 36

empiricism, 11
encounters, 150
epistemologies, 22
epistemology, 21
    feminist standpoint, 127
ethic of ultimate ends, 57
ethical decisions, 54
ethics
    British Sociological Association Code
        of, 55
    defined, 54
    professional, 56
ethnocentrism, 193

ETHNOGRAPH, 126
ethnographer as instrument of data
        collection, 138
ethnographic analysis, 126
ethnography, 136
    critical realist method, 137
    data collection, 138
    doing, 139
    postmodern, 152
ethnomethodology, 39
    idealism of, 34
Europe in Figures, 66
European Union, 179
Eurostat, 66
evaluation research, 183
explanatory variables, 94
exploration, 118

fact gathering, 36, 51
factor
    endogenous, 187
    exogenous, 187
factorial scales, 97
facts
    criminal, 71
    empiricism and, 10
    social, 65
feminisms, 17
feminist
    approaches to interviewing, 121
    criticisms
        of research, 17
        of science, 18
    epistemologies, 21
    standpoint epistemology, 22, 127
field notes, 144
formalism, 134
Frankfurt School, 36
funding intentions, 45

gatekeepers, 54
General Household Survey, 66
General Register Office, 65
globalization, 180
grand theory, 29
grounded theory, 125
group
    comparison, 183
Guttman Scale, 97
gynopia, 20

hermeneutic principles, 14

iceberg phenomenon, 75
ideal speech situations, 37
ideal type welfare, 188
idealism, 13
ignorants, 184
import mirror view, 185
independent variable, 102
induction, 30
informed consent, 55
Institutionalist School, 74
internet, 66
interpretative analytics, 15, 40
interpretative paradigm, 38
intersubjectivity, 14, 38
interval scale, 101
interview
    biographical, 112
    face to face, 89
    focused, 112
    group, 113
    life history, 112
    oral history, 112
    restructured, 113
    semi-structured, 111
    as social encounter, 116
    unstandardized, 112
    unstructured, 112
interviewer errors, 92
interviewing
    chronological method of, 120
    developmental, 126
    feminist approaches to, 121
    in-depth, 123
    objectivity, 114
    sequential, 120
    subjectivity, 114
interviews
    analysis of, 124–8
        ETHNOGRAPH, 126
        NUDIST, 126
    biographical, 112
    computer assisted, 92
    conducting, 114
    developmental, 126
    feminist approaches to, 121–4
    focused, 112, 118
    group, 113
    informal, 112

life history, 112
oral history, 112
rapport, 117
restructured, 113
semi-structured, 111
as social encounter, 116
structured, 110
telephone, 93
unstandardized, 112
unstructured, 112

knowledge
    proven, 8
    scientific, 8

laws, covering, 10
Library of Congress, 162
Likert Scale, 96, 101
logical sequence, 101

macro theory, 39
male bias, 17
MARSBARS (Methods are Resembling
    Saloon Bar Sociology), 120
meaning equivalence, 191
measures
    accretion, 161
    erosion, 161
    unobtrusive, 160
metanarratives, 181
method of interpretation, 39
micro theory, 39
motivation, 116
multimethod approach, 88

nationalism
    resurgence of, 181
natural science, 10
naturalism, 135, 153
news sources, 168
normal science, 32
NUDIST, 126

objectivism, 51
objectivity, 9
observational studies, 173
Office of Population Censuses and
    Surveys (OPCS), 67
official inquisitor, 123

official statistics, 65
   Admiralty papers, 166
   birth and death, 65
   British Crime Survey, 69, 77
   British Social Attitudes Survey, 66
   Census of Population, 66, 87, 166
   Central Office of Information, 66
   compilation, 71–2
   crime statistics
      construction of, 67
      and discretionary procedures, 70
      reliability of, 68
      validity of, 68
   electronic access, 66
   Eurostat, 66
   General Household Survey, 66
   General Register Office, 65
   and iceberg phenomenon, 75
   institutionalists, 74
   and internet, 66
   Public Records Office, 162, 166
   radicalists, 74
   realists, 74
   as secondary sources, 66
   Social Trends, 67, 91
   Treasury papers, 166
ontology, 21
open archival, 162
open published, 162
operationalization, 93
orientating theory, 143
Osgood semantic differential scale,
   97

participant
   complete, 140
   as observer, 140
participant observation, 133
   access, 141
   aims of, 133
   complete participant, 140
   data logging, 144
   defined, 136
   and feminism, 151
   field notes, 144–5
   fieldwork role, 139–43
   natural state, 135
   and naturalism, 153
   observer as participant, 140–1
   origins, 133

   participant as observer, 140
   postmodern, 152
   researcher as research instrument,
      138
   and social anthropology, 133
   writing, 152–3

Penal Affairs Consortium, 73
people view, 39
phi, 103
pluralist theory of power, 75
police, 70
positivism, 9, 10
   logical, 44
postmodern
   ethnography, 152
   research strategies, 151
postmodernism, 15
postmodernity, 16
poststructuralism, 15
poverty, 186
power relations, 45
practical reasoning, 129
primary sources, 161
professional ethics, 56
proven knowledge, 8
psychoanalytic theory, 12
Public Records Office, 162, 166
purists, 184
purposive sampling, 87

qualitative analysis, 125
questionnaires, 84
   analysis, 101
   attitude scales, 96–7
   CAPI, 91
   CATI, 91
   coding, 95–6
   computer mediated, 89, 92
   design, 92–3
   face-to-face, 89
   interviewer
      errors, 92
      influence, 91–2
   mail
      response rate, 90
      strengths, 90
      weaknesses, 90
   pre-coded, 95
   purpose of, 82
   sampling

questionnaires (*cont.*)
  self-completion, 89
  telephone, 89, 90–1
    advantages of, 91
  wording, 98–101
questions
  classification, 94
  closed, 95, 104
  descriptive, 118
  explanatory, 94
  factual, 94
  non-directive, 116
  open, 95, 125
    coding of, 125
  opinion, 94
  structural, 119
  verification, 119
  wording, 98
  writing, 98

radical perspective, 75
radical school of thought, 74
random number tables, 86
realism, 11
realist school of thought, 74
reliability, 68, 84
replicability, 84
representativeness, 170
representatives, 85
research
  case study, 166
  feminist criticisms of, 17
  malestream, 23
  process, 42
  psephological, 31
  sponsorship of, 45
  and values, 42

samples, 85, 87
  characteristics, 85
  non probability, 87, 119
  population, 85, 86
  probability, 85
  proportionate quota, 87
  random, 85
  random number tables, 86
  snowball, 119
  stratified random, 86
  systematic random, 86

sampling
  bias in telehone surveys, 91
  frame, 86
  multi-method approach, 88
  multistage cluster, 86
  non-probability, 87, 119
  purposive, 87–8
  quota, 94
  ratios, 86
  snowball, 119
  systematic random, 87
  theoretical, 144
scale
  factorial, 97
  Guttman, 97
  interval, 101
  Likert, 101
  Osgood Semantic Differential, 97
  Thurston, 97
science of society
  production of, 32
scientific
  knowledge, 8
  paradigms, 33
  practice, 42
  progression, 32
  revolutions, 33
  theories, 8
  truth, 9
secondary
  analysis defined, 66
  sources, 159
selectivity, 48
semiotic approach, 165
sequence
  logical, 101
  social psychological, 101
sequential analysis, 151
social
  consensus, 146
  exclusion, 186
  life, 10
  world, 150
Social and Community Planning
    Research, 95, 105
Social Trends, 67, 91
specific semiotics, 174
SPSS (Statistical Package for the Social
    Sciences), 101
standardization, 84

statements
  normative, 43
  positive, 43
statistical
  association, 84
  error, 86
  generalization, 85
  package for the social sciences (SPSS),
    101
statistics
  criminal, 67
  judicial, 67
  prison, 67
  probation, 67
structured interviewing, 84
subjective adequacy, 145
subjectivity, 12
surveys
  longitudinal, 104
  origin, 83
  telephone, 89
    advantages, 91

theoretical
  sampling, 144
  saturation, 144
theory
  grand, 29
  philosophization of, 29
  role of, 27
theory development view, 185
Thurstone Scale, 97
totalists, 184

Treasury papers, 166

ultimate values, 52
unobtrusive measures, 160

validity, 68, 84
  external, 154
value
  consensus, 46
  freedom, 52
  judgements, 42, 45
    appraising, 49
    characterizing, 49
    defined, 42
  neutrality, 49
values, 42
  and research, 42
  and scientific research, 42
  ultimate, 52
variables
  dependent, 102
  exogenous, 183
  independent, 102
  interval, 101
  nominal, 101
  ordinal, 101
  relationship between, 102
view
  difference, 185
  import mirror, 185
  prediction, 185
vocabularies of motive, 127